Apprenticeship Companion

Level 3: Business Administrator

Tim Webb
PGCE, FBII, FInstLM

The Choir Press

Titles in the Apprenticeship Companion series

Level 3: Business Administrator

Level 3: Customer Service Specialist

Level 3: Team Leader/Supervisor

Level 5: Operations / Departmental Manager

Copyright © 2022 Tim Webb

All rights reserved. No part of this publication may be reproduced or transmitted in any form or by any means, electronic or mechanical including photocopying, recording or any information storage or retrieval system, without prior permission in writing from the publishers.

The right of Tim Webb to be identified as the author of this work has been asserted by him in accordance with the Copyright, Designs and Patents Act 1988

First published in the United Kingdom in 2022 by
The Choir Press

ISBN 978-1-78963-287-3

Foreword

Foreword

Having already written a couple of books you might think the endless hours of writing, researching and proof reading would deter any attempt to repeat the process. Given that this is now the third book in the series, that clearly hasn't happened! This time the challenge has been a little easier. The benefit of 20:20 hindsight and a great deal of the research done previously, whilst it has been no walk in the park, it has certainly been very rewarding.

The time, effort and endeavour will all be worth it though, if just one of today's Business Administrators finds it a beneficial and effective support resource as they work towards the End Point Assessment of their Apprenticeship.

I have taken the materials and resources I have used and developed over the years I have taught management studies and recompiled it into a format which, I hope, will be of benefit to all who have the stamina to wade through the detail it contains. I have tried to steer clear of the traditional, drab, textbook style and have striven to lighten what can be a rather mundane subject being so entrenched in theory.

It is no coincidence the book follows the Standard for the Level 3 Business Administrator Apprenticeship and has been designed to provide the reader with support through each module of the programme.

I hope that everyone who delves into this documents finds something of interest and reward, and for those who use it to support their efforts to develop themselves and their career, I wish you every success.

Remember – you only get out, what you put in!

Contents

Contents

Foreword 3
Chapter 1: Personal & Professional Development 7
   Professional Development 8
   Personal Development 10
   Key Stages in Development Planning 12
   Self-Reflection 16
   360-Degree Feedback 18
   Skills Audits 19
   SWOT Analysis 23
   Setting Objectives 25
   Learning Styles 29
      Learning and Development Activities 30
   Personal Development Plan (PDP) 31
   Continuing Professional Development Log (CPD) 35
      The Cost of Personal and Professional Development 36
Chapter 2: The Organisation 37
   The Organisational Purpose 38
   Mission, Vision and Value Statements 40
      The Vision Statement 40
      The Mission Statement 41
      The Values Statement 42
      Customer Service Statement 43
      Organisational Strategies 44
      Strategic Plans 44
      SWOT Analysis 46
      PESTLE Analysis 47
Chapter 3: Value of Skills 53
   Organisational Structure 54
      Mechanistic vs. Organic Organisational Structures 55
      Organisational Roles 63
      Roles in a Team 66
      Team Leadership 67
      Team Training and Learning 68
Chapter 4: Stakeholders 71
   Stakeholders 72
      Internal and External Stakeholders 73
      Identifying Stakeholders 74
      Stakeholder Analysis 76
      Stakeholder Needs and Expectations 78
      Managing Stakeholder Expectations 80
      Communication Channels 87
      Communication Tools 90
      Building Relationships with Stakeholders 91
      Active Listening 93
      Managing Stakeholder Meetings 96
Chapter 5: Governance and Compliance 103
   Aims of Governance and Compliance 104

Contents

Compliance 106
The Six Pack 111
    Health and Safety Policy Statements 114
    Employment Legislation 115
    The Human Rights Act 1998 119
    Equality Act 2010 120
    Working Time Regulations 1998 124
Operational Legislation 127
    The Data Protection Act 2018 127
    The General Data Protection Regulation 2016 128
    Freedom of Information Act 2000 130
    Digital Economy Act (2017) 131
    Copyright, Designs and Patents Act (1988) 132
    The Computer Misuse Act (1990) 134
Consumer-Related Legislation 136
    The Consumer Rights Act 136
Governance 138
    Implications of unresolved governance and compliance issues 145
Policies 147

Chapter 6: Fundamentals of Business Practice 151
Business Sectors 153
Business Principles 155
Business Change Management and Project Management 157
    Change Management 159
    Business Change Manager 162
    Change Management Models 167
    Project Management 178
    The Project Manager 185
    Key Project Documentation 189
    Project Management Tools 192
    Evaluating Project Performance 204
    Managing Project Risks and Issues 205
    Identifying and Mitigating Risks 207
    Managing Issues 209
    A Framework of Rules and Practices 216
    How governance and compliance relate to financial management 217
    Governance and Compliance Processes 218
    Audits 220
    Delivering Value for Money 222
Marketing 227
    Marketing and Advertising 235

Chapter 7: Processes 243
Policies 244
Business Policies 245
Internal Policies 245

Chapter 8: Project Management 261
Project Management 262
    Project Governance 271

Contents

The Project Plan *275*
Project Management Methodology *281*
Key Project Documentation *283*
Managing Resources *286*
Managing Project Risks and Issues *289*

Chapter 9: Project Planning 299
Planning for a Project *300*
Producing the Project Plan *314*

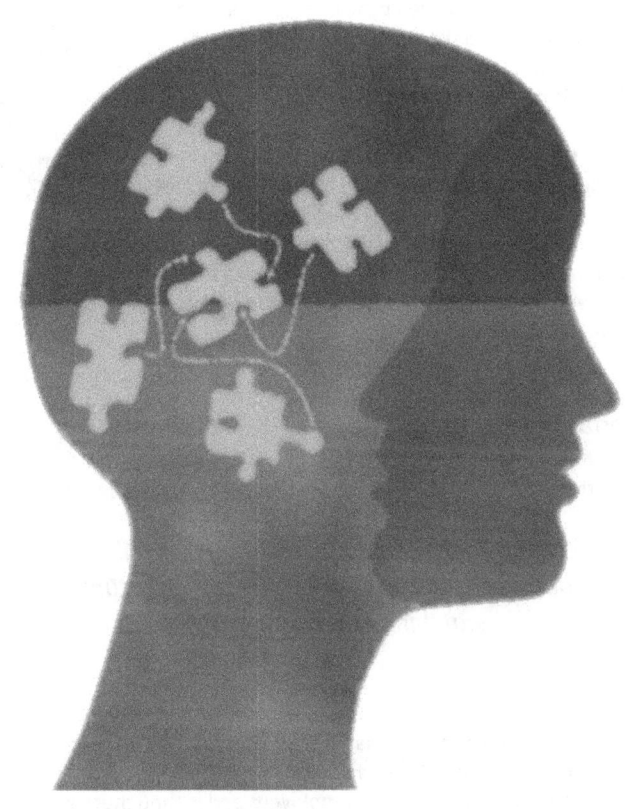

Chapter 1: Personal & Professional Development

Personal & Professional Development

Personal and Professional Development

There was a time when personal and professional development was provided and managed by the employer. You went on a few courses chosen by your employer, said yes when you were offered the chance to take on a new project and waited until the time was right to move up, or move on. But it is not like that anymore.

These days, **you** are responsible for your personal and professional development and **you** need to identify and look for your own opportunities. In order to achieve this, you need to know what needs to be changed and what needs to be developed. The only way to do this is to take a deep and thorough look at yourself, not just at work, but personally too. How can you manage and direct others if you do not have knowledge of your own weaknesses and inadequacies?

Professional Development

Can be defined as:

> *"the process of improving and increasing capabilities of employees through access to education and training opportunities or through watching others perform the job."*

Professional Development is focused on gaining new capabilities and experience and improving the knowledge and skills that improve potential in the work environment. These skills make staff more efficient and effective at their job. It is also suggested that it helps build and maintain the morale of employees and is thought to attract higher quality staff to an organisation.

> *"professional development is either related to a current role or a role you want to do in the future"*

With changes to our working lives happening every day, it is important to develop your skillset to remain effective in your career.
Effective professional development involves ensuring your knowledge and understanding of your area of expertise is always at the highest possible level. It is the acquisition of skills and knowledge for career advancement, but inevitably, it also includes an element of personal development.

Broadly speaking, it may include formal types of vocational education or training that leads to a career related qualification. It can also include informal training and development programmes, which may be delivered on the job in order to develop and enhance skills.

Personal & Professional Development

Some examples of professional development are:

- *IT training*
- *Health and Safety*
- *Accountancy or budgeting*
- *Legal knowledge or expertise*

Benefits of Professional Development

Investing in employees is beneficial to the whole organisation and can boost the bottom line. Listed below are some of the organisational benefits which can be expected because of effective professional development training initiatives:

Increase the collective knowledge of the team.
Encouraging employees to train in relevant subjects and applications — an advanced course in a software package they use daily, can have an immediate effect on productivity. Professional development can also help raise overall staff expertise when employees with vastly different backgrounds and levels of experience are required to work together such as on projects.

Boost employees' job satisfaction
When staff members can do their jobs more effectively, they become more confident. This leads to greater job satisfaction and improved employee retention. There are a range of low-cost professional development training options to choose from, including mentorships, job shadowing and cross training.

Make the organisation more appealing.
When providing training and development opportunities, it builds a positive reputation as an employer that cares about its workforce and wants to employ only the best. Customers and clients will benefit too, from the high level of efficient service they receive. Employees are your brand ambassadors. When they attend conferences and seminars, they represent and reflect all that is good about the organisation.

Attract the right kind of job applicants
Organisations want to attract the most highly driven and career-focused candidates when they advertise a job. By offering them an enticing picture of how they can grow professionally or expand the career avenues available to them if they come to work for you is an attractive add on to an attractive salary.

Help retain staff
Employees want to feel like they are appreciated and making a difference. But they also want to feel like they are developing expertise and becoming more well-rounded. If your team members do not feel challenged, or they sense stagnation in their careers, they will look for advancement opportunities elsewhere. Lifelong learning exposes your employees to new experiences and keeps them engaged in their work. Professional development helps build and maintain enthusiasm, but it also inspires loyalty.

Personal & Professional Development

Make succession planning easier.
Professional development programs are tools for developing future leaders for the organisation. The ability to promote existing staff to managerial positions in the future using targeted training now, can help ensure the best and brightest are readied to move up.

Personal Development

> *"the process of improving oneself through activities such as enhancing employment skills, increasing consciousness and building wealth."*

Personal development is about improving talents and potential, both in and out of the workplace.

Personal development sits alongside professional growth —to progress in a career, personal; development will be needed first.

It helps with handle fears, take on more responsibility, and succeed with greater challenges. Personal Development requires broadening of knowledge, improvement and development of skills and develop and refinement of behaviours to ensure performance with the utmost professionalism.
You may have experienced something like this:

> There are two people in your team, both of whom are great at managing budgets. They are both accurate, detail-oriented and deliver the results needed. However, one of them is a real people person. Their interpersonal and communication skills are fantastic, and, because of this, they have no problem getting the information they require quickly from colleagues at any level. The other person does not have this skill and often encounters conflict from colleagues, for many possible reasons.

Which of these people do you think needs personal development?

Both can do their jobs. Both have the skills required on a professional level to deliver results, however, with the benefit of excellent relationship building skills one of them will always be one step ahead.

Personal & Professional Development

Some examples of personal development are:

- *Leadership training*
- *Management training*
- *Time management*
- *Handling difficult situations and conflict management*
- *Communication skills*

Personal development relates to life skills. These are what is needed to achieve life goals. It focuses on helping to improve talents, whether they are related to work or not.

Personal and professional development courses can improve motivation and help to develop excellence in your domain.

Benefits of Personal Development

Personal development offers many different benefits.

- *Boosting self-awareness*
- *Increasing self-knowledge*
- *Developing your existing skills or learning new ones*
- *Renewing or building your self-esteem or identity*
- *Developing pre-existing talents or strengths*
- *Enhancing your employability*
- *Improve the quality of your life.*
- *Positively affecting your social status and wealth*

All these activities can help make a major difference in life. When feeling helpless, these are skill sets which can help turn the odds in your favour. By focusing on personal development, it ensures the right skill sets are available.

Activities suitable for Personal and Professional Development

Personal Development	*Professional Development*
Emotional Wellbeing	Management Training
Health and fitness	Skill-based training
Communication	Internal Assessment
Motivation	Conflict Resolution
Spirituality	Online Education
Self-belief	Networking
Journaling	Research

Personal & Professional Development

Difference between Personal and Professional Development

It is clear from the definition that professional development relates to enhancing the workforce and/or an individual within that workforce. The objectives will usually be specific to the organisation and its goals at a specific time and the skills that would be required to deliver the products/services.

The definition of personal development suggests it is used when individuals, seek to update their own knowledge and learn skills that they would like to have. This means the activities are more unique to the individual and their personal objectives.

When contrasting personal development against professional development, it is easier to see that there is a connection rather than trying to identify differences.

Both professional and personal development are similar in that they both represent a drive towards improvement, greater understanding and increased effectivity (either an individual or a group).

Both require effort, time and resources (often money) to get involved in and both regularly reoccur for all individuals and not just professionals.

Whilst personal development might seem to be separate from the professional life, it could be a great way to achieve career objectives. It is not just what is learnt that could help at work; making a commitment to personal development clear to an employer, will demonstrate dedication and the ability to learn and grow.

Personal development makes a difference in life on a daily basis. At almost every stage of life, something new will be learnt which will help development as a person.

The key to managing personal development is knowing one's strengths and areas for improvement. Knowing these can help you to develop your weaknesses and turn them into strengths.

Finally, neither Personal nor Professional development can be completed satisfactorily without a depth of self-awareness which is far greater than we currently have. By having a thorough understanding of what you need to achieve and how to achieve it, you can develop the necessary skills by way of a solution.

Key Stages in Development Planning

There are several stages to go through to plan personal and professional development. These can be defined as:

Personal & Professional Development

- *analyse current skills, knowledge and experience* – to identify skills gaps and where we are now.
- *identify development needs and set objectives* – to focus on where we need to be.
- *identify learning styles.*
- *arrange resources and support mechanisms to meet the objectives* – the basis of how we are going to achieve our goals.
- *monitor and review progress and overcome barriers to learning* – to make sure we are still going the right way.

At the heart of the process, there are three questions:

Where am I now?
To answer this question, we need to have a look at our current, personal, situation – e.g., our skills, knowledge and experience; qualifications; job description and tasks; salary package; grade or position at work.

Where do I want or need to be?
Where we would like to be in the future. This can be six months ahead, a year, five years or a period that fits into our future plans. We need to consider our goals, the things we want or need to achieve – e.g., a higher salary; promotion; increased knowledge and skills in specific areas at work; greater job satisfaction; improved job security; improve employability prospects.

How will I get there?
The route achieving this is what will be recorded in our Personal Development plan. We need to identify the steps we need to take to begin to work towards our goals.

This may include qualifications, a career review, do voluntary work to gain specific experience, ask to broaden experience within current work role, shadow colleagues to learn from them, consider the best learning options for you personally.

Remember! This is about focussing on your personal goals and set targets that are specific to you and your needs.

Identifying Personal and Professional Development Requirements

Self-awareness is your ability to recognise your own emotions and their effects on you and others. Without being aware of, and understanding your own emotions, it will be difficult for you to deal with the other emotional competencies like self-management, social awareness, or team leadership.

Personal & Professional Development

Self-awareness is:

> *the conscious knowledge of ourselves – our character, desires, beliefs, qualities, motives and feelings*

When you look in a mirror – what do you see?

> *Do you see the person you are?*
> *The person you want to be?*
> *The person you think other people see?*

The first step on the road to self-development is to recognise that the image we see is simply a reflection of the packaging we come in! That packaging is about as relevant as the cardboard box your breakfast cereals are delivered in!! – You don't eat the box – it's what is inside the box that matters!!

We seldom look inside the packaging because we are afraid of what we might find. Without absolute honesty, you will never recognise what is really inside.

We are not inclined to spend much time on self-reflection. Even when personal feedback is presented to us, we are not always open to it, because honest feedback is not always flattering. Consequently, many of us have a pretty low level of self-awareness.

> ***Self-awareness is being aware of oneself including one's traits, feelings and behaviours.***

It is quite difficult today to find time to think about who we are, what our strengths and weaknesses are, personality type, habits and values. We are just not inclined to spend much time on self-reflection.

Consequently, many of us have low level of self-awareness. An increased level of self-awareness is the essential first step toward maximising management skills. It can improve judgment and help identify opportunities for professional development and personal growth.

This first step on the road to personal development, therefore, is to take a long hard look at ourselves and be brutally honest about our true targets and expectations in life.

> ***If you cannot be totally honest with yourself – you will never be honest with anyone.***

Self-awareness is also associated with soft skills – There are thought to be five elements to this – Personality, Values, Habits, Needs and Emotions.

Personal & Professional Development

These are considered below:

Personality: – Personalities cannot be changed, but values and needs are based on what we learn about ourselves. Understanding our own personality can help us find in what environment we can be successful. Awareness of our personality helps us analyse such a decision.

Values: – It is important that we know and focus on our personal values. When we focus on our values, we are more likely to accomplish what we consider most important.

Habits: – Our habits are the behaviours that we repeat on a daily basis and often, automatically. Although we would like to possess the habits that help us interact effectively with and manage others, we can all identify at least one of our habits that decrease our effectiveness.

Needs: – Maslow and other scholars have identified a variety of psychological needs that drive our behaviours such as needs for esteem, affection, belonging, achievement, self-actualisation, power and control.

Emotions: –Understanding your own feelings, what causes them, and how they impact our thoughts and actions is emotional self-awareness. Persons with high emotional self-awareness understand the internal process associated with emotional experiences and, therefore, has greater control over them.

Having a good sense of these aspects of ourselves can help us in the workplace, and in our private lives. We can assess personal growth and understanding through self-awareness by, for example:

- *being aware of how people and other things influence us.*
- *learning how to influence and interact with others.*

Developing self-awareness, and understanding our own psychology, is a skill that is part of our personal and professional development.

Self-awareness can be applied in our working lives to help us to, for example:

- *understand emotions more clearly* – ours and other people's
- *improve our communication skills* – and interact with others in the workplace and resolve conflict more effectively
- *improve leadership skills* – and our general operational performance
- *improve job satisfaction* – by focusing on job roles and tasks that truly motivate us
- *maximise career development opportunities*

Personal & Professional Development

Techniques that can help us learn about how to reveal, recognise, evaluate and understand the different attributes and qualities that make us unique include, for example:

> *psychometric tests*
> *management tools*
> *coaching tools*
> *self-reflection tools*

Self-Reflection

Self-reflection helps to develop skills and review their effectiveness, rather than just carry-on doing things as you have always done them. It is about questioning, in a positive way, what you do and why you do it and then deciding whether there is a better, or more efficient, way of doing it in the future.

In any role, whether at home or at work, reflection is an important part of learning. You would not use a recipe a second time around if the dish did not work the first time! You would either adjust the recipe or find a new one.

When we do our job, we can become stuck in a routine that may not be working effectively. Thinking about your own skills can help you identify changes you might need to make.

Reflective questions to ask yourself:

- **Strengths** – What are my strengths? Am I well organised? Do I remember things?
- **Weaknesses** – What are my weaknesses? Am I easily distracted? Do I need more practise with a particular skill?
- **Skills** – What skills do I have? What am I good at?
- **Problems** – What problems are there at work/home that may affect me? For example, responsibilities or distractions that may impact on study or work.
- **Achievements** – What have I achieved?
- **Happiness** – Are there things that I am unhappy with or disappointed about? What makes me happy?
- **Solutions** – What could I do to improve in these areas?

Although self-reflection can seem difficult at first, or even selfish or embarrassing, as it does not come naturally, you will find it becomes easier with practise and the end result could be a happier and more efficient you.

Identifying Development Needs

Personal & Professional Development

From Feedback

There are many sources of feedback and it can be collected from, for example:

- **line managers** – e.g., in formal appraisals or informal chats
- **customers** – e.g., in surveys, comments or complaints
- **team members and other colleagues** – e.g., during appraisals or informal discussions
- **training providers** – e.g., in reports and debriefing sessions after completing a unit of a training course or following an observation session
- **coaches and mentors** – e.g., as part of a question and answer session after a learning activity or discussion

It is important to look at the feedback in detail and be objective about the comments. Some feedback will be reliable, useful and easily interpreted. For example, structured and informed feedback from a line manager, coach or training provider will be valuable as they have the skills to give useful and constructive criticism.

Good-quality feedback is likely to be based on good knowledge about, for example:

- *the individual*
- *the workplace environment*
- *observations of the situation and task being reviewed*
- *the organisation's standards and requirements*

Some feedback is not reliable, however, due to the inexperience of some of those taking part. There may be emotional and over-critical comments from some people due to personal reasons, which may not be honest, valid or useful. For example, customers sometimes leave feedback that is biased, emotional and subjective. When this happens, it is important to interpret the feedback in context, check facts very carefully and look for useful and valid information that can be used as a guide for improving performance.

Personal & Professional Development

Gathering Feedback

There are many sources of information which can be used to help with ascertaining the development needs of an individual.

Information can be obtained from sources as diverse as job descriptions for more senior roles to resources offered and provided by professional bodies and organisations.

These can be broken down into internal and external sources.

Internal sources could include:

- *training department*
- *manager*
- *colleagues*
- *intranet*
- *coach/mentor*

External sources could include:

- *industry sources*
- *training provider/college*
- *on-line training*
- *social media platforms*
- *journals*

360-Degree Feedback

Some organisations use a 360-degree model for formal appraisal, where performance feedback is given from a full circle of people at work – senior managers, line managers, colleagues, team members, customers and the person being appraised.
The idea is to give a rounded view of performance from many angles that gives more valuable and detailed feedback than might be gained from just one-line manager. It considers the importance of a wider circle of work relationships.

This mechanism is particularly useful when evaluating skills, experience and knowledge connected with self-awareness. To maximise its effectiveness, it can be beneficial to compare self-appraisal with comments from other people to gain a more objective view.

Personal & Professional Development

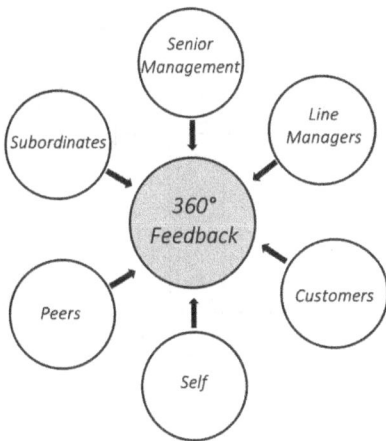

By gathering feedback from different sources, as happens in the 360-degree appraisal, we can:

- *have access to a three-dimensional picture of ourselves from other people's perspectives*
- *have access to reliable feedback from certain sources – so that we can gain useful and valid insight and information*
- *see how some feedback is unreliable – and should not be taken too seriously or personally*

Skills Audits

Skills audits can be used to list the skills that are relevant to a role, then assess one's ability using a scoring system. The skills tested can be for a current role, to see where improvement is needed, or on a role we want to aim for in the future.

In the example below, an experienced departmental manager in a supermarket wants to apply for promotion to deputy store manager.

The following skills audit is based on the skills and attributes shown in the organisation's job description for the deputy manager position. This helps them to identify skills gaps that will need to be addressed if their application for promotion is to be successful.

Personal & Professional Development

They show their current skills in these areas, with 1 = poor and 5 = excellent

Skills and attributes	1	2	3	4	5	Action to be taken
Experience of all departments within the store			✓			Need to work in other store areas – see line manager
Evaluating competitors' stores and managing advantage			✓			OK for fresh produce, useful to try other areas competitive
Leadership skills				✓		OK
General staff management skills				✓		OK
Communication skills				✓		Usually very good, but need more at senior management level – ask line manager
Training and coaching skills					✓	One of my strengths
Purchasing and negotiating delivery and discounts	✓					Do not have to do this in current role – Ask procurement team if I can shadow them for a day/week?
Ability to promote and generate sales – demonstrations, displays					✓	One of my strengths
Customer service skills					✓	One of my strengths
Budgeting/finance skills			✓			Only have to do a bit – need to shadow someone
Working to the organisation's and industry's standards					✓	OK
Maintaining health and safety -e.g., fire evacuation, first-aid cover, risk awareness, minimising hazards, dealing with dangerous chemicals correctly			✓			OK in my area, do not really need to worry about chemicals here – find out a bit more for rest of store

The audit now reveals the areas that this manager needs to address before or when preparing to apply for promotion.

Personal & Professional Development

Analyse your current skills, knowledge and experience.

The normal process for analysing current skills, knowledge and experience is to use a skills audit. This is a simple process which identifies what you are good at what you are not so good at as well as things you may not have done before.

An audit is:

a simple process to identify your strengths and weaknesses.

The skills audit will help to analyse your current position – where I am I now? – and reveal areas that are strong and those that need attention. These can be entered onto a Personal Development Plan, so that we can see our strengths and skills gaps, then start to decide what we need or want to consolidate or improve.

Preparing a Skills Audit

A definitive and comprehensive list is made of the skills that are relevant to the role covering all the relevant criteria. When deciding what skills are necessary to audit, the details can be taken from a variety of sources – the job description and person specification should go some way to providing most of the criteria for this, but can be supplemented by criteria from the organisation's own policies, procedures and standards; national occupational standards; essential standards; professional bodies' standards, etc. The final list should be checked by all parties concerned or involved.

The existing skill set is then compared to the list and a simple rating system applied which shows the level of skill for each criterion.

The rating can be from self-evaluation or be done with someone else, such as the line manager.

These are just two samples of skills audits:

Personal & Professional Development

Professional Skills Audit		
Skills required	Rating (1–5)	Action to be taken
Computing skills	4	Undertake short courses (if possible) to enhance computing skills
Leadership skills	4	Get more involved in communities/societies
Numeracy skills	4	Discuss with lecturers and fellow students on ways to improve
Revision and exam techniques	3	Learn from lecturers and fellow students on techniques to revise and answer exam questions.
Time-management and organisation skills	2	Jot down all activities that need to be done accordingly in a diary
Oral presentation skills	4	Learn to fully utilise and use other presentation aids that are available besides PowerPoint
Critical analysis and logical argument skills	3	Get more involved in group discussions
Selecting and prioritising information when reading	3	Listen to lectures and identify which are the important points
Referencing skills	3	Write more essays and get used to the Harvard referencing style
Summarising skills	4	Need to fully understand the topic
Developing appropriate writing style	3	Read more articles and journals to get used to the writing style so that it can be implemented
Search skills (library and e-resources)	3	Fully utilise the library's 'resources and support' section
Utilising and comprehension	5	Listen more to the way people converse with each other and try and pick up whatever necessary
Proofreading and editing	3	Take another look at the work

Personal & Professional Development

Personal Audit		1	2	3	4	5
1	Lack confidence in expressing my needs		✓			
2	Manage time effectively			✓		
3	I am competent to lead		✓			
4	I cope with stress well				✓	
5	I do not have the confidence to give presentations			✓		
6	I am patient when teaching and coaching others		✓			
7	I can handle a number of tasks		✓			
8	I do not have the confidence to influence others			✓		
9	I can motivate others			✓		
10	I do not make people do tasks			✓		

SWOT Analysis

As well as doing a skills audit and reflecting on your choices, you can also do a **SWOT** analysis to focus your attention on your strengths and weaknesses. These are the things which you are good at and things you are not so good at or need additional support or training to achieve a higher level of competence.

SWOT stands for Strengths, Weaknesses, Opportunities, and Threats.

The strengths and weaknesses are factors which affect you personally. Strengths are things you are good at, things you can do without support or help. This could include literacy or numeracy. It could include being well organised, etc.

Weaknesses are things you need help or support to achieve. It may be that you can happily read a newspaper, but a textbook may be more challenging. You can maybe deal with personal finance including paying bills and managing credit cards, but departmental budgets and cost management you find difficult and need help with. It may also be that you are simply disorganised! These are your strengths and weaknesses!

Opportunities and threats are not about you personally, but about society in general. Opportunities are the things that help you to achieve your targets such as free training courses, help with childcare whilst studying, work shadowing opportunities, etc. Threats are the things which may prevent you from achieving your targets such as the economic

Personal & Professional Development

climate, lack of opportunities, etc. Both opportunities and threats are matters outside of your control, but you should be aware of these issues.

- **S** Strengths
- **W** Weaknesses
- **O** Opportunities for improvement
- **T** Threats to such progress – *things that may stop progress.*

The next stage is to prepare a SWOT analysis to identify development needs in more detail. This shows what is needed to be able to develop skills, experience and knowledge to be in a good position to apply for promotion or a new role.

SWOT

Strengths	Weaknesses
Personal finance *Paying bills* *Managing credit cards*	*Departmental budgets* *Cost management* *Disorganised*
Free training courses *Help with childcare.* *Work shadowing opportunities*	*Economic climate* *Lack of opportunities*
Opportunities	**Threats**

Personal & Professional Development

Setting Objectives

Having analysed where you are now, you can then work out where you want to be and set personal objectives to plan how to improve your performance at work.

When setting personal work objectives, it is important to have a realistic number of goals. If overloaded, people feel overwhelmed and are more likely to fail, give up and lose confidence. Honesty about achievements and expectations is important.

It can be useful to support this process with personal reflection and discussions with senior colleagues, maybe during the appraisal process. Once you have established your needs, you can set objectives that support your strengths, address your weaknesses and help you to improve your performance.

SMART Objectives

Once areas for personal development have been identified, it is important to set targets.

By having our goals and objectives clearly in mind, there is a much greater chance of success. One good way to set goals is to use SMART objectives:

SMART is an acronym that you can use to guide your goal setting.

To make sure your goals are clear and reachable, each one should be:

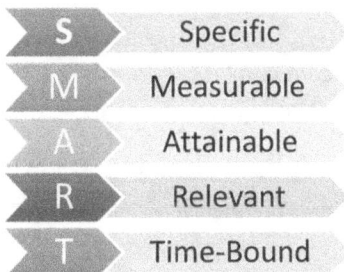

- S — Specific
- M — Measurable
- A — Attainable
- R — Relevant
- T — Time-Bound

Some theorists have expanded it to include extra focus areas.

SMARTER, for example, includes Evaluated and Reviewed.

Personal & Professional Development

S	Specific	What are the details of the learning activity, task or training course that I want to do? What qualifications do I need for that promotion? Which job am I aiming for?
M	Measurable	Is there a certificate or report that can show my progress? Can I count the number of units I am covering so that I can see my progress?
A	Achievable	Can I do it? What support do I need to find to make sure that I can achieve these goals?
R	Realistic	Is it realistic to do the training or tasks in the time that is allowed? Is it realistic to work full time and do all of this study quickly, or do I need to study over a longer period of time?
T	Time-bound	What are the deadlines? Do I need to have completed this task before my tutor comes next time, or in time for my annual review?

How to Use SMART objectives

1. Specific
Your goal should be clear and specific, otherwise you will not be able to focus your efforts or feel truly motivated to achieve it. When writing your goal, try to answer the five "W" questions:

- *What do I want to accomplish?*
- *Why is this goal important?*
- *Who is involved?*
- *Where is it located?*
- *Which resources or limits are involved?*

Example:
Imagine that you are currently a marketing executive, and you would like to become head of marketing. A specific goal could be, "I want to gain the skills and experience necessary to become head of marketing within my organisation, so that I can build my career and lead a successful team."

2. Measurable
It is important to have measurable goals, so that you can track your progress and stay motivated. Assessing progress helps you to stay focused, meet your deadlines, and feel the excitement of getting closer to achieving your goal.

Personal & Professional Development

- *A measurable goal should address questions such as:*
- *How much?*
- *How many?*
- *How will I know when it is accomplished?*

Example:
You might measure your goal of acquiring the skills to become head of marketing by determining that you will have completed the necessary training courses and gained the relevant experience within five years' time.

3. Achievable

Your goal also needs to be realistic and attainable to be successful. In other words, it should stretch your abilities but still remain possible. When you set an achievable goal, you may be able to identify previously overlooked opportunities or resources that can bring you closer to it.
An achievable goal will usually answer questions such as:

- *How can I accomplish this goal?*
- *How realistic is the goal, based on other constraints, such as financial factors?*

Example:
You might need to ask yourself whether developing the skills required to become head of marketing is realistic, based on your existing experience and qualifications. For example, do you have the time to complete the required training effectively? Are the necessary resources available to you? Can you afford to do it?

4. Relevant

This step is about ensuring that your goal matters to you, and that it also aligns with other relevant goals. Everyone needs support and assistance in achieving our goals, but it is important to retain control over them. So, make sure that your plans drive everyone forward, but that you are still responsible for achieving your own goal.

A relevant goal can answer "yes" to these questions:

- *Does this seem worthwhile?*
- *Is this the right time?*
- *Does this match our other efforts/needs?*
- *Am I the right person to reach this goal?*
- *Is it applicable in the current socio-economic environment?*

Example:
You might want to gain the skills to become head of marketing within your organisation, but is it the right time to undertake the required training, or work toward additional

Personal & Professional Development

qualifications? Are you sure that you are the right person for the head of marketing role? Have you considered your spouse's goals? For example, if you want to start a family, would completing training in your free time make this more difficult?

5. Time-bound
Every goal needs a target date, so that you have a deadline to focus on and something to work toward. This part of the SMART goal criteria helps to prevent everyday tasks from taking priority over your longer-term goals.

A time-bound goal will usually answer these questions:

- When?
- What can I do six months from now?
- What can I do six weeks from now?
- What can I do today?

Example:
Gaining the skills to become head of marketing may require additional training or experience. How long will it take you to acquire these skills? Do you need further training, so that you are eligible for certain exams or qualifications? It is important to give yourself a realistic time frame for accomplishing the smaller goals necessary to achieve your final objective.

Advantages and Disadvantages of SMART

SMART is an effective tool that provides the clarity, focus and motivation you need to achieve your goals. It can also improve your ability to reach them by encouraging you to define your objectives and set a completion date. SMART goals are also easy to use by anyone, anywhere, without the need for specialist tools or training.

When you use SMART, you can create clear, attainable and meaningful goals, and develop the motivation, action plan, and support needed to achieve them.

Personal & Professional Development

Learning Styles

Once objectives have been set and agreed, it helps to be aware of different learning styles so that we can focus on the most suitable learning activities.

Everyone has a preferred learning style that they use to develop their skills, experience and knowledge. Some like to learn by reading about things, others need to see a demonstration to understand something, and others need to try the activity themselves before they remember everything.

People have favourite ways of learning and training needs to be adapted to accommodate these preferences where possible.

These four styles are:

- **Visual** – seeing and watching – e.g., seeing pictures of how to make the product, or watching instruction videos
- **Auditory** – listening and speaking – e.g., being told how to make the product
- **Reading/writing** – e.g., reading instructions and writing personal notes
- **Kinaesthetic** – touching and doing – e.g., touching the components and actually making the product under supervision

According to this model, people have a dominant or preferred learning style.

When training team members, managers need to be prepared to use a combination of all four styles so that everyone's preferred learning style can be met.

- A visual learner will learn about a subject by looking at graphs, pictures and diagrams, or watching videos or demonstrations. Just being told about what to do will not register. Touching and doing the new activity will help to reinforce the learning at a basic level, but they will need to observe and read up on the details.

- A reading/writing learner will learn best from reading instructions, research and information about the subject, and writing notes to help them remember important details.

- An auditory learner will absorb the information by listening to their tutor or colleague, asking questions, then listening carefully to the answers.

- A kinaesthetic learner needs to touch and do the activity. They may absorb a reasonable amount of information from listening to the tutor or watching a demonstration, but they will not truly understand the subject or activity until they do it for themselves.

Personal & Professional Development

Learning and Development Activities

We can use a variety of learning and development activities, based inside or outside the workplace. It is better to choose a learning activity which is more closely associated with your preferred learning style.

A combination of activities can be put together to suit the individual's needs, goals and areas of weakness.

Activities may include, for example:

delegation – e.g., offering tasks to challenge the individual and give them the opportunity to develop their skills and experience.
demonstrations – e.g., watching demonstrations about how a new piece of equipment is used, then trying it out
role-play – e.g., to practise how to deal with angry customers' complaints.
job rotation – e.g., training people in a wide variety of tasks to aid flexibility and motivation.
shadowing – e.g., arranging for a trainee to follow an experienced member of staff for a week.
coaching and mentoring – e.g., giving intensive one-to-one support and guidance; having a senior member of staff as a role model
project work – e.g., expanding knowledge and experience by following through all aspects of a project, and not just isolated tasks.
classroom-based training courses – e.g., a first-aid course at the local college
computer-based training – e.g., induction courses to give an overview of the organisation and its policies and procedures.
Internet-based e-training – e.g., food safety knowledge, followed by an exam at an assessment centre to gain the full certificate.
blended learning – a mixture of different methods – e.g., a computer-based course in Spanish as well as conversation lessons at the local college
distance learning – e.g., a course done at work or at home, with the assistance of an assessor or a tutor who may be based miles away.
workplace training – e.g., internal training sessions on equality and diversity given by colleagues or external trainers.

You should identify the activities which suit your learning style and then identify the development opportunities available including the cost, duration, level, availability, etc.

Personal & Professional Development

Personal Development Plan (PDP)

A PDP is a document that is based on awareness, values, reflection, goal setting and planning for personal development. This can be at work, in education or in the context of self-improvement.

Employees who are taking part in personal, professional, development are typically asked to record their development by completing a PDP.

A Personal Development Plan is a written account of self-reflection and improvement, which doubles up as a detailed action plan used to identify ways to achieve academic, personal, or career-based goals.

It is usually created within the workplace or when studying (with guidance from your manager or tutor), and works by allowing you to establish your aims, recognise your strengths and weaknesses, and identify the need for improvement.

Objectives are put in place, based on the areas you would like to improve, and the plan consists of your own personalised actions that will help you to achieve them.

When creating a Personal Development Plan, it is essential to make sure it accurately outlines your personal goals, why they are important to you, and how you plan to achieve them.

Although all PDPs are specific to each individual, the plan will generally detail your ideal future based on your short and/or long-term ambitions. Areas of development will be specific to you, and could be centred on work, education, or self-improvement.

It should also always recognise the potential obstacles you might face, and how you propose to overcome them – and if the roadblocks cannot be tackled, include a contingency plan to help your career keep moving forward.

The PDP can also contain SWOT analyses, SMART objectives and other action plans about how to develop skills, knowledge, understanding and experience in the future.

When preparing a PDP, you will need to have identified:

- **clear SMART objectives** – Specific, Measurable, Achievable, Realistic and Time-bound
- **resource requirements** – e.g., learning activities, training materials or courses.
- **timescales and finances** – e.g., work and study deadlines or course fees
- **support mechanisms** – e.g., line manager, course tutor, workplace mentor or coach

Personal & Professional Development

Below is an example of a PDP:

Personal Development Plan

Name: Alex Smith	Job title: Senior Supervisor

Relevant Professional and Vocational qualifications:

- A level business studies, GCSE economics.
- Qualified first aider
- PTTLS (training qualification), qualified H&S induction trainer
- Level 2 team leading
- Level 2 customer service
- Level 3 diploma in management (part of the way through)

Date: 1 April 2021

Part 1 – Personal Analysis

Strengths	Weaknesses
Good listener, good communicator with team and customers Organised and able to meet deadlines. Planning and allocation of tasks Training – new and established team members Coordinating and planning resources needed by team. Confident following recruitment process Dealing with customer complaints (when team members need to escalate)	Can get distracted by interruptions – e.g., colleagues wanting something. Do not enjoy repetitive routine. Get frustrated when people waste my time. Feel that team members take advantage of me sometimes. Spending too much of my free time doing work jobs to catch up – e.g., emails and reports for 1-2 hours each evening at home

Personal & Professional Development

Opportunities	Threats
This is a good role to show my ability to work under pressure, solve problems and make decisions. Can demonstrate a good range of management and leadership skills. Team has 30 members now (24 last year), further 10-15 to be recruited and trained at end of 2017 – good opportunity to develop my M&L skills further, especially strategy and planning. Can consolidate current role and skills and start to think about going for promotion next year. I can ask for coaching and mentoring from line manager. My annual appraisal will give focus and be a source of guaranteed feedback	Time-management skills Work-life balance

Part 2 – Setting Objectives

Objective	Action	Resources and support mechanisms	How to measure success	Timescale and review dates
Finish L3 apprenticeship in leadership and Management	5 more units to go – complete 1 per week	Approx. 70 hours of study needed to finish – plus review time. Computer and Internet access Ask course tutor for extra feedback and support if necessary	Finish each assessment. Tutor feedback – work on weak areas & resubmit if necessary. L3 awarded	10 study hours per week if possible – so end of May, mid-June at the latest. Course tutor review booked next week
Improve my time management	Arrange coaching and self-study	Next unit on L3 course covers this. Ask line manager for coaching afterwards if needed	Less chaotic diary Reduction in stress Less work at home in the evenings	Next L3 unit will be done by mid-April. Review & ask for coaching if needed end June

Personal & Professional Development

Develop planning and strategy skills	Review records and data to track team changes. Develop plan for next stage of change	Recruitment, training and performance records for last 12 months Recruitment & training plans for next 12 months Customer and team feedback reports Line manager for support and feedback	Smooth transition to next stage with new staff Team members' performance records – to check quality, output and skills gaps	Review past records – by mid-June. Develop plan – by end June. Review team's progress & performance – ongoing
Maintain my motivation, enthusiasm and energy	Find ways to avoid too much repetitive work – e.g., delegate some tasks once they are established. Set new goals every so often. Discuss with line manager	Good team members Allocating sufficient time Discussion time with line manager	Job satisfaction will be maintained. Feedback from manager will help me to focus	Ask for extra appraisal review end July (approx. a month after L3 study has finished)

Part 3 – Personal Objectives

Short-term goals (next 3 months)

Finish L3 leadership and management
Start to prepare for having larger team.
Improve time management and stop working at home so much

Medium-term goals (next 12 months)

Consolidate current role this year and develop management skills with the larger team.
Start to discuss and plan promotion opportunities for next year

Long-term goals (beyond 12 months)

Promotion to customer services manager
Do a level 4 course – check funding nearer the time

Personal & Professional Development

Continuing Professional Development Log (CPD)

CPD stands for Continuing Professional Development (CPD) and is the term used to describe the learning activities professionals engage in to develop and enhance their abilities. It enables learning to become conscious and proactive, rather than passive and reactive. It may include life-long learning, maintaining the currency of skills and knowledge, developing occupational effectiveness, impact and achievement.

CPD is the holistic commitment of professionals towards the enhancement of personal skills and proficiency throughout their careers.

A CPD log combines and records the different methodologies undertaken for learning, such as training workshops, conferences and events, e-learning programs, best practice techniques and ideas sharing, completed by an individual over a period of time.

Development recorded in the PDP is transferred to the CPD Log when it has been satisfactorily completed.

Engaging in Continuing Professional Development ensures that both academic and practical qualifications do not become out-dated or obsolete, allowing individuals to continually 'up skill' or 're-skill' themselves, regardless of occupation, age or educational level.

Benefits of CPD.

For individuals
Continuing Professional Development helps individuals to regularly focus on how they can become a more competent and effective professional. Training and learning increase confidence and overall capability, and compliments career aspirations.

CPD enables individuals to adapt positively to changes in work/industry requirements. Recording CPD properly provides evidence of professional development (this can be useful for supervision and appraisals).

CPD log shows the individuals commitment to self-development and professionalism.

For organisations
Providing learning benefits the organisation by promoting a healthy learning culture leading to a more fulfilled workforce and retaining valuable staff.

Staff may have CPD obligations as members of professional bodies.

Personal & Professional Development

Allocating Time for CPD

Most institutes provide their members with Continuing Professional Development requirements generally as a minimum annual number of hours. These targets are defined by the accrual of CPD hours through training, seminars & workshops, events & conferences as well as other structured forms of CPD learning. These CPD hours are sometimes converted to points, units or credits. Most institutions allow members to choose subjects of relevance to them as individuals, a minority also require their members to seek CPD on a range of core subjects.

Recording CPD

An individual must keep a track of their annual Continuing Professional Development activities on a CPD log and must ensure it is correct, up to date and meets the requirements of their professional body or association.

The CPD activity is recorded in terms of learning outcomes and practical application of the knowledge obtained.

The Cost of Personal and Professional Development

Anything which is beneficial in our lives almost always comes at a cost and that is also true of Development. There can be a personal cost as well as a cost for the organisation. It is, however, true to say that the cost of development is often far outweighed by the benefits it brings.

The costs of development can include any or all of the following:

- *Financial cost of the training*
- *Time spent on training.*
- *Expenses involved in attending the training.*
- *The cost of providing mentors and coaches.*
- *Loss of production whilst training.*
- *Cost of replacement staff.*

There may also be additional cost regarding resources. It maybe that new software or machinery needs to be purchased to facilitate the development. It may be that structural alterations may be needed to facilitate this or additional resources such as PPE may need to be purchased. It may require that other staff need to be trained first to bring them to a standard whereby they can perform the task being left vacant by another staff member taking up their development.

ORGANISATION

Chapter 2: The Organisation

The Organisation

The Organisational Purpose

The Organisational Purpose does not explain what it does, but rather defines why it exists – what purpose does it serve.

Rather than asking the question - What do you do? it asks the question Why is the work you do important? The organisational purpose of a fast-food outlet might be to serve the public quickly and safely. It does not consider how it will achieve profits, set goals or targets, but simply states why it exists, what is it there to do.

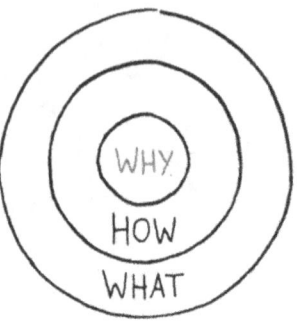

Purpose is fundamental to an organisation because it is the basis for all aspects of the business.

The management and employees must agree on the organisation's Purpose.

Employees must genuinely believe that the purpose is meaningful. If the purpose is not supported by employees, then a key factor in gaining employee engagement is missing.

In the bigger picture of any organisation, the purpose is at the very heart of its existence, everything else sits around this core purpose.

The table below contains some examples of purpose statements.

Organisation	Purpose
Facebook	We bring the world closer together
IKEA	We make everyday life better
Private Healthcare	We help people on their path to better health
Virgin Group	Changing Business for Good
Kellogg's	Nourishing families so they can flourish and thrive

The statement should be meaningful for employees, and easily understood. It must be more than just a cliched set of words. It must capture the emotion of the business. It must encourage employees to feel part of something positive and inspire them with the energy to achieve more. It should also be directed but improving society as a whole.

Purpose becomes even more important when you think about the world today and the challenges we all face. Organisations today are part of communities, societies and the planet. Purpose focusses on how the organisation makes a difference and this is a goal that can be extended to achieving a better world.

The Organisation

The understanding and use of organisational purpose has changed over the years.

Organisations used only to view their purpose as way to make money. Managers believed that making money was the only reason they were in business. They believed employees would be motivated and engaged with this narrow view.

Organisations must make money to stay in business, and employees need to make money to support themselves and their families. However, once a worker has sufficient money to live, making money as a purpose is no longer valid and therefore the purpose ceases to be of importance.

Organisations also view their purpose from their customers perspective. If what the organisation does made things better in some way for those they serve, then that too is a meaningful purpose. It does not take long to realise that purpose is not just a contribution to external issues. It must also be a contribution for the people who work there.

If an organisation chooses improving health and well-being as its purpose, it would be wrong if the company only sought to improve the health and wellbeing of their customers. Employees cannot be expected to work each day to improve the health of "others" when the company neglects the health and well-being of its employees. The focus of purpose has grown from just being customer focused to also being employee focused.

Today, the visionary organisations have expanded their view on Purpose still further. An organisation is more than a vehicle for serving employees and customers. Organisations today recognise they must also make a meaningful impact on the communities it serves, to the society at large, and even to the planet.

If you are creating a purpose statement, you must - inspire your staff to do good work for you, find a way to express the organisation's impact on the lives of all stakeholders and make sure it has an emotional impact so they can "feel" it.

The Organisation

Mission, Vision and Value Statements

In the latter part of the 20th century organisations began to introduce Statements or Charters which were aimed at telling people why the organisation existed, what it did and how it did it. Today, successful businesses have moved on from issuing lengthy, wordy, statements that no employee can understand, never mind remember.

Today it is common to have three concise company statements:

The Vision Statement

A vision statement is a statement of an organisation's overarching aspirations of what it hopes to achieve or to become. Here are some examples of vision statements:

> **Disney:** To make people happy
> **IKEA:** To create a better everyday life for the many people
> **British Broadcasting Company (BBC):** To be the most creative organisation in the world
> **Avon:** To be the company that best understands and satisfies the product, service and self-fulfilment needs of women—globally
> **Sony Corporation:** To be a company that inspires and fulfils your curiosity

The vision statement does not provide specific targets. Notice that each of the above examples could apply to many different organisations. Instead, the vision is a broad description of the value an organisation provides. It is a visual image of what the organisation is trying to produce or become. It should inspire people and motivate them to want to be part of and contribute to the organisation.

Vision statements should be clear and concise, usually not longer than a short paragraph.

The Organisation

The Mission Statement

The vision statement and mission statement are often confused, and many companies use the terms interchangeably. However, they each have a different purpose. The vision statement describes where the organisation wants to be in the future – the dream! the mission statement describes what the organisation needs to do now to achieve the vision – the how!

The vision and mission statements must support each other, but the mission statement is more specific. It defines how the organisation will be different from other organisations in its industry. Here are examples of mission statements from successful businesses:

> **Adidas:** We strive to be the global leader in the sporting goods industry with brands built on a passion for sports and a sporting lifestyle.
> **Amazon:** We seek to be Earth's most customer-centric company for four primary customer sets: consumers, sellers, enterprises, and content creators.
> **Google:** To organise the world's information and make it universally accessible and useful

Each of these examples indicates where the organisation will compete (what industry it is in) and how it will compete (what it will do to be different from other organisations). The mission statement conveys to stakeholders why the organisation exists. It explains how it creates value for the market or the larger community.

Because it is more specific, the mission statement is more actionable than the vision statement. By describing why, the organisation exists, and where and how it will compete, the mission statement allows leaders to define a coherent set of goals that fit together to support the mission.

> ***The mission statement leads to the creation of strategic goals.***

Strategic goals are the broad goals the organisation will try to achieve.

Today, most businesses have a Mission Statement – whether it is a formal statement emblazoned on publicity materials, websites, etc or an informal statement which is used in house as a reference.

It is important for every organisation to have its mission and vision statements as it serves as a guide when it comes to decision making and alignment.

The Organisation

The Values Statement

The values statement, also called the code of ethics, differs from both the vision and mission statements. The vision and mission statements define where the organisation is going (vision) and what it will do to get there (mission). They direct the efforts of people in the organisation toward common goals.

The values statement defines what the organisation believes in and how people in the organisation are expected to behave—with each other, with customers and suppliers, and with other stakeholders. It provides a moral direction for the organisation that guides decision making and establishes a standard for assessing actions. It also provides a standard for employees to judge exceptions.

> ***Managers cannot just create a values statement and expect it to be followed.***

For a values statement to be effective, it must be reinforced at all levels of the organisation and must be used to guide attitudes and actions. Organisations with strong values follow their values even when it may be easier not to. Levi Strauss & Co is an excellent example of a company that is driven by its values.

> *When Levi Strauss began to outsource its manufacturing overseas, the company developed a set of principles for overseas operations and suppliers. One of the principles covered the use of child labour:*
>
> *Use of child labour is not permissible. Workers can be no less than 15 years of age and not younger than the compulsory age to be in school. We will not utilise partners who use child labour in any of their facilities. We support the development of legitimate workplace apprenticeship programs for the educational benefit of younger people.*
>
> *Levi Strauss found that one of its contractors was employing children under 15 in a factory in Bangladesh. The easy solution would be to replace the contractor, but in Bangladesh, the children's wages may have supported an entire family. If they lost their jobs, they may have had to resort to begging on the streets.*
>
> *Levi Strauss came up with a different solution, one that supported its values of empathy, originality, integrity, and courage: it paid the children to go to school. Levi Strauss continued to pay salaries and benefits to the children and paid for tuition, books, and supplies. Even though it would have been easier to just fire the child laborers and consider the problem settled, Levi Strauss was driven by its values to find a better solution.*

Together, the vision, mission, and values statements provide direction for everything that happens in an organisation. They keep everyone focused on where the organisation is going and what it is trying to achieve. They define the core values of the organisation and how people are expected to behave. They are not intended to be a straitjacket that restricts or inhibits initiative and innovation, but they are intended to guide decisions and behaviours to achieve common ends.

The Organisation

Customer Service Statement

In the 21st century, competition has never been greater, customer choice has never been wider and the needs and demands of customers is constantly changing. As a result, these three statements are no longer enough – today a business must also address Customer Service with a clear statement about Customer Service within the organisation.

In some instances, this may be included in the Mission Statement, but increasingly organisations are producing separate statements which detail exactly what type of customer service you want your company to provide to its customers.

Think of a mission statement for a football team – it may be "to win the Premier League title". However, that is not what the defenders or midfielders will say to each other at the start of the match!

Winning the Premier League is a result, not the action. The Customer Service Statement would be how the game would be played. This one statement is the one every employee in the organisation must be able to understand and know it backwards and forwards.

The Customer Service Statement is what each and every employee, regardless of department, level, or wage, must deliver to every Customer, every time. It provides a meaningful purpose for the employees.

The Customer Service Statement is never shared with the outside public, i.e., Customers. It is only used by the employees.

The Disney vision: – *To make people happy – is just that - a vision. It is the Customer Service Statement which will define how the employees can achieve that.*

The Organisation

Organisational Strategies

Organisational strategy is a combination of a clear vision, coupled with a meaningful mission and purpose, underlined with some clear steps to make sure the right resources and plans are in place to achieve outcome-based goals.

An organisational strategy is the sum of the actions a company intends to take to achieve long term goals, and these will help to form a strategic plan.

The strategic plans will need involvement from all levels within the organisation. Whilst managers at the top will create the organisational strategy, middle and lower management will help by looking at the step-by-step actions that are needed to fulfil the goals to achieve the overall strategy. This collaboration is like a journey, where each step must be satisfied to enable the journey to continue which leads to the ultimate destination.

> *Building a culture where employees understand the organisational strategy and purpose, have buy-in to the business and team objectives, and want to develop ideas that creates continuous improvement, is a culture that has the 'hearts and minds' of the people.*

Together, these actions make up the organisation's strategic plan.

Strategic Plans

Strategic plans take at least a year to complete, requiring involvement from all company levels. Top management creates the larger organisational strategy, while middle and lower management adopt goals and plans to fulfil the overall strategy step by step.

This unified effort can be likened to a journey. The journey starts at the point we are at today and ends at the ultimate destination. The route to get there will be formulated and the road conditions encountered on the journey are the challenges which need to be overcome to complete each stage of the journey, which will eventually lead to the ultimate destination.

Effective planning usually results in a written strategic plan. This is a formalised document that describes the business' goals, and the actions needed to achieve them.

The Purpose of Strategic Planning

Strategic planning is a systematic process that helps to set an ambition for the business' future and determine how best to achieve it. Its primary purpose is to connect three key areas:

The Organisation

the mission - *defining your business' purpose*
the vision - *describing what you want to achieve*
the plan - *outlining how you want to achieve your ultimate goals*

Importance of Strategic Planning

Strategic planning is necessary to determine the direction for your organisation. It focuses your efforts and ensures that everyone in the business is working towards a common goal. It also helps you:

- *agree actions that will contribute to business growth*
- *align resources for optimal results*
- *prioritise financial needs*
- *build competitive advantage*
- *engage with your staff and communicate what needs to be done*

Another significant purpose of strategic planning is to help to manage and reduce business risks.

Growing a business is inherently risky. Detailed planning may help to:

- *remove uncertainty*
- *analyse potential risks*
- *implement risk control measures*
- *consider how to minimise the impact of risks, should they occur*

There are a variety of models and approaches which can be beneficial in strategic planning. Many businesses include a SWOT analysis or a PESTLE analysis as key elements of their strategic plan.

The Organisation

SWOT Analysis

Managers can produce these quickly and simply to help to clarify their thinking and focus their attention on all aspects of the problem. A SWOT analysis is particularly useful for gathering, interpreting and analysing information. For each realistic possible solution, managers can analyse the following:

- S – *Strengths*
- W – *Weaknesses*
- O – *Opportunities*
- T – *Threats to success*

If your car has been causing you problems, a SWOT analysis could show, for example:

	Option A – *have it fixed every time to keep it going for as long as possible – maybe another year*	**Option B** – *replace the car with a brand-new, up-to-date version that should last ten years*	**Option C** – *replace it with a second hand, model that should last five years*
Strengths	Not too expensive to run The problems are well-known and familiar	Good reliability Up-to-date technology Good warranty support	Reasonable cost Its service history should indicate reliability Know how to operate it
Weaknesses	Cost of repairs Frequent disruption of your life that cannot be planned Drop in your efficiency and performance	Very expensive May have to make sacrifices Will be difficult to look after properly	Does not benefit from the most up-to-date technology and design Only a short warranty Could develop problems at any time
Opportunities	Easy to arrange with garage for repairs	Three possible suppliers Available in about two months	Plenty available if researched online Could be bought quickly as changes to storage arrangements not needed
Threats to success	Garage staff may refuse to repair it when it breaks again. Repair costs are high. Wages could be lost due to delays	Cost and budget constraints Might be outdated after a few years Personal benefits may not justify cost	Cost might not be justifiable if planning to keep it for less than five years

Although a SWOT analysis does not give a magic answer to the problem, it does help managers to identify the pros and cons of each option. Once they know their budget

The Organisation

constraints and the long-term targets, the decision makers would be able to identify the best solution to the problem.

PESTLE Analysis

Another system that could be used when wishing to make well-informed decisions is a PESTLE analysis.

This can be particularly useful when there are areas of concern, outside of the control of the organisation, and for gathering, interpreting and analysing information.

For example, if the problem is that the company has outgrown its present site and is considering solutions to the problem, it will have to consider many things that are outside its control. When doing a PESTLE analysis, managers would look at these areas:

P	Political	e.g., government funding for expanding in the same area or setting up in a different location
E	Economic	e.g., the overall economic climate and whether stakeholders would support investment and expansion if the economy is slow or in recession
S	Social	e.g., the effect on the local population if the company moves away/stays put and expands
T	Technological	e.g., the scope for using new technology as part of the expansion plans
L	Legal	e.g., legal requirements about redundancies or relocation of staff
E	Environmental	e.g., the regulations on emissions and waste management in the current area and the potential new area

You may also want to include an implementation schedule, key performance indicators (KPIs) and other accountability measures.

Factors Affecting an Organisation

You may often hear the term *trend* in relation to the way an organisation of the economy is performing. These trends are often caused by a variety of influences which might include:

- *Governments*
- *International trading activity*
- *Speculation and expectation*
- *Supply and demand*

The Organisation

These are known as Market Forces and are the factors that influence the price and availability of goods and services in a market economy, i.e., an economy with the minimum of government involvement.

Market forces push prices up when supply declines and demand rises and drive them down when supply grows or demand contracts. When demand equals supply for a product or service, the market is said to have reached equilibrium

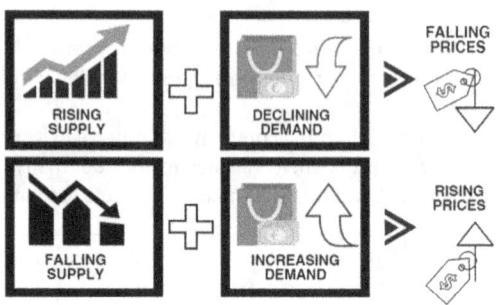

Government
Governments across the World have a great deal of influence how business trades both within their own borders and more widely at an international level. The fiscal and monetary policies that governments and the central banks put in place will have a profound effect on the economy.

The Government will increase or decrease taxes as it sees necessary. If it needs to raise money, it will raise taxes. If it wants to stimulate the economy, create jobs and encourage investment, it will reduce taxes, freeing up money to be spent thus boosting the economy. This is known as monetary policy.

The Bank of England has the power to set and adjust interest rates and these are used as a brake or accelerator on the UK economy. Lower interest rates mean it is cheaper to borrow money and therefore there is an inclination to spend. This will lead to an upturn in trade as people buy goods and services meaning the volume of trade increases and business becomes mor profitable.

Conversely, when interest rates are increased, it causes the economy to shrink. Money becomes more expensive to borrow and because repayments against debts is increasing, there is a reduced amount of money available for spending elsewhere and so the economy contracts. This is known as monetary policy.

International Trade
The way in which money flows between countries affects the strength of a country's economy and its currency. The more money that is leaving a country, the weaker the country's economy and its currency becomes. Countries that are predominantly exporters of goods and services are continually bringing money into their countries.

The Organisation

This money can then be reinvested and can stimulate the financial markets within those countries.

Prior to Brexit, the United Kingdom traded goods and services around the World under trade agreements which were agreed by the European Union. This meant that the international trade helped to support the Euro as well as the Pound. Now the UK has left the European Union, it is now seeking trade agreements around the World to enable independent trade which will boost the UK economy and strengthen the value of the pound against other international currencies.

Speculation and Expectation
Speculation and expectation are integral parts of the financial system. Huge amounts of money are made on the international money markets by trading in foreign currencies and shares. News of a major takeover of an organisation will prompt dealers to buy shares because such activity is a sign the business is doing well, and the share value will rise. Likewise, the money markets will respond in a similar way to the news that Governments are to reduce taxes or lower interest rates, indicating that the economy is buoyant. Future action is dependent on current activity and this type of speculation shapes both current and future trends.

Supply and Demand
Supply and demand has long been a key theme for economists' organisations which manufacture or sell goods or services. The greater the demand, the higher the price that can be charged for an item. If there is no demand for a product the price will be reduced to tempt people to buy something which is far less popular than other items on the marketplace. This is true for everything from consumer goods to aeroplanes! Who wants to buy a Turkey in January? Think about new cars = how many people are still buying petrol- or diesel-powered cars when we know that they will be banned in the near future and fuel may become difficult and expensive to buy.

If something is in demand and supply begins to shrink, prices will rise. If supply increases beyond current demand, prices will fall. If supply is relatively stable, prices can fluctuate higher and lower as demand increases or decreases.

Policy and Regulatory Change
Policy and regulatory change means that the government are changing the rules. These changes will impact heavily on organisations across all sectors and because the change is a government action, they must be complied with businesses must change to meet their new requirements.

This may be changes to taxation such as increases to VAT, corporate taxation, personal taxation or a range of other levies and duties which the government is able to apply. All of this will have an impact on the businesses which it affects.

One of the most common examples of policy and regulatory change is the annual change to the national minimum wage. Each year the government decides what the national minimum wage should be based on a number of criteria including the retail

The Organisation

price index, inflation, etc. and then sets the minimum amount of money an employer must pay an employee per hour for the next 12 months.

There may also be changes to tariffs and training policies. This is currently affecting the United Kingdom as, following Brexit, the United Kingdom must renegotiate trade deals with other countries across the world otherwise there is a requirement to trade under World Trade Organisation rules which apply fixed tariffs to the import and export of goods.

Free trade agreements allow all such trade to take place without there being any tariffs applied. The United Kingdom now has a limited trade policy with the European Union whereby the majority of goods may be traded free of tariff, providing that certain quotas are not exceeded, or the other policy changes do not make those particular goods more favourable than those available in the EU states.

Another example of policy and regulatory change is the use of subsidies. Governments may choose to subsidise certain sectors or industries using government money to allow the goods or services to be sold internationally or locally at discounted prices. It is common for Governments to subsidise the cost of public transport to encourage people to use it rather than using their own personal transport to reduce congestion or emission. This is a practise which is also being used in China where the government subsidises the cost of production of some goods and in some cases, the cost of postage to other countries around the world for goods which are sold online from China.

GDPR is another example of regulatory activity which is impacted on businesses. GDPR was introduced to protect data which is being collected and stored in every increasing quantities, from abuse or misuse by other organisations or countries. The impact on business has been significant.

Many organisations have had to introduce new policies, procedures and methods of working to ensure compliance with GDPR and others have also had to make major changes to the information they collect from websites, social media and other platforms in common use today. This has not only affected businesses in the UK, the GDPR regulations were part of European law, which has further impacted across the World as the regulations apply to data which is collected from citizens of the nations who fall under the GDPR regulations. This means other continents have also had to accommodate these changes, but more importantly, it serves as a warning that they too may soon be subject to similar policy changes to ensure data protection within their borders as well.

Supply Chain
The supply chain of an organisation is critical. In its most basic form, the supply chain is all the activities required by an organisation to deliver goods or services to its customer.

The Organisation

The supply chain focuses on the core activities of the organisation which are required to convert raw materials or component parts through manufacturing to the finished product or service and onward to its customers who will sell into the marketplace.

Even a simple supply chain will have a significant number of stages to it and at every stage there is the possibility of problems arising which could disrupt the steady flow of production of goods from raw materials to finished goods and delivery to the point of sale.

Even the production of a simple loaf of bread has a supply chain more complex that might initially be imagined. At each stage, the process can be frustrated by situations and circumstances which are totally beyond the control of the organisation. As a result, the production of the item could be slowed or even stopped whilst a totally unrelated issues is resolved elsewhere.

Organisations today work on a just in time stock holding basis where they may only hold sufficient stock for about one to two hours production before they are unable to continue. This is commonly used on car production lines, so if they run out of a single component because the supply chain is disrupted, it will bring the whole production line to a halt. The scale and severity of the problems this type of supply chain disruption can cause needs no explanation.

Take a look at the supply chain task below for a loaf of bread and try to identify the possible frustrations which could arise at each stage. Remember! This supply chain is just for one ingredient, there are four others used in a loaf of bread without considering packaging, etc!

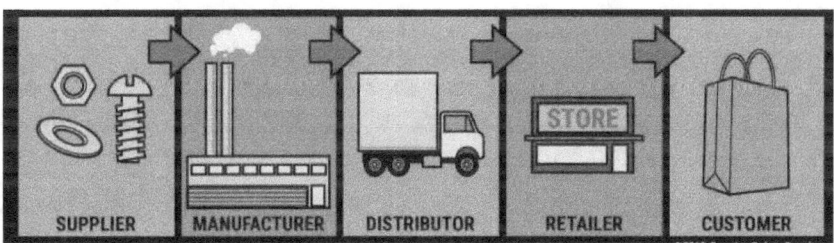

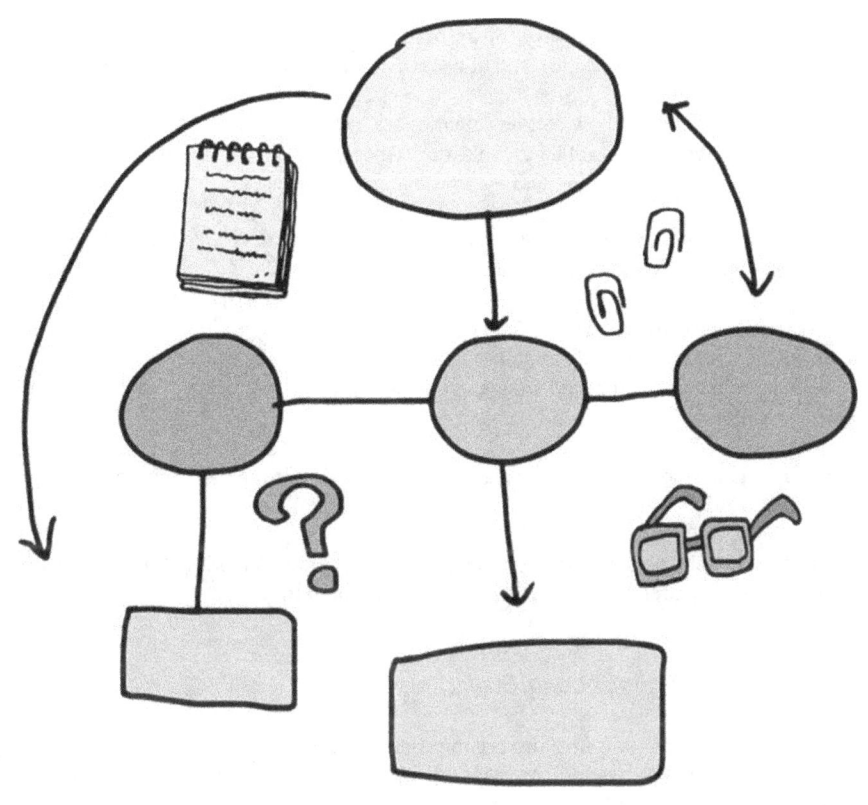

Chapter 3: Value of Skills

Value of Skills

Organisational Structure

An organisational structure is a visual diagram of a company that describes what employees do, who they report to, and how decisions are made across the business.

It is a system that outlines how certain activities are directed to achieve the goals of an organisation. These activities can include rules, roles, and responsibilities.

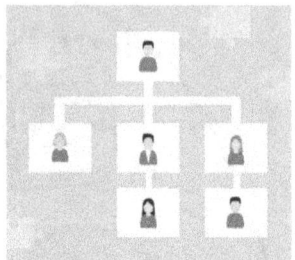

The organisational structure also determines how information flows between levels within the company.

In a centralised structure, decisions flow from the top down, while in a decentralised structure, responsibility for decision-making is distributed among various levels of the organisation.

Having an organisational structure in place allows companies to remain efficient and focused.

The organisational structure also identifies where an individual sits within the organisation and indicates the people who report to them and to whom they report.

Understanding Organisational Structures

Businesses of all shapes and sizes use organisational structures. They define the hierarchy within an organisation. A successful organisational structure defines each employee's job and how it fits within the overall system. At its simplest level, the organisational structure lays out who does what in order that the company can meet its objectives.

This structuring provides a company with a visual representation of how it is shaped and how it can best move forward in achieving its goals. Organisational structures are normally illustrated in some sort of chart or diagram like a pyramid, where the most powerful members of the organisation sit at the top, while those with the least amount of power are at the bottom.

Not having a formal structure in place may prove difficult for certain organisations. For instance, employees may have difficulty knowing who they should report to. That can lead to uncertainty as to who is responsible for what in the organisation.

Having a structure in place can help with efficiency and provide clarity for everyone at every level. That also means departments can be more productive, as they are likely to be more focused on energy and time.

Value of Skills

Mechanistic vs. Organic Organisational Structures

Organisational structures lie on a scale, with "mechanistic" at one end and "organic" at the other.

The mechanistic structure represents the traditional, top-down approach to organisational structure, whereas the organic structure represents a more collaborative, flexible approach.

Mechanistic Structure

Mechanistic structures, also called bureaucratic structures, are known for having narrow spans of control, as well as high centralisation, specialisation, and formalisation. They are also quite rigid in what specific departments are designed and permitted to do for the company.

This organisational structure is much more formal than an organic structure, using specific standards and practices to govern every decision the business makes. While this model does hold staff more accountable for their work, it can become a hindrance to the creativity and agility the organisation needs to keep up with random changes in its market.

As daunting and inflexible as mechanistic structure sounds, the chain of command, whether long or short, is always clear under this model. As a company grows, it needs to make sure everyone (and every team) knows what is expected of them. An informal structure where Teams are collaborating with others might help get a business off the ground in its early stages but sustaining that growth -- with more people and projects to keep track of will eventually require some policymaking and formalisation. It is therefore advisable to keep plans for a mechanistic structure in reserve as you never know when you will need it.

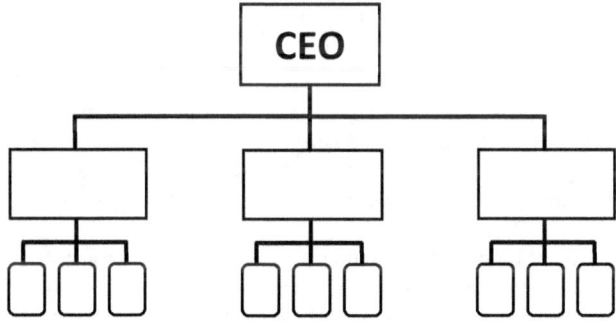

Value of Skills

Organic Structure

Organic structures (also known as "flat" structures) are known for their wide spans of control, decentralisation, low specialisation, and loose departmentalisation. This model may have multiple teams answering to one person and taking on projects based on their importance and what the team is capable of -- rather than what the team is designed to do.

This organisational structure is much less formal than a mechanistic structure and takes a bit of an ad-hoc approach to business needs. This can sometimes make the chain of command, whether long or short, difficult to decipher. As a result, leaders might give certain projects the green light more quickly but cause confusion in a project's division of labour.

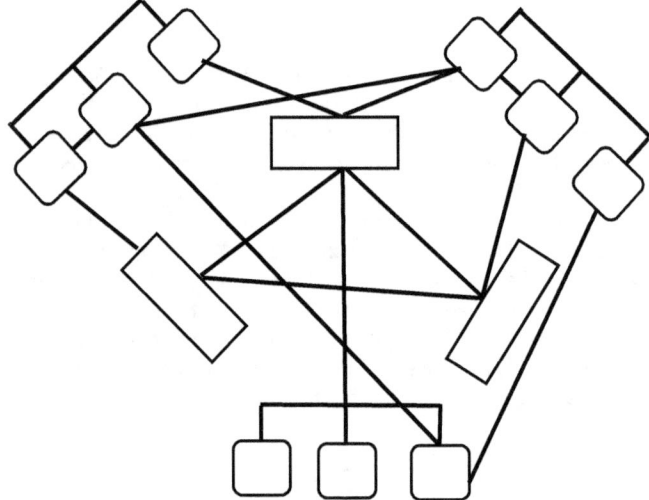

Nonetheless, the flexibility that an organic structure allows for can be extremely helpful to a business that is navigating a fast-moving industry, or simply trying to stabilise itself after a difficult period. It also empowers employees to try new things and develop as professionals, making the organisation's workforce more powerful in the long run.

Start-ups are often perfect for organic structures as they usually comprise only a few employees at the outset and as new staff join the haphazard organic structure is formed. Whilst the organisation remains small, there is little justification for changing the structure but as more people are engaged the diversity of roles will increase and a formal structure will begin to form naturally at which point a formal structure should be implemented.

Value of Skills

Types of Organisational Structure

In between the Mechanistic and organic structures on the spectrum discussed above, there are a range of different structures which impose differing degrees of control. Some of these are considered below.

Functional Structure
The choice of structure for each organisation is dependent very much on what they do and the activities they undertake. The Technology industry works under a very different organisational structure to that of the manufacturing industry of fifty years ago. The most common is a functional structure. This is also referred to as a bureaucratic or mechanistic organisational structure and breaks up a company based on the specialisation of its workforce.

A functional organisational structure is based on each job's duties.

Most small-to-medium-sized businesses implement a functional structure. Dividing the firm into departments consisting of marketing, sales, and operations is the act of using a bureaucratic or mechanistic organisational structure.

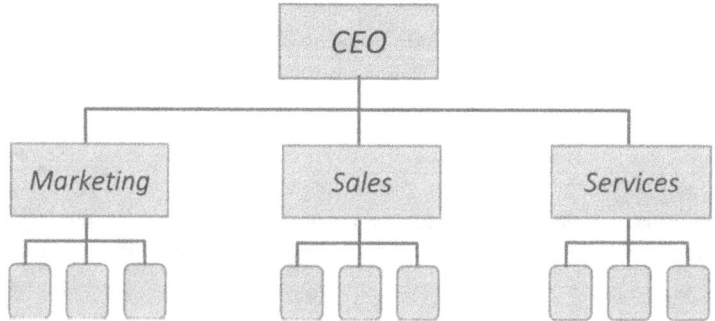

The functional structure allows for a high degree of specialisation for employees and is easily scalable should the organisation grow. Also, this structure is mechanistic in nature -- which has the potential to inhibit an employee's growth -- putting staff in skill-based departments can still allow them to delve deep into their field and find out what they are good at.

Disadvantages
A Functional structure also has the potential to create barriers between different functions -- and it can be inefficient if the organisation has a variety of different products or target markets. The barriers created between departments can also limit peoples' knowledge of and communication with other departments, especially those that depend on other departments to succeed.

Value of Skills

Divisional or Multi-divisional Structure

Divisional structures are common among large companies with many business units. A company that uses this method structures its leadership team based on the products, projects, or subsidiaries they operate. A good example of this structure is Johnson & Johnson. With thousands of products and lines of business, the company structures itself, so each business unit operates as its own company with its own president.

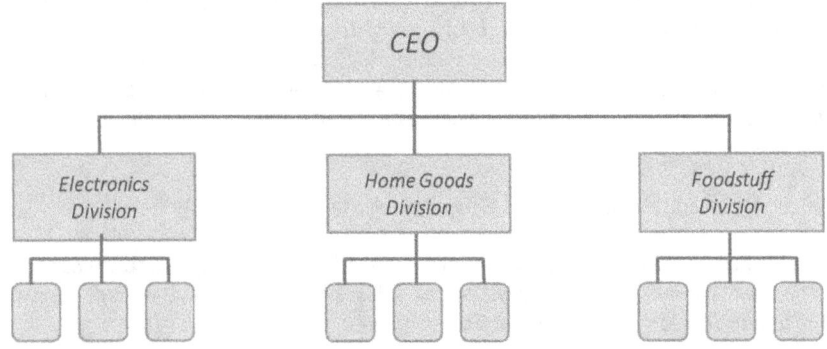

This type of structure is ideal for organisations with multiple products and can help shorten product development cycles. This allows small businesses to go to market with new offerings fast.

Disadvantages

It can be difficult to scale under a product-based divisional structure, and the organisation could end up with duplicate resources as different divisions strive to develop new offerings.

Market-Based Divisional Structure

A variant of the divisional organisational structure is the market-based structure, where the divisions of an organisation are based around markets, industries, or customer types.

The market-based structure is ideal for an organisation that has products or services that are unique to specific market segments and is particularly effective if that organisation has advanced knowledge of those segments. This organisational structure also keeps the business constantly aware of demand changes among its different audience segments.

Value of Skills

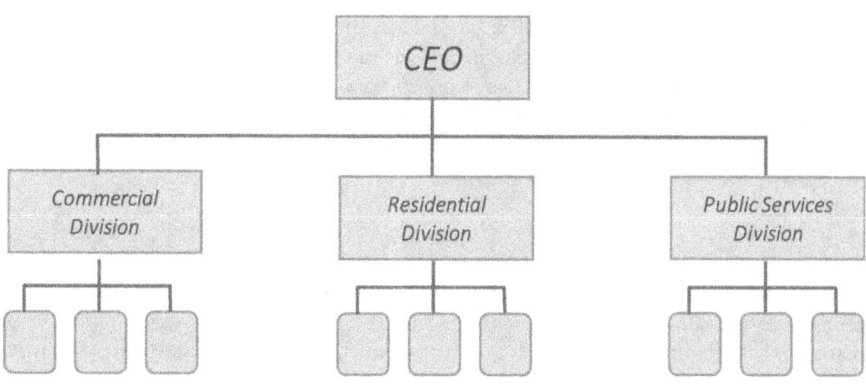

Disadvantages
Too much autonomy within each market-based team can lead to divisions resulting in systems that are incompatible with one another. Divisions might also end up inadvertently duplicating activities and resources that other divisions are already handling.

Geographical Divisional Structure
The geographical organisational structure establishes its divisions based on location. More specifically, the divisions of a geographical structure can include territories, regions, or districts.

This type of structure is best suited to organisations that need to be near sources of supply and/or customers (e.g., for deliveries or for on-site support). It also brings together many forms of business expertise, allowing each geographical division to make decisions from more diverse points of view.

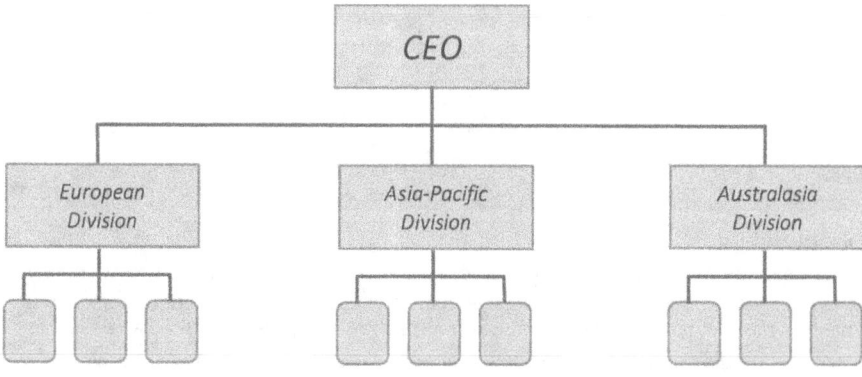

Value of Skills

Disadvantages
The main downside of a geographical organisational structure is that it can be easy for decision making to become decentralised, because the geographic divisions (which can be hundreds, if not thousands of miles away from corporate headquarters) often have a great deal of autonomy and independence. Likewise, when you have a marketing department for each region, you run the risk of creating campaigns that compete with (and weaken) other divisions across your digital channels.

Flat Structure
While a more traditional organisational structure might look more like a pyramid -- with multiple tiers of supervisors, managers and directors between staff and senior management, the flat structure limits the levels of management, so all staff are only a few steps away from leadership. It also might not always take the form or a pyramid, or any shape for that matter. As we mentioned earlier, it is also a form of the "Organic Structure" identified above.

This structure is probably one of the most detailed, it is also thought that employees can be more productive in an environment where there is less hierarchy-related pressures. The structure may also make staff feel like the managers they have are more like equals or team members rather than intimidating superiors.

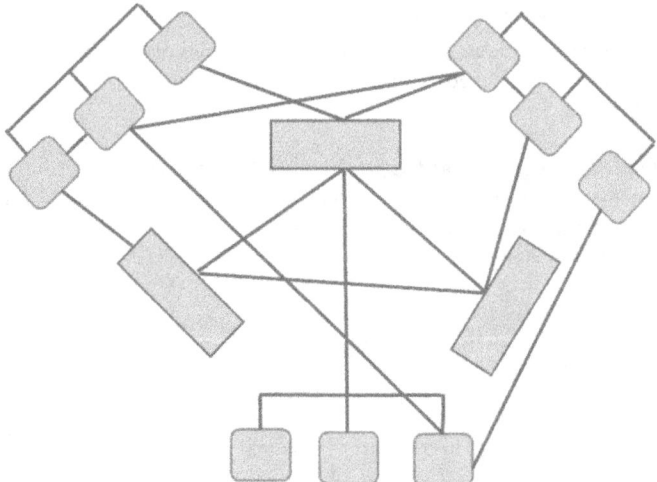

Disadvantages
When teams in a flat organisation disagree on something, such as a project, it can be hard to realign and get back on track without executive decisions from a leader or manager. The complicated structure's design makes it difficult to determine which manager an employee should go to if they need approval or an executive decision for something. When using a flat organisation, there should always be a clearly marked tier of management or path that employers can refer to when they run into these scenarios.

Value of Skills

Matrix Structure

The matrix structure is the most confusing and the least used. This structure matrixes employees across different superiors, divisions, or departments. An employee working for a matrixed company, for example, may have duties in both sales and customer service.

The main appeal of the matrix structure is that it can provide both flexibility and more balanced decision-making (as there are two chains of command instead of just one). Having a single project overseen by more than one business line also creates opportunities for these business lines to share resources and communicate more openly with each other -- things they might not otherwise be able to do regularly.

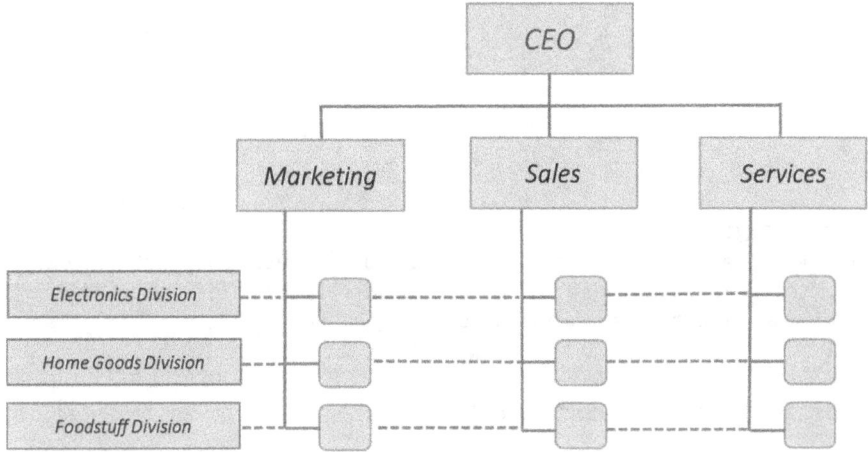

Disadvantages

The primary pitfall of the matrix organisational structure is its complexity. The more layers of approval employees must go through, the more confused they can be about who they are supposed to answer to. This confusion can ultimately cause frustration over who has authority over which decisions and products -- and who is responsible for those decisions when things go wrong.

Circular Structure

Whilst it appears markedly different from the other organisational structures. The circular structure still relies on hierarchy, with more senior employees occupying the inner rings of the circle and lower-level employees occupying the outer rings. The leaders or executives in a circular organisation should not be seen as sitting at the top of the organisation, sending directives down the chain of command, instead, they are at the centre of the organisation, spreading their vision outward.

The circular structure is meant to promote communication and the free flow of information between different parts of the organisation. A traditional structure shows different departments or divisions as occupying individual, semi-autonomous branches, the circular structure depicts all divisions as being part of the same whole.

Value of Skills

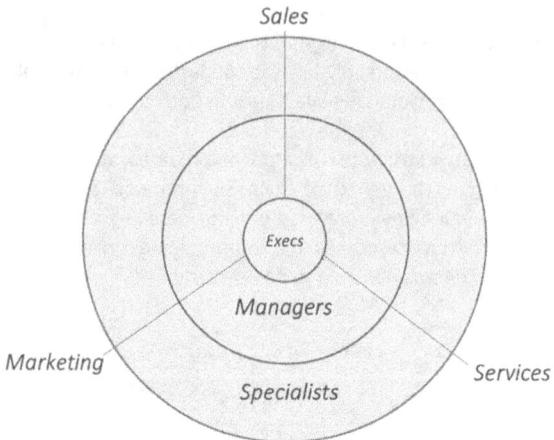

Disadvantages

From a practical perspective, the circular structure can be confusing, especially for new employees. A circular structure can make it difficult for employees to figure out who they report to and how they are meant to fit into the organisation.

Benefits of Organisational Structures

Putting an organisational structure in place is beneficial to a company. The structure not only defines a company's hierarchy, but it also allows the firm to set out the pay structure for its employees. The structure also makes operations more efficient and much more effective. By separating employees and functions into different departments, the company can perform different operations at once seamlessly.

Job Descriptions to Allow for Growth

When an organisational structure is implemented, job descriptions can be developed to not only meet the organisation's goals but allow for organisational and employee growth. Internal equity and employee retention are a key to successful operations. Recruitment is also one of the highest investments for organisations, so ensuring employees have promotional opportunities and job security can assist in reducing recruitment costs.

Allow for Organisational Expansion

If an organisation expands, the organisational structure allows room for growth. This can include adding additional layers of management, new divisions, expanding one or several functional areas or appointing additional top executives. When the structure is reorganised for expansion, it provides the mechanism to edit salaries and job descriptions quickly and efficiently with minimal disruption to an organisation's operations. Within these structures, management will have a variety of roles and functions and these will differ depending on the structure chosen for the organisation.

Value of Skills

Organisational Roles

Management roles may include but are not limited to responsibility, accountability, authority, autonomy, reporting structures, inter-dependences between functional areas (e.g., HR, finance, marketing, customer services and production), teams, colleagues, customers, suppliers, contractors, partnerships, communication, managing budgets and resources, procurement, input into strategic planning.

Roles in the Team

In the past thirty years or so, team working has grown in importance. Until relatively recently, roles at work were well-defined. In the traditional factory, for example, there was strict division of responsibilities and most job titles conveyed exactly what people did. With advances in technology and education, employers began to place a growing emphasis on versatility, leading to an increasing interest in team working at all levels. The gradual replacement of traditional hierarchical forms with flatter organisational structures, in which employees are expected to fill a variety of roles, has also played a part in the rise of the team.

What is a team?
There are numerous definitions, but a team can be simply defined as:

a limited number of people who have shared objectives at work and who co-operate, on a permanent or temporary basis, to achieve those objectives in a way that allows each individual to make a distinctive contribution.

Types of Team

There are many types of teams. What follows is not a comprehensive list, and there are other typologies or classifications.

> **Production and service teams** - examples are in production, construction, sales and health care. They have a relatively long lifespan, providing an ongoing product or service to customers or the organisation.
>
> **Project and development teams** - including research and product development teams. They are dedicated to a particular objective and have limited lifespans and a clear set of short-term objectives. They are often cross-functional, with members selected for the contribution their expertise can make.

Value of Skills

Advice and involvement teams - with the aim of improving, for example, working conditions or quality. Members will not devote a great deal of time to them, and once they have achieved their objectives they should be disbanded.

Crews - such as airline crews, who may be formed from people who have rarely worked together but through prior training clearly understand their respective roles.

Action and negotiation teams - such as surgical and legal teams, consist of people who tend to work together regularly. They have well-developed processes and clear objectives.

Virtual teams - who work in separate buildings and who may even be in different countries. Such teams may also fit into one of the above categories, such as project and development. They may need to communicate by telephone, e-mail and tele-conferencing rather than face-to-face.

Managing virtual teams is particularly difficult, not least because remote working can exacerbate misunderstandings.

Self-managed teams - where much decision-making is devolved from line managers to team members. (Also known as semi-autonomous or fully autonomous teams according to the degree of self-management.) Again, such teams may also fit into one of the above categories. The 1998 Workplace Employee Relations Survey suggested that the positive benefits of team working may be largely associated with such teams, rather than teams in general. Fully or semi-autonomous teams tend to have higher than average levels of labour productivity; a lower rate of voluntary resignations; lower levels of employee dismissals, and a better than average employee relations climate.

Normally, teams will consist of people from the same employer, but sometimes there may be teams from different employers: examples are design project teams in construction, which bring together architects and engineers from different firms, or teams which include customers or suppliers.

Benefits of Team Working

Organisations have introduced team working for the following reasons, among others:

- *to improve productivity*
- *to improve quality of products or services*
- *to improve customer focus*
- *to speed the spread of ideas*
- *to respond to opportunities and threats and to fast-changing environments*
- *to increase employee motivation*
- *to introduce multi-skilling and employee flexibility.*

Value of Skills

There can be benefits for employees too. The most quoted outcomes are greater job satisfaction and motivation, and improved learning. But the introduction of team working needs skilful management and resources devoted to it, or initiatives may fail.

Characteristics of Effective Teams

An effective team has the following characteristics:

- *a common sense of purpose*
- *a clear understanding of the team's objectives*
- *resources to achieve those objectives*
- *mutual respect among team members, both as individuals and for the contribution each makes to the team's performance*
- *valuing members' strengths and respecting their weaknesses*
- *mutual trust*
- *willingness to share knowledge and expertise*
- *willingness to speak openly*
- *a range of skills among team members to deal effectively with all its tasks*
- *a range of personal styles for the various roles needed to carry out the team's tasks.*

Value of Skills

Roles in a Team

A team made up of people with the same ability, skills, beliefs and attitudes might be considered ideal, as their needs would be the same and therefore easily satisfied. The absolute opposite, however, is true.

Team members need to very different to each other as it is these differences in skills, capability, ideals, cultures, etc. which helps to make the team a strong independent unit with team members looking after and supporting each other. The goal when creating a team is to find people with complimentary skills. What one team member does not know, another one will.

It has been argued that the optimal team with have this level of diversity and Dr Meredith Belbin conducted some pioneering work on team roles in the 1970s. He identified nine team roles in addition to the necessary technical and specialist skills which need to be satisfied to achieve successful teamwork. He identified:

Role	Characteristic
Plant	creative, imaginative, unorthodox. Solves difficult problems.
Resource investigator	extrovert, enthusiastic, exploratory. Explores opportunities. Develops contacts.
Co-ordinator	mature, confident, a good chairperson. Clarifies goals, promotes decision making.
Shaper	dynamic, challenging. Has drive and courage to overcome obstacles.
Monitor evaluator	sober, strategic, discerning. Sees all options.
Team worker	co-operative, mild, perceptive, diplomatic. Listens, builds, averts friction.
Implementer	disciplined, reliable, conservative. Turns ideas into practical action.
Completer	painstaking, conscientious, anxious. Searches out errors and omissions, delivers on time.
Specialist	single-minded, self-starting, dedicated. Provides knowledge and skill in rare supply.

Belbin's work has been criticised on the grounds that individuals rarely fit neatly into these categories – most fit into more than one, and arguably the best team workers will adapt their behaviour to fill different roles as circumstances require. However, knowing that one

Value of Skills

tends to fit a certain profile arguably has value in understanding one's own and others' strengths and weaknesses.

Team selection is not an exact science and instinct should come into play as well. A mix of types is necessary, as is a mix of skills – for example, selecting a team of IT specialists to look at an IT project would be wrong (although it happens!); users of the IT system will need to be included in the team.

Teams can include senior and junior people (for the latter, team membership may also be a development opportunity) and someone relatively junior may be a team leader. To reiterate, what is most important is the team's mix of skills and types.

Team Size

Most commentators suggest that between five and eight people is the ideal size for teams. Teams need to be large enough to incorporate the appropriate range of expertise and representation of interests, but not so large that people's participation, and hence their interest, is limited.

Team Leadership

Leadership is vital for successful teams.

There is no one recipe for successful team leadership. Like other team members, team leaders have their own personal styles, which they need to understand and work within.

Some people, by instinct, will be directive – they will want to tell people what to do. Those with directive tendencies will need to temper their approach to avoid causing resentment; otherwise, other team members may ask 'If he knows all the answers, why are we involved?'.

Others will be democratic and ask questions to gain commitment and get people on board, even if they themselves have clear ideas about how things should be done. Leaders with democratic tendencies will need to be aware that there is a danger of drift and lack of direction if there is too much debate.

Some leaders will be more involved, while others will let team members get on by themselves.

Whatever their personal styles, leaders should:

- *listen to team members*
- *question them to understand their points of view*
- *be responsive to feedback.*

Value of Skills

In this way they act as facilitators or coaches to get the most out of team members, and to encourage learning and creativity. The roles that leaders play, and hence the ways in which they behave, may differ at different stages of team development. Helping to overcome conflict in the early stages may develop to setting tasks at a later stage. It can also be argued that successful team leaders need a high degree of emotional intelligence.

In some situations, leadership may rotate. Different individuals may take the lead at different stages of a project for which a team is responsible. Some semi-autonomous or fully autonomous teams may also appoint their own leaders as they see fit.

Team Training and Learning

Team building training is often necessary to assist the move from working in a traditional hierarchy to being part of a team, and in circumstances where team members have not worked together previously and may not even know each other. Such training may consist of exercises carried out jointly under a facilitator, sometime outdoors to enable people to get to know each other and to work together, understanding each other's strengths and weaknesses.

Communications, knowledge-sharing and problem-solving may often be on the agenda, but the areas covered will depend on the nature and role of the team, so it is impossible to generalise.

Social events may also be used to get team members to know each other. Separate training may take place for team leaders. As projects develop, there may be additional training that emerges from the team's needs. An important role of the team leader is to act as a coach or facilitator to encourage learning.

Team Reward

It is a criticism of traditional appraisal systems that they do not give sufficient weight to individual contributions to teams, but this is starting to change. A few organisations have introduced team pay systems, aimed at encouraging group endeavour rather than individual performance. Research has found that such schemes are less important for success than management style, culture and the working environment. If team pay is to be introduced, it should be done with great care, and the complementary impact of non-financial reward should always be acknowledged.

The importance of working together in a team

The principle of working together in a team should underpin how an individual operates. Managing or leading people does not just mean acting as overseer, to see that they get their work done satisfactorily. It means involving people throughout the team in a creative role, to ensure that together you are all able to succeed.

Value of Skills

Involving people on broad issues is motivational. Never underestimate people. Their views can enhance everything from methods, standards, processes to overall effectiveness.

Managers are not paid to have all the ideas that are necessary to keep their section working well in a changing world, but they are paid to make sure that there are enough ideas to make things work and go on working.

Chapter 4: Stakeholders

Stakeholders

Stakeholders

A stakeholder is anybody who can affect or is affected by an organisation, strategy or project. They can be internal or external and they can be at senior or junior levels.

Stakeholders are crucial to the success of an organisation. Neglect them and they will actively work against you. Manage them well and they will actively promote you and the organisation.

The Importance of Stakeholder Management

As your career develops, and you become more successful, the actions that you take and the decisions you make start to affect more and more people. The more people you affect, the more likely it is that some of them will have significant power and influence over your work.

These people are your stakeholders. They could be strong supporters of your projects – or they could block them, so you need to identify who your stakeholders are and win them over as soon as possible.

You can do this by conducting a Stakeholder Analysis – an effective three-step process for identifying, prioritising and understanding your stakeholders

A stakeholder-based approach gives you four key benefits:

Getting an organisation into shape
You can use the opinions of your most powerful stakeholders to help define your operation at an early stage. These stakeholders will then more likely support you, and their input can also improve the quality of your project.

Winning resources
Gaining support from powerful stakeholders can help you to win more resources, such as people, time or money. This makes it more likely that your operation will be successful.

Building understanding
By communicating with your stakeholders early and often, you can ensure that they fully grasp what you are doing and understand the benefits your organisation may be able to offer. This means that they can more actively support you when necessary.

Stakeholders

Getting ahead of the game
Understanding your stakeholders means that you can anticipate and predict their reactions to your operation as it develops. This allows you to plan actions that will more likely win their support.

Internal and External Stakeholders

It has been commonplace to deal with external stakeholders politely, efficiently and effectively, however, this has not always been the case with Internal stakeholders. To create a more proactive environment employees have been urged to consider other internal stakeholders within the organisation as customers. The idea being that the internal stakeholders become "internal customers" and should be regarded in the same way a customer would.

The concept of stakeholders being external customers is straightforward, but the internal customer is more difficult to understand. The notion that all departments are a customer of each other can be difficult to comprehend. It becomes easier though if we think of everyone being part of the same team.

If all the internal stakeholders work closely together, helping and supporting each other, that group will achieve far more than one which works against each other. To win, a Tug o' War team must all pull at the same time and in the same direction. They would never win if half the team were pushing and the other half were pulling!!

Look at the hierarchy below for a hotel. Think about a situation where the Pot washer's wages are incorrect - he will go to the Finance & HR department to resolve it, similarly the Finance and HR department will go to the maintenance dept. when they need something repairing and so, they become a customer of each other.

In this case, some of the internal stakeholders are using the goods and service from other departments. The restaurant is selling the food it gets from the kitchen. Room service delivers the food and drink it gets from the kitchen and bars. The chef obtains food from the stores and they obtain the food by arranging with the accounts department to buy it and so the relationships go on. Internal departments therefore become suppliers and customers of each other

Although no money changes hands in these internal transactions, the transaction still takes place, and it can become frustrated just as a sale to an external customer can cause complaints to arise.

Stakeholders

It is as important therefore that the relationship between the organisation and internal stakeholders is as good as the one it has with external stakeholders. If not, service levels will drop, the internal stakeholder relationship will be compromised and the delivery of goods and services to external stakeholders will be compromised. It is imperative that everything possible is done to manage the relationship between internal stakeholders in just the same way the external stakeholder's relationship is managed.

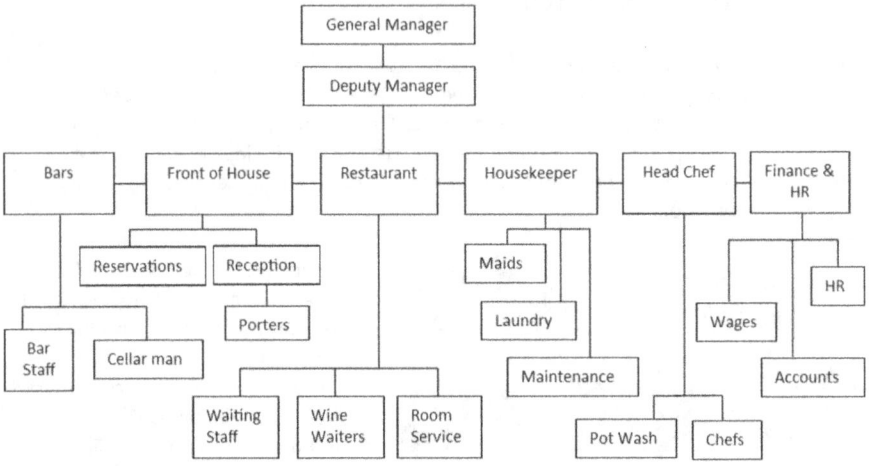

Identifying Stakeholders

The first step in stakeholder management is to identify your stakeholders. List everybody that you can think of who is, or will, be affected by the organisation. Ask as many people as possible and capture every name, organisation or type of stakeholder you can think of. Common examples of stakeholders include employees, customers, shareholders, suppliers, communities, and governments.

Types of Stakeholders

Customers
Many would argue that organisations exist to serve their customers. Customers are stakeholders of an organisation; in that they are impacted by the quality of service/products and their value. For example, passengers traveling on an airplane literally have their lives in the company's hands when flying with the airline.

Stake / Interest held: Product/service quality and value

Employees
Employees have a direct stake in the company in that they earn an income to support themselves, along with other benefits (both monetary and non-monetary). Depending

Stakeholders

on the nature of the organisation, employees may also have a health and safety interest (for example, in the industries of transportation, mining, oil and gas, construction, etc.).

Stake / Interest held: Employment income and safety

Investors
Investors include both shareholders and debtholders. Shareholders invest capital in the organisation and expect to earn a certain rate of return on that invested capital. Investors are commonly concerned with the concept of shareholder value. Lumped in with this group are all other providers of capital, such as lenders and potential acquirers. All shareholders are inherently stakeholders, but stakeholders are not inherently shareholders.

Stake / Interest held: Financial returns

Suppliers and Vendors
Suppliers and vendors sell goods and/or services to an organisation and rely on it for revenue generation and on-going income. In many industries, suppliers also have their health and safety on the line, as they may be directly involved in the company's operations.

Stake / Interest held: Revenues and safety

Communities
Communities are major stakeholders in large organisations located near to them. They are impacted by a wide range of things, including job creation, economic development, health, and safety. When a big company enters or exits a small community, there is an immediate and significant impact on employment, incomes, and spending in the area. With some industries, there is a potential health impact, too, as companies may alter the environment.

Stake / Interest held: Health, safety, economic development

Governments
Governments can also be considered a major stakeholder in an organisation, as they collect taxes from the company (corporate income taxes), as well as from all the people it employs (payroll taxes) and from other spending the company incurs (sales taxes). Governments benefit from the overall Gross Domestic Product (GDP) that companies contribute to.

Stake / Interest held: Taxes and GDP

Stakeholders

Stakeholders may be further grouped into internal and external and each will have different interests, and organisations often face trade-offs in trying to please all of them.

A list might typically include:

Internal Stakeholders	External Stakeholders
Team Members	Potential Employees
Line Managers	Customers
Senior Managers	Suppliers
Board Members	Pressure Groups
Consultants	Government Agencies
Subject Experts	Regulatory Organisations
	General Public
	Shareholders
	Partners
	Contractors

Stakeholder Analysis

Before an organisation can consider the needs and expectations of its stakeholders during its planning, it must identify those stakeholders and sort them in their order of importance to the organisation.

One method to accomplish this is to list the stakeholders and then determine the degree of their interest and influence in the organisation. If stakeholders have a high degree of interest, the organisation needs to communicate with them on a regular basis and keep them informed about its activities. The organisation also needs to keep them placated.

Prioritising Stakeholders

Having produced a list of people and organisations that have an interest in the organisation, some of these may have the power either to obstruct the organisations progress or to advance it. Some may be interested in what you are doing, while others may not care, so you need to work out who you need to prioritise.

You can map out your stakeholders and classify them according to their power over your work and their interest in it, on a Power/Interest Grid.

The position that you allocate to a stakeholder on the grid shows you the actions you need to take with them:

Stakeholders

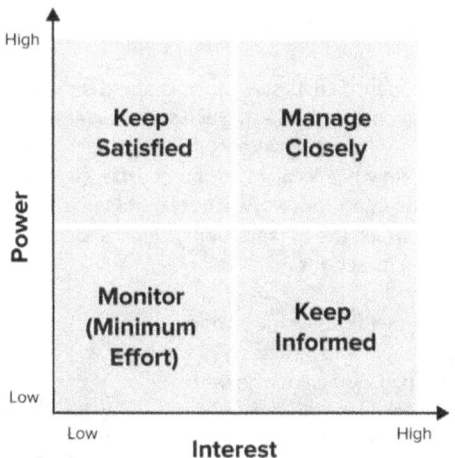

High power, Highly interested people (Manage Closely): you must fully engage these people and make the greatest efforts to satisfy them.

High power, Less interested people (Keep Satisfied): put enough work in with these people to keep them satisfied, but not so much that they become bored with your message.

Low power, Highly interested people (Keep Informed): adequately inform these people and talk to them to ensure that no major issues are arising. People in this category can often be very helpful with the detail of your project.

Low power, Less interested people (Monitor): again, monitor these people, but do not bore them with excessive communication.

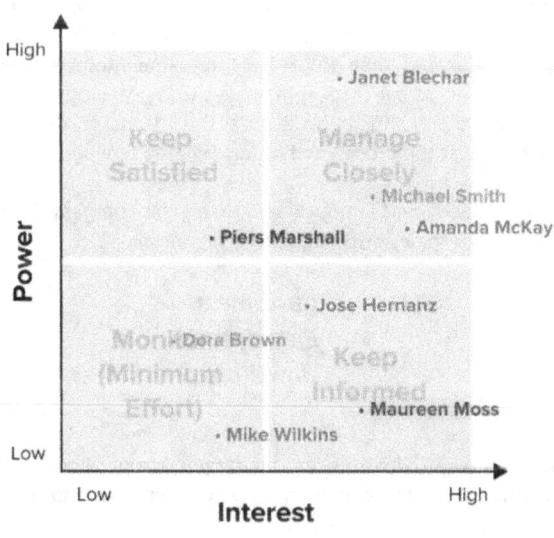

Level 3: Business Administrator

Stakeholders

Stakeholder Needs and Expectations

Once the organisation has identified its stakeholders and their importance, it can begin to plan based on their needs and expectations. Each stakeholder has needs that it expects to be met by the organisation. The organisation's owners expect it to be profitable and to distribute that profit to them while local government expect it to obey the law and pay its business rates on time. The importance of each stakeholder to the organisation determines the degree to which the organisation attempts to accommodate the stakeholder when planning its actions.

The impact of stakeholder needs and expectations on organisations is inescapable and affects all aspects of the organisation. Organisations exist to meet the expectations of each specific stakeholder. Every organisation is set up and operated to produce profit for its owners and investors. However, organisations must also consider the needs and expectations of all the other stakeholders because of their ability to help or hinder their operations e.g.

An organisation should be considerate of the local community because it improves its reputation and strengthens its market presence. On the other hand, if the organisation chooses to ignore its local community, that disregard becomes a black mark on its reputation and can result in significant opposition if relations become bad enough.

The only stakeholders that organisations can ignore are the ones with very little interest and influence on their operations.

Organisations often struggle to prioritise stakeholders and their competing interests. Where stakeholders are aligned and have similar needs and expectations the process is easy. However, in many cases, they do not have the same interests. If the company is pressured by shareholders to cut costs, it may have to lay off employees or reduce their wages, which presents a very difficult trade off as the internal stakeholders (the staff) are likely to become hostile at the prospect of losing their job or wages.

Jack Ma, the CEO of Alibaba, has famously said that, in his company, they rank stakeholders in the following priority sequence:

Customers
Employees
Investors

Much of the prioritisation will be based on the stage a company is in. If it is a start-up or an early-stage organisation, then customers and employees are more likely to be the

Stakeholders

stakeholders considered top priority. If it is a mature, publicly traded company, then shareholders are likely to be front and centre.

At the end of the day, it is up to a company, the CEO, and the board of directors to determine the appropriate ranking of stakeholders when competing interests arise.

Successfully managing stakeholders mean you will be better able to maintain focus, understand where there is potential risk, and mitigate issues that would otherwise be detrimental to the organisation.

By properly managing the stakeholders' expectations from the outset, the chances for a smoother journey are much greater.

Identify the stakeholder's preferred method of communication.
Using the most effective method of communication will help ensure the stakeholder remains content. If you make the mistake of using the wrong method (or non-preferred method) it will cause frustration and lack of confidence. It will show their initial direction was ignored.

Keep stakeholders engaged throughout the process with timely updates.
Ask the right questions, of the right people, at the beginning and throughout the relationship.

Accurately map expectations.
Be crystal clear on the expectations from the stakeholder's point of view. Inevitably you will discover conflicting definitions of success. Some will consider meeting a final deadline their number one priority. Another might consider functionality of the final product as most important. These conflicting expectations can be resolved by meeting all stakeholders (where practical) and helping them come to mutually acceptable agreements.

Classify the level of communication for each stakeholder.
Identify those who require hand holding and insist on receiving all details, those who prefer a basic, occasional overview and those who want daily or weekly communication?

Identify which stakeholders will be advocates and which will be obstructive.
Map your strategy accordingly.

Engage the stakeholders in decision making.
Every stakeholder believes they are important. It is important to present reports in such a way that stakeholders feel they have been involved in the process. Stakeholders will remember the overall mood of the entire process. Their measure of success is not just the finished product, but the way you attained the end goal.

Stakeholders

Managing Stakeholder Expectations

The most important part of operational management may be getting the business done, but the way stakeholder expectations are managed will directly affect those results.

- *Staff expect they will have all the time, tools and support they need to get their job done without burning out*
- *Top management expect the job to be completed successfully*
- *Clients expect requirements followed and executed.*
- *Plenty will be expected from your role too.*

Sometimes, communication falls short and one side is left expecting more than the other side can offer.

The trick to making sure that the organisation runs smoothly is in managing stakeholder expectations.
Around 57% of organisations fail because communication was not up to standard; there was not enough transparency on either end, client or delivery team.

Not managing expectations leads to obstacles such as:

- *Stakeholder disengagement*
- *Unclear objectives and goals*
- *Poor prioritisation*
- *Inadequate risk management*
- *Performance issues.*

It is much easier to manage an organisation when everyone is on the same page, and that's exactly what expectation management is all about.

Fortunately, managing stakeholder expectations does not have to be complicated.

There are 9 key areas you should focus on:

1. *Engage from the beginning and plan well*
   Planning is the key to success. Unfortunately, most organisations rush through planning, eager to get to work and get the clients off their backs. This is often what leads to expectation mismanagement, as the rules, objectives, and metrics have not been properly outlined.

   To manage everyone's expectations in the planning phase, you should communicate clearly and transparently with the clients, operational teams, and top management regarding:

Stakeholders

- *Objectives*
- *Goals*
- *Scope*
- *Changes*
- *Expectations.*

Make sure you fully understand what their expectations are, and that you are clear on which expectations you will and will not meet.

Then record it in the planning documents. Later, if there is any confusion, you can simply reference them.

You should put in the maximum amount of effort and attention into the planning. If you have done everything properly, the rest of your work will be much easier.

2. *Manage internal stakeholder expectations*
   It is best to include employees in the planning phase. If that is not possible, the issue should still be discussed with them.

   When requirements and roles are unclear, staff often feel like they are taking on too much. To avoid any confusions and unrealistic expectations, you should:

   - *Define roles and responsibilities clearly and early*
   - *Define schedules and task dependencies across the organisation*
   - *Establish KPIs and metrics that will be used*
   - *Set up a communication plan.*

3. *Understand stakeholder expectations*
   When dealing with stakeholders, you also have to be a psychologist who constantly asks:

   ## "Why do they want what they want?"

   It is vital to understand why stakeholders have expectations they have. The most important part of managing expectations is understanding them. Everyone has clear goals they state, but it is essential it is fully understood what they are really hoping to get.

   For a staff member, that might be a rise. For top management, improved public esteem. Whatever it is, understand it, and then approach those expectations accordingly.

Stakeholders

4. *Define levels of engagement*
   Some stakeholders will naturally be more engaged with the organisation. Some, however, may want to be engaged more or less than may be anticipated. It is just as important to define levels of engagement, as well, and create a communication plan for each stakeholder group.

   Encourage stakeholders to be proactive. If they have questions, provide a platform for them to ask them. Schedule time for status updates.

5. *Changes and escalation*
   It is important that the task is fully scoped. This should be defined at the outset. It should be clearly stated:

   - What type of changes to the task would be acceptable?
   - What type of change are there no resources for?

   Similarly, if an issue gets out of hand, there should be an escalation route.

6. *Manage conflict*
   When there is conflict, your natural reaction may be to stop it immediately and decide on the course of action. However, it is much better to manage it, keeping the goals of each stakeholder in mind. If internal departments are arguing, take the time to sit down with them and understand what the problem really is.

   Discuss the pre-set expectations to see if the conflict is a professional or a personal issue.

   Encourage team members to communicate and offer their feedback on everything from progress to suggestions.

7. *Record issues, changes and activity*
   When managing expectations, it is very important to record issues, changes and stakeholder activity. Not only will recording them help understand stakeholders' motivations, but it will also help assess team performance.

   Learning from what did and did not work will create better strategies in the future.

8. *Manage perceptions*
   Your perception of the organisation is one thing. The way the stakeholders perceive the organisation is an entirely different thing. Ideally everyone's perception of the organisation must be similar, if not the same.

Stakeholders

It is important to communicate with stakeholders to ensure their perception is realistic. This will avoid a lot of disappointment and conflict, while securing approval.

9. **Do not micromanage (but manage)**
   A team may be taking on more than they can handle, especially at the start of the project which is why it is important not only to manage what they are doing, but also help them manage time as well.

   Let them know you are there to help them and keep an eye on their workload to ensure they are not pushing harder than they can.

   In the long term, this will earn their respect and communication will improve significantly.

After all, it all comes down to communication. Understand everyone's expectations, and then plan to meet them, or be honest about why you cannot.

The Organisation will be all the better for it

Benefits of Effective Stakeholder Engagement

Learning
Engaging with different perspectives provides opportunities for learning and potentially changing the approach to ensure it fits the needs of stakeholders.

Decision-making
Understanding the views and interests of stakeholders can lead to more effective decision-making.
This is more than just getting the language right. In understanding issues and concerns, it provides an opportunity to reflect on what will and will not work, and why.

Saving time and money
Engaging early can lead to savings of both time and money in the long term. Stakeholder engagement is not only critical to developing a robust policy or product, but to develop a real understanding of needs.

Risk management
Being open to different methodologies can improve risk management through potentially highlighting issues you may not have been aware of and help you prioritise.

Stakeholders

Accountability
Engaging with stakeholders is central to improving accountability within the organisation as well as to the wider market. Transparency is important – be clear about the outcomes it is hoped to achieve and the steps on the way.

Understand needs
Understanding the full range of needs and views can let to better policy making and better outcomes.

Communicating with Stakeholders

The way to manage stakeholders depends on:

- ***The size and complexity of the organisation.***
- ***The amount of help you needed to achieve the desired results.*** This could include sponsorship, advice and expert input, physical resources, reviews of material to increase quality, and so on.
- ***The time available to communicate.*** Consideration of the time to be spent on communication must be made, particularly if the organisation requires a lot of stakeholder input. It is often better to allocate more time to communicating with stakeholders, rather than trying to "get by" without all the help or input that is necessary.

Plan for communicating with your stakeholders once they have been mapped them on a Power/Interest Grid.

Establishing ground rules for effective stakeholder communication will save time, remove obstacles and ultimately, put the organisation in the place it seeks to be. There are several communication methods which should be implemented when communicating with stakeholders.

All methods of communication described below have their upsides and downsides, so it is important to select the right one depending on the message being sent to stakeholders.

Schedule a meeting
Stakeholder meetings are the most common communication method in place for organisations especially since they can save time in conveying the message to many people. The best way to communicate the message at a meeting might be PowerPoint, Prezi or any of the mind mapping software solutions available online. Being in the same room with stakeholders should avoid misinterpretation issues.

It should be noted that as teams become larger and more remote, scheduled meetings are becoming a thing of the past. With growing online platforms that ensure real-time transparency, stakeholders are no longer passive consumers of information. Delivering periodic reports without supporting communication is not acceptable anymore.

Stakeholders

Send out a newsletter
Using the organisations intranet or collaboration platform already in place, you can act proactively and define a newsletter to be sent out to stakeholders at given time periods. It can be great for including even those stakeholders who are not directly involved with a specific part of the organisation. E-mail is a one-way communication channel, so you should avoid it for issues that require immediate feedback.

Separate online "screen to screen" meetings
As time-consuming as they can be, separate face to face meetings are the best way to get the message across stakeholders. Not everyone responds to a presentation the same way, so by meeting stakeholders separately, their concerns can be addressed in more detail and with greater control. As a result of the pandemic geographically dispersed teams "screen to screen" is becoming the new "face to face", since so many of the meetings are held via online communication and collaboration platforms. Having a presentation is optional; you are better off focusing on the dialogue.

Summary report
A summary report is usually sent out in predefined periods (weekly, monthly). The protocol is already agreed so if there are no issues, there should be no concerns. Supported by data and statistics it should highlight the top performing aspects and reassure the stakeholders the situation under control.

Schedule a conference call
Conference calls, whether by telephone or video conferencing, are commonly used in situations where the issue is too urgent for a formal meeting. When there is an obstacle that needs to be resolved immediately a conference call can be arranged in the matter of minutes.

Lunch meetings
Lunch meetings would fall into the informal communication category of stakeholder meetings. They would be a great idea for getting honest feedback or getting stakeholders to sign off on a particular idea in mind. Informal meetings can be just as effective as the official ones.

Approach the choice of communications channels with an open mind. Consider which channels will be most effective to reach and engage the audience. Resist the impulse to revert automatically to channels that have been used previously, or that are most familiar unless they are known to be the right channel for the audience.

There are three questions that can guide your choice of communications channels:

What channels do the target audiences already use and trust?
Think about their existing behaviour. What sources of information do they already use/respond to? Do not invest in channels that your audience do not, or will not, use and trust.

Stakeholders

What is the purpose of the communication?
Some channels lend themselves to communicating complex information; some are efficient ways of delivering short pieces of relevant information. The model below illustrates this on a spectrum.

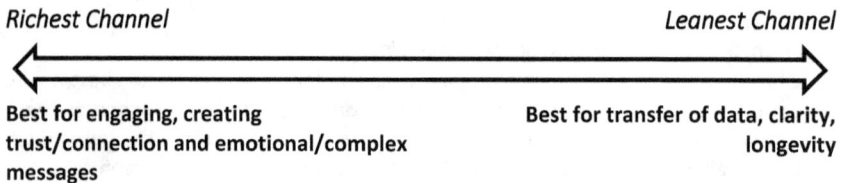

Richest Channel — Best for engaging, creating trust/connection and emotional/complex messages

Leanest Channel — Best for transfer of data, clarity, longevity

Physical presence (one-to-one meetings, events)	Personal interactive (phone, webinar, targeted social media)	Impersonal interactive (email, social media)	Impersonal static (letter, report, e-news updates, newsletters)

If there is a need to communicate a complex issue, the best channels will be on the left of the spectrum. However, do all channels lie at one end of the spectrum? One-to-one meetings may need to be reinforced by regular e-news updates. Mass social media communications may be augmented by carefully targeted events.

What resources do you have?
Social media and 'owned' media that may be available (existing organisational websites, e-news, newsletters, etc.) are free to use but will need a combination of set-up time and regular maintenance.

Events, printed materials, videos and media coverage will need time and budget, and specialist skills may be needed. The choice of channels will need to match the resources available.

The channels used to reach and engage people should depend on what needs to be achieved with the communications, the preference of the target audience and the resources and budget available.

It may be necessary to use a range of channels to achieve all objectives. Some channels for consideration are set out in the table below:

Stakeholders

Communication Channels

Channel	Good For	Consider
Group meetings, workshops, conferences	Listening, brainstorming, relationship building, building and sharing purpose, exchange of complex learning and information, building trust and loyalty, engaging early adopters.	Time and cost resource; do participants have sufficient time/ motivation to attend? Timing and location: make it easy/ appealing to attend or piggyback on existing meetings.
Launch events	Internal morale, stakeholder awareness, can provide a hook for media coverage.	Time and cost resource; do target audiences have sufficient interest/ motivation to attend? Timing and location: make it easy/ appealing to attend. Media coverage: do you have something genuinely newsworthy?
1:1 meetings	Engaging influencers/stakeholders; building knowledge and trust; building or maintaining key relationships.	The messages you want to give in the meeting and how to follow up to ensure the relationship is maintained.
Email	Low cost, regular updates; driving traffic to website or blog.	Writing style and visuals: emails are easy to delete. Ensure that content and look of yours is audience-focused and stands out from crowd.
Webinars	Exchange of complex information or learning; maintaining relationships; project management among dispersed teams.	Scheduling: think of a time likely to be convenient to most participants. Promoting: make sure people know about it and remind them. Organising: give it some leadership and structure. Ensure the content is engaging.
Social media (e.g., Twitter, Facebook, LinkedIn)	Finding or creating networks with niche specialisation or interests; building a profile; directing to other communications (website or blog); brief, real-time updates; maintaining relationships; exchange of information/learning; place for like-minded to interact; reaching early adopters.	Content: who will post and regularly update/respond. Need to focus more time on reacting/ responding to others to build relationships. How can you use this to cross-promote other comms (i.e., an online blog)?

Stakeholders

Channel	Good For	Consider
Media coverage (professional and consumer media)	Credibility (a third-party endorsement) and reputation; internal morale; improving awareness; influencing debates and agendas.	Time and skills required; need to be able to respond to any interest in very short timeframes; lack of ability to 'control' the message. Plan any media activity with the knowledge of senior sponsors and their comms leads.
Film/ animation	Creating an emotional connection with a cause; telling stories that can illustrate complex issues; longevity (can be used more than once).	Resource and budgets; how will you promote/distribute/make it available to ensure return on investment. Length: online films should be as short as possible (one–three minutes as a rule).
Website (and/or intranet sites)	Credibility; demonstrating full range of work; attracting new members/audiences; information exchange; accessibility.	Time and cost resource for initial and ongoing development; ability to keep up to date; analytics for evaluating use/impact. Consider creating a web page hosted on the web site of the sponsor organisation / partners.
Blogs	Demonstrating expertise, learning and knowledge transfer; content for social media; can boost traffic to website; place for like-minded to interact.	Content: a catchy title; a subject your audience cares about; a central point, argument or call to action. Promoting the blog through social media channels. Blogging through existing sites with an established audience.
Letter	Now more unusual/distinctive than email; easy to personalise if small print run.	Language, layout, audience focus – all usual principles for good communications apply.
Leaflet, brochure, flyer, quick reference cards	Longevity; visual impact; means of communicating quite detailed information; control of message/s.	Resource for production and effective distribution (too often they are produced without sufficient thought/budget for distribution).
Merchandise or display materials (posters, mouse mats, wall charts, screensavers, pens, certificates, infographics)	Longevity; visual impact; thanking and recognising supporters and celebrating success.	Budget: is the cost justified? How will it be perceived by others? Developing tools that combine your message with useful content for your audience in a format they will use.

Stakeholders

Channel	Good For	Consider
Online network	Facilitating information exchange; building a community.	Cloud-based technology make this possible and affordable. Easy to set up groups through social media, e.g., LinkedIn, but they need to be actively maintained.
Advertising	Communicating a strong, clear sales message; controlling how your message is received.	Can you measure its effectiveness and justify the costs involved? Can the channel owner demonstrate good return on investment and data on the readership among your audience?
Newsletters (e-news/hard copy)	Keeping a defined group of people up to date with your activities; keeping in touch.	Can you achieve more impact submitting content to existing newsletters run by others?
Mobile technology/ SMS/mobile apps	Flagging new content. Quick delivery of short, simple messages or tools.	Is the content valued and does it address a genuine need?

Stakeholders

Communication Tools

Here are some digital and online multimedia tools and channels to consider using in your communications.

Format	Uses, Benefits and Considerations
Video	Good for showing at meetings and events and provides a legacy for the project. Brings life to ideas and concepts and an engaging way of telling a story and sharing the perspective of staff/patients. Combinations of film locations – as opposed to a 'talking head' – generally more engaging. Increasingly produced by amateurs - can be expensive if involving a film production company – around £1,500 for 'talking head', up to maybe £4,000 if location filming (e.g., in workplace) is included. You can create very short (6 seconds) video clips using Vine (a free app) – they have a 'homemade' feel to them provide a visual snapshot. People are increasingly used to watching video online, especially with rise of mobile and tablet use. Upload films to YouTube which increases visibility of content in Google searches.
Audio slideshow	Quick-win content, especially if a presentation has already been prepared for offline use (e.g., at a conference). Cheap to produce (around £300) and a fairly quick to turn around. Can help to explain and illustrate ideas at the same time (through voice and visual). Slideshows can also be uploaded to SlideShare (open-source software) which increases visibility of content.
Audio clip	Cheap to produce (around £300) and quick to turnaround. Should not be too long (max 5 mins) unless it is very engaging. You can create free audio clips using the Audioboom app (on all platforms, www.audioboom.com).
Animation	Can be creative with visual to convey complex ideas, especially when you are doing lots of referring to and interpreting of figures. Expensive and resource-intensive to produce. Around £7,000 and upwards.
Infographic	Visual way of communicating data rather than simple chart or written copy – great for illustrating what data means, quickly. Can be flat infographics or interactive Good for sharing on social media, especially Facebook where image-led updates get highest levels of engagement. Costs would be around £300 for non-interactive but increase significantly for interactive.

Stakeholders

Building Relationships with Stakeholders

Regardless of whether it is a small organisation or a multinational organisation, there should be no underestimation of the importance of building effective stakeholder relationships. To conduct business and manage successfully there is a need to establish and maintain relationships with employees, suppliers and other internal and external stakeholders. Successful stakeholder relationships can enhance the organisation profile, create potential career opportunities, create additional services and lead to overall business success.

The key steps to creating effective working relationships with stakeholders can be summarised into five stages.

1. *Build trust*
   Successful and influential partnerships are built on trust. Give stakeholders a reason to trust you by always doing what you say you are going to do. Be honest and open about progress and never over-promise or feel pressurised to say yes to unreasonable demands. Stakeholders will respect you more for being transparent about situations and this will ultimately build trust.

2. *Think in 'win/win' solutions*
   Being able (and willing) to show empathy (putting yourself in another person's shoes and understand how they feel) is key to building strong stakeholder relationships. Try to view organisation situations from your stakeholder's perspective and be committed to sourcing solutions that will benefit all parties. The idea of a win/win solution is not based on compromise but on the understanding that mutual benefit can be drawn from every situation.

3. *Respond*
   Whether a potential supplier has made contact, or the largest and most important client has been in touch, always respond. Communications should be prioritised in order of importance, so you do not need to respond to all contacts straight away, but simply ignoring people shows you have little or no regard for building strong relationships. You never know whether that supplier or client might be useful in the future so always send a quick email response or phone call to acknowledge contact. It is vital.

4. *Ask questions*
   The most effective stakeholder relationships are built on people asking purposeful questions whether it be to check understanding of a particular project or prompt discussion. Asking questions, in particular open questions, also develops rapport and encourages conversations. It also gives stakeholders a sense of ownership over particular projects. So, ask away!

5. *Continuously demonstrate your competence*
   Building great stakeholder relationships is by no means a one-off exercise. You should continuously develop these relationships by demonstrating your competence and reliability, keeping updates on track and communicating key agreements and

Stakeholders

decisions. Try treating stakeholders like you would a valued client; take time to have one-to-one conversations and engage with them regularly. Take interest in their world and you will earn respect, demonstrate your competence and ultimately build strong, meaningful stakeholder relationships

Stakeholders

Active Listening

Listening is one of the most important skills you can have. How well you listen has a major impact on your job effectiveness, and on the quality of your relationships with others.

For instance:

- *We listen to obtain information.*
- *We listen to understand.*
- *We listen for enjoyment.*
- *We listen to learn.*

Given all the listening that we do, you would think we would be good at it! In fact, we are not good at it and research suggests that we only remember between 25 percent and 50 percent of what we hear, as described by Edgar Dale's Cone of Experience. That means that when you talk to your boss, colleagues, customers, or spouse for 10 minutes, they pay attention to less than half of the conversation.

Turn it around and it reveals that when you are receiving directions or being presented with information, you are not hearing the whole message either. You hope the important parts are captured in your 25-50 percent, but what if they are not?

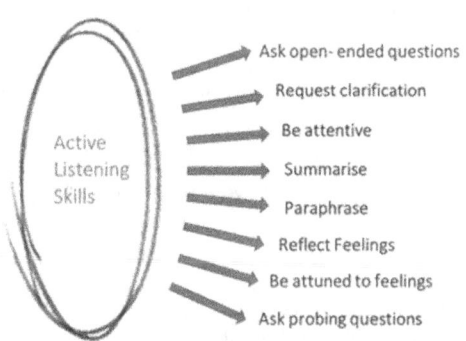

Clearly, listening is a skill that we can all benefit from improving. By becoming a better listener, you can improve your productivity, as well as your ability to influence, persuade and negotiate. What is more, you will avoid conflict and misunderstandings. All of these are necessary for workplace success!

Good communication skills require a high level of self-awareness. Understanding your own personal style of communicating will go a long way toward helping you to create good and lasting impressions with others.

The way to improve your listening skills is to practice "active listening." This is where you make a conscious effort to hear not only the words that another person is saying but, more importantly, the complete message being communicated.
To do this, you must pay attention to the other person very carefully.

You cannot allow yourself to become distracted by whatever else may be going on around you, or by forming counter arguments while the other person is still speaking. Nor can you allow yourself to get bored and lose focus on what the other person is saying.

Stakeholders

If you are finding it particularly difficult to concentrate on what someone is saying, try repeating his or her words mentally as he says them – this will reinforce his message and help you to stay focused.

To enhance your listening skills, you need to let the other person know that you are listening to what she is saying.

To understand the importance of this, ask yourself if you have ever been engaged in a conversation when you wondered if the other person was listening to what you were saying. You wonder if your message is getting across, or if it is even worthwhile continuing to speak. It feels like talking to a brick wall and it is something you want to avoid.

Acknowledgement can be something as simple as a nod of the head or a simple "uh huh." You are not necessarily agreeing with the person, you are simply indicating that you are listening. Using body language and other signs to acknowledge you are listening can also help you to pay attention.

Try to respond to the speaker in a way that will encourage them to continue speaking, so that you can get the information you need. While nodding and "uh uhing" says you are interested, an occasional question or comment to recap what has been said also communicates that you are listening and understanding his message.

Be aware that active listening can give others the impression that you agree with them even if you do not. It is also important to avoid using active listening as a checklist of actions to follow, rather than really listening. It may help to practice Mindful Listening if you find that you lose focus regularly.

Becoming an Active Listener

There are five key active listening techniques you can use to help you become a more effective listener:

1. **Pay attention**
   Give the speaker your undivided attention and acknowledge the message. Recognise that non-verbal communication also "speaks" loudly.

   - *Look at the speaker directly.*
   - *Put aside distracting thoughts.*
   - *Do not mentally prepare a rebuttal!*
   - *Avoid being distracted by environmental factors. For example, side conversations.*
   - *"Listen" to the speaker's body language.*

2. **Show that you are listening**
   Use your own body language and gestures to show that you are engaged.

Stakeholders

- Nod occasionally.
- Smile and use other facial expressions.
- Make sure that your posture is open and interested.
- Encourage the speaker to continue with small verbal comments like yes, and "uh huh."

3. **Provide feedback**
Our personal filters, assumptions, judgments, and beliefs can distort what we hear. As a listener, your role is to understand what is being said. This may require you to reflect on what is being said and to ask questions.

- *Reflect on what has been said by paraphrasing. "What I am hearing is...," and "Sounds like you are saying...," are great ways to reflect back.*
- *Ask questions to clarify certain points. "What do you mean when you say...." " "Is this what you mean?"*
- *Summarise the speaker's comments periodically.*

If you find yourself responding emotionally to what someone said, say so. Ask for more information: "I may not be understanding you correctly, and I find myself taking what you said personally. What I thought you just said is XXX. Is that what you meant?"

4. **Defer judgment**
Interrupting is a waste of time. It frustrates the speaker and limits full understanding of the message.

- *Allow the speaker to finish each point before asking questions.*
- *Do not interrupt with counter arguments.*

5. **Respond appropriately**
Active listening is designed to encourage respect and understanding. You are gaining information and perspective. You add nothing by attacking the speaker or otherwise putting her down.

- *Be candid, open and honest in your response.*
- *Assert your opinions respectfully.*
- *Treat the other person in a way that you think she would want to be treated.*

Stakeholders

Managing Stakeholder Meetings

Every organisation has individuals and groups who are interested in the activities of the organisation and have a stake in its success. Keeping stakeholders informed is the best way to keep them engaged and up to date on topics having a potential impact on the organisation. By involving stakeholders in decision-making and communicating regularly through meetings and other channels, it will be easier to get their approval for new ideas and their support if problems do arise.

Meeting Participants
When a general stakeholder meeting is scheduled, a representative from each of the stakeholder groups is invited to attend. Others from the stakeholder group also might participate depending on their need to know and ability to contribute to the discussion. One or more staff members from the department responsible for stakeholder relations should also be present to facilitate the discussion, take notes and attend to meeting logistics. Internal or external subject-matter experts are invited to give presentations on a specific topic or answer questions.

Meetings
The frequency of stakeholder meetings depends on the nature of overall stakeholder communication. When stakeholders are kept informed through newsletters, email and periodic reports through a website, a meeting might only be necessary for an annual progress report or to vote on a specific topic. Meetings also are held when stakeholders need to be made aware of a new program or give feedback on an issue. Standing committees made up of stakeholders are sometimes created to meet on a regular basis and serve as decision-making bodies or advisory boards to an organisation.

Topics
Stakeholder meetings cover a broad range of topics. Negotiation sessions between unions and companies are one type of stakeholder meeting. Community members, local councils and local businesses are stakeholders in local legislation and would attend a meeting involving planning for a new construction. A department planning to revise the company website would meet with content owners and others who rely on the Internet for business purposes to get their input about the process.

Meeting Outcome
Meeting proceedings typically are recorded and distributed to all stakeholder groups and individuals in attendance at the meeting. Effective meeting minutes include when and where it was held, participants and their roles, topics discussed, decisions reached, action items and responsibilities, and items carried over for future discussion.

Stakeholder meetings give all of those with an interest in the organisation a chance to stay involved in the operations of the company. The meetings are typically targeted at the most influential stakeholders, such as shareholders, executives or partnering companies.

Stakeholders

Meetings for different types of stakeholders are also an option so the information presented can be tailored to how the stakeholder influences the company. Meetings are often educational and informational, covering general topics or new changes coming to the company. A well-organised meeting is key to make a positive impression on stakeholders.

Identify the specific purpose of the stakeholder meeting, as well as the specific audience. For example, plan a meeting for your suppliers to address changes in your purchasing process or a meeting with shareholders to keep them updated on an upcoming corporate merger. Use this purpose and the specific audience as a planning tool for the meeting.

Write an agenda that covers each portion of the meeting. Determine how you will start the meeting, present the information and wrap up the meeting. Include key points on the agenda that you plan to cover to serve as an outline for yourself and the meeting attendees.

Write a list of questions or discussion topics that enables you to gain feedback from the stakeholders. Determine what type of information you want to learn from them beforehand. An example of information you might seek is feedback on your current products or services, as well as suggestions for how to improve them going forward.

Assemble documents you plan to pass out to stakeholders at the meeting. Provide handouts for relevant information, such as the past year's financial information for shareholders or investors.

Schedule the meeting for a time and location that works for most of the stakeholders involved. Choose a location with enough space to comfortably hold the number of people and facilitate the type of activities you plan to do.

Call the meeting to order on time so it does not run long. Follow the agenda and stay on schedule as much as possible while allowing stakeholders the chance to provide input.

Send out a copy of the minutes to all who attended the meeting as a method of following up. Encourage the participants to contact you with any questions or concerns after the conclusion of the meeting.

Stakeholder Feedback

The term 'feedback' is used to describe the helpful information or criticism about prior action or behaviour from an individual, communicated to another individual (or a group) who can use that information to adjust and improve current and future actions and behaviours.

Feedback occurs when an environment reacts to an action or behaviour. For example, 'customer feedback' is the buyers' reaction to an organisations products, services, or policies; and 'employee performance feedback' is the employees' reaction to feedback

Stakeholders

from their manager – the exchange of information involves both performance expected, and performance exhibited.

Who would dispute the idea that feedback is a good thing? All can benefit from feedback. Both common sense and research make it clear – feedback and opportunities to use that feedback helps to improve and enhance, whether an individual, group, business, business unit, company, or organisation – and that information can be used to make better informed decisions. It also allows us to build and maintain communication with others.

Feedback, whether positive or negative, is beneficial.

Feedback is valuable information that will be used to make important decisions. Top performing companies are top performing companies because they consistently search for ways to make their best even better.

For top performing companies 'continuous improvement' is not just a showy catchphrase. It is a true focus based on feedback from across the entire organisation – customers, clients, employees, suppliers, vendors, and stakeholders. Top performing organisations are not only good at accepting feedback, but they also deliberately ask for feedback. They know that feedback is helpful only when it highlights weaknesses as well as strengths.

Effective feedback has benefits for the giver, the receiver, and the wider organisation. Here are five reasons why feedback is so important.

1. *Feedback is always there*

    If you ask someone in your organisation when feedback occurs, they will typically mention an employee survey, performance appraisal, or training evaluation. Feedback is around us all the time. Every time we speak to a stakeholder, we communicate feedback. In fact, it is impossible not to give feedback.

    Organisations do not need to go through a lot of hassle to gather feedback. It is always available for them and they just need to look for a way to gather and manage feedback in an appropriate manner. Organisations can also gather feedback in many different ways. It is up to the organisation to think about the most convenient method that needs to be followed to gather feedback.

2. *Feedback is active listening*

    Feedback can be gathered in different ways. Collecting verbal feedback via a survey is one of the most popular techniques out of them. In fact, collecting verbal feedback is like active listening. The organisations owners can gather a lot of information from feedback, which can help them to focus on future development.

    Whether the feedback is done verbally or via a feedback survey, the stakeholder providing the feedback needs to know they have been understood (or received) and they need to know that their feedback provides some value. When conducting a survey, always explain why stakeholder feedback is important and how their feedback will be used.

Stakeholders

3. *Feedback can motivate*
   Feedback has the potential to motivate organisations owners as well. Through feedback, they will be able to identify where they are not doing well. Then they can think of making required changes in the organisation to adapt accordingly and provide more value to stakeholders. This is one of the most convenient methods available for the organisations to increase the potential customer base as well, because it can help the organisation meet the specific needs and requirements of the customers.

   By asking for feedback, it can motivate employees to perform better. Employees like to feel valued and appreciate being asked to provide feedback that can help formulate business decisions. Feedback from stakeholders can be used to motivate to build better working relationships.

4. *Feedback can improve performance*
   Most organisations do not have a clear understanding whether they are performing in an effective manner or not. Feedback can assist them to get to know about it. However, the organisation owners need to be careful not to ignore feedback as criticism. What is viewed as negative criticism is actually constructive criticism and is the best kind of feedback that can help to formulate better decisions to improve and increase performance.

5. *Feedback is a tool for continued learning*
   For an employer/employee relationship to work well, both parties need to be willing to learn from each other. Seizing learning opportunities can provide an exceptional springboard for business and personal growth. It is possible to get feedback from stakeholders on a regular basis. Therefore, it can be considered as an excellent tool for the organisation to engage with continuous learning. In other words, organisations can develop new products or services or rebrand the existing products based on feedback.

Regular feedback sessions, both scheduled and impromptu, allows reflection on behaviours, and, if appropriate, upgrade or change the way things are done. Seeing ourselves from someone else's point of view can be a truly enlightening experience.

Negative feedback, however, can have the opposite effect. Using feedback as a tool to berate a colleague or staff member, should never be employed as a leadership tactic. If someone is awful at their job, making them feel horrible about themselves will only serve to make things worse. In cases of poor performance, a more formal feedback stance or training route should be considered.

Feedback fuels change

Business processes need to change for many reasons; to make cost savings, to create efficiencies, to provide better service to clients... the reasons for change are endless.

Stakeholders

When an organisation is experiencing a period of change, feedback is a crucial element of the change process. If change is not the direct result of external feedback, then it is important to source opinions from those stakeholders who matter to the organisation.

Invest time in asking and learning about how stakeholders experience working with the organisation.

Most of the world's most prominent organisations use stakeholder feedback to make improvements to their products and services. No matter what the size of organisation, never lose sight of the opinion of those that spend their time, money and resources with you.

Value of Stakeholder Feedback

Understanding stakeholders is vital in business today. This includes listening to the views and beliefs of stakeholders as well as seeking their feedback. These are the people who will shape and influence future successes (or failures).

The key to keeping stakeholders on-side is consultation. This involves the development of constructive and productive long-term relationships. Stakeholder consultation aims to build relationships based on mutual trust and benefits. Listening to and understanding the views and feedback from stakeholders can help shape and improve the overall operations of an organisation.

Stakeholder consultation can be project-based or on-going. Specific project-based consultation is generally used for the development of new products and services. An organisation may consult with customers to establish specific needs of the target market. On-going consultation, however, is generally used to track the progress of a company in regard to stakeholder expectations and to maximise buy-in. An organisation may consult with stakeholders regarding changes to the company's direction or its branding.

Benefits of Stakeholder Feedback

The benefits of stakeholder consultation are clear, with some of the most significant reasons listed below:

- *Enable more informed decision making*
- *Lead to greater stakeholder satisfaction*
- *Improves chances of project/initiative success*
- *Promote open, two-way communication*

Stakeholders

Gathering Stakeholder Feedback

Gathering feedback from internal stakeholders in your organisation is fundamental to developing a successful product. Remember that team members are also internal customers, and will likely be as or more vocal than your external customers about your product — they have a lot to say, but where and how should they say it? Let us look at some ways to gather feedback from stakeholders.

While product teams rely on a combination of several communication channels to share feedback with colleagues, others find it better to pick one and stick with it.

Here are a few common feedback communication channels and a brief look at the pros and cons of each so you can make a considered choice about what works best for you:

Channel	Pros:	Cons:
Email & Chat Share feedback via email and use labels or folders to stay organised, or if your organisation uses a chat platform internally, create a room specifically for feedback.	Convenient for customer teams to use. Feedback can be shared virtually anytime. You can search feedback later.	Neither option scales well for the Product Manager. Chat and email can be distracting. Does not aggregate data or provides analytics. Requires extra manual work to extract the feedback.
Team Meetings Consider holding bi-monthly or monthly feedback meetings with customer teams to let folks share and discuss what they have been hearing.	Opportunity to provide product updates/share what is next on your roadmap. Allows you to ask follow-up questions. You can clarify feedback with those who have shared it.	Can lead to confusion if customer teams must hold onto feedback for a month before relaying it. (Think of the game "telephone.") Getting everyone in the room at the same time can be hard and inconvenient.
Feedback Reports In lieu of (or in addition to) facilitating a feedback meeting, have every team generate a customer feedback report every two weeks or so and share it with your team.	Contains both qualitative and quantitative data. It is a resource you can return to for information when you need it.	Time-consuming and possibly inconvenient for customer teams to produce. Does not look at long-term feedback trends.

Stakeholders

Channel	Pros:	Cons:
Collaborative Spreadsheets You can ask customer-facing teams to enter feedback directly into a spreadsheet within Google Sheets or a similar tool.	Customer teams can share feedback at any time. Good for gathering and both qualitative and quantitative feedback.	May be inconvenient for customer teams to use, which could result in them sharing less feedback. Hard for customer teams to know whether the product team is reading their feedback.
Feedback Collection Platforms You can take advantage of software tools designed to collect user feedback and route it to the correct party.	Highly scalable. Can aggregate qualitative and quantitative data from every feedback source in one place, making it easy to access and use to make decisions.	Cost may be a con if your budget is tight. Customer teams may require a bit of training to help them understand how the system works.

All these communication channels come with their benefits and disadvantages, and the right approach is probably some combination of several. It is up to you and your team to decide which combination of channels works best for you.

Chapter 5: Governance and Compliance

Governance and Compliance

Governance and Compliance

All businesses must have Policies, Processes and procedures which apply Governance and Compliance to its operations.

Compliance is the term used for the way the organisation complies with the legal aspects of its operation, whilst governance refers to the systems by which it is directed and controlled.

Aims of Governance and Compliance

Organisations need to operate in compliance with a wide variety of financial rules, regulations and legislation that vary according to the type of organisation and the activities it undertakes.

There will be internal governance to ensure compliance with the requirements set out in the organisation's policies and procedures, for example:

- *how sales need to be recorded*
- *how often reports need to be generated*
- *how to use systems that track banking activities*
- *information needed for monthly reports sent to head office*
- *how to prepare quarterly reviews for shareholders*
- *systems to check and monitor compliance*

Issues that governance and compliance aim to avoid and mitigate

Broadly speaking, governance and compliance aim to avoid and mitigate issues such as:

- **fraud** – *e.g., procedures to shred documents to prevent identity theft*
- **theft** – *e.g., using CCTV to monitor staff using a cash till*
- **tax evasion** – *e.g., procedures to make sure that cash payments are declared*
- **criminal activity** – *e.g., taking bribes or trafficking workers*
- **misuse of funds and resources** – *e.g., monitoring budgets closely to reduce waste and unnecessary spending*
- **inefficiency** – *e.g., from not monitoring waste or opportunities to steal cash or goods*
- **money laundering** – *e.g., disposal of large sums of money which have been derived from illegal activity*

Governance and Compliance

Sometimes actions are deliberate and have a criminal intent – e.g., knowingly employing people who are illegal immigrants or those who have been trafficked, stealing products or cash.

Some actions are due to negligence and ignorance – e.g., from someone not realising that they need to provide workplace pensions for their employees; under-declaring VAT due to lack of knowledge about the rules.

There many legal requirements imposed by external stakeholders which must be complied with. It is a requirement of all organisations to satisfy these legal requirements by, for example:

- **paying the right amounts of tax** – *e.g., PAYE tax and national insurance, VAT or corporation tax*
- **paying the correct level of minimum wage**
- **making contributions to workplace pensions** – *e.g., to comply with the Pension Regulator's requirements*
- **keeping adequate records** – *e.g., audited accounts for large companies*
- **using, storing and disposing of financial information correctly** – *e.g., in accordance with the General Data Protection Regulations 2018 (GDPR)*
- **submitting accurate returns on time** – *e.g., to HMRC or Companies House*
- **avoiding making bribes** – *e.g., to conform with the Bribery Act 2010*
- **satisfying industry-specific requirements** – *e.g., FCA requirements for financial services organisations*

There can also be costs associated with compliance – e.g., accountancy fees for preparing and submitting accounts; consultancy fees for compliance advice and strategy making and audit fees for verification.

In order to achieve compliance with legislation, organisations need good governance – the systems by which organisations are directed and controlled, imposed by management such as a board of directors or trustees.

Financial governance is necessary to enable organisations to:

- **keep up to date with new legislation and stakeholder expectations**
- **increase efficiency and revenue**
- **lower the costs of compliance**
- **avoid fines and penalties**
- **avoid damage to their reputation**

Governance and Compliance

Compliance

All organisations must comply with the laws and regulations which relate to its industry, environment, legal entity and circumstances. Financial compliance must be demonstrated through the accounts of the business and the financial returns it makes to the necessary enforcement bodies.

The following are just a small sample of the laws which apply to every business in the UK.

- Health and Safety Act
- Financial Laws including tax laws
- Employment law
- General data Protection Regulations (GDPR)
- Freedom of Information Act
- Privacy and Electronic Communications Regulations
- Copyrights, Design and Patents Act
- Human Rights Act
- Equality Act

In addition, there is also the legislation which defines how a business should conduct itself.

These can include:

Legislation	Purpose
Companies Act	Defines the duties of the Directors of all companies registered in the UK
Financial Services and Markets Act	Regulates shares and securities
Financial Services Act	Applies criminal offences for making false claims or misrepresentation and creating false impressions
Insolvency Act	Governs the winding up of companies including liquidation and bankruptcy
Consumer Credit Act	Protects credit cards, loans and hire purchase agreements
Consumer Rights Act	Protects and assigns rights to the consumer including the right to compensation
Misrepresentation Act	Protects consumers from false or fraudulent claims
Payment Services Regulations	Protects consumers who are victims of fraud
Unfair Terms in Consumer Regulations	Defines the terms which are considered unfair in consumer agreements
Consumer contracts Regulations	Protects customers when buying items online

Governance and Compliance

The type and nature of the legislation which must be complied with, will vary from organisation to organisation. Not all legislation will apply to all business, however, a few do and include employment law, equality law, data protection and health and Safety.

The Health and Safety Act 1974

The thought of being hurt at work is not very appealing but on average, 300 people a year lose their lives at work in Britain. In addition, around 158,000 non-fatal injuries are reported each year and an estimated 2.2 million people suffer from ill health caused or made worse by work. Some £16 billion is lost each year through accidents and injuries.

Accidents don't happen. They are caused!

The Health and Safety Executive (HSE) was set up under the Health and Safety Act and it is the HSE who enforces workplace health and safety and apply.

The Act contains powers for the HSE to enforce these employer duties and apply penalties for non-compliance.

The Health & Safety at Work Act 1974 applies to all employees, the self-employed, government offices and in some circumstances the general public.

When it was introduced, the Act did three things.

- *Introduced the concept of criminal liability.*
- *Introduced the concept of you are guilty until proven innocent.*
- *Gave wide, sweeping, powers to Health & Safety Inspectors to enter businesses at any time that work is in progress, carry out inspections and if necessary, serve notice that practices are dangerous.*

Its main concept is that employers have a duty to protect their employers and members of the public affected by their work and must inform them about matters relating to their health, safety and welfare.

The employer's duty under the Health and Safety at Work Act is to provide staff with a safe and healthy workplace, and this includes:

- *a safe system of work*
- *a safe place of work*
- *safe equipment, plant and machinery*
- *safe and competent people working alongside you, because employers are also liable for the actions of their staff and managers*

Governance and Compliance

- *carrying out risk assessments as set out in regulations, and taking steps to eliminate or control these risks*
- *informing workers fully about all potential hazards associated with any work process, chemical substance or activity, including providing instruction, training and supervision*
- **appointing a 'competent person' responsible for health and safety** *(competent persons, such as a head of health and safety, oversee day-to-day safety management, oversee safety inspections, and liaise with staff safety reps)*
- **consulting with workplace safety representatives** *(if a union is recognised, your employer must set up and attend a workplace safety committee if two or more safety reps request one)*
- *providing adequate facilities for staff welfare at work*

The Health and Safety at Work Act 1974 states:

"All employers are required to have a health and safety policy, carry out risk assessments and provide health and safety training for their employees."

The Health and Safety at Work Act allows the government to issue regulations, guidance and Approved Codes of Practice (ACOPs) for employers. These set out detailed responsibilities for an employer in every aspect of workplace health and safety, from working safely with computers, to stress and hazardous chemicals.

Approved Codes of Practice (ACOPs) are guidance with specific legal standing. They deal with a wide range of hazardous materials and working practices.

Employers who are prosecuted for a breach of health and safety law, who have not followed an ACOP, are likely to be found at fault by the courts.

A failure to follow an Approved Codes of Practice is not an offence in itself, but an employer will need to be able to show that equally effective methods have been adopted to demonstrate compliance with the law.

Governance and Compliance

Safety Regulations

The Health and Safety at Work Act is a huge piece of legislation as it covers all industries and sectors. To address this diversity, the Act is underpinned by Regulations which are designed to meet the needs of different industry sectors.

Safety regulations are the strongest form of official advice that employers have to follow, and they are legally enforceable. Regulations are made by government ministers, often following proposals from the Health and Safety Executive (HSE) and approved by Parliament.

They broadly cover the general management of health and safety at work, work processes (e.g., manual handling, use of display screen equipment) and specific standards (e.g., exposure to chemicals).

The main set of regulations is the Management of Health and Safety at Work Regulations 1999, also known as the 'Management Regs'. They place a legal duty on employers to carry out a risk assessment as a first step in ensuring a safe workplace and lie at the heart of the modern approach to health and safety at work.

The Management of Health and Safety at Work Regulations 1999

The Management of Health and Safety at Work Regulations 1999 were introduced to reinforce the Health and Safety Act 1974.

Also known as the 'Management Regs', these came into effect in 1993. Main employer duties under the Regulations include:

- *making 'assessments of risk' to the health and safety of its workforce, and to act upon risks they identify, so as to reduce them (Regulation 3).*
- *appointing competent persons to oversee workplace health and safety.*
- *providing workers with information and training on occupational health and safety*
- *operating a written health and safety policy.*

They explicitly outline what employers are required to do to manage health and safety and apply to every work activity. The regulations place a set of duties on both employers and employees to maintain a safe and healthy workplace.

Risk Assessments

The main duty placed on employers by the Management of Health and Safety at Work Regulations is to undertake risk assessments to identify potential hazards to employee

Governance and Compliance

health and safety and anyone who may be affected by their work activity. Employers with five or more employees must record in writing any significant findings.

Separate risk assessments should be conducted for young people (under the age of 18) – taking their inexperience and immaturity into consideration – and new and expectant mothers.

As a result of conducting a risk assessment, employers must then make arrangements for implementing health and safety measures to control the hazards identified by the risk assessment.

Where the risk assessment has identified that health surveillance of an employee is needed, it is necessary for a system of regular checks to be carried out. These are used to detect ill-health due to working conditions such as noise, vibration, solvents or dust early to prevent severe damage or deterioration caused by the workplace.

Finally, the risk assessment should determine the procedures required to manage serious and imminent danger. For example, an evacuation procedure in the event of a fire or other emergency situations. It also needs to advise how and when an employee should contact the emergency services.

Competent Persons
Employers are required to appoint at least one competent person (preferably from within the organisation) to oversee, supervise and assist in all matters of health and safety and complying with legislation.

Information and Training
Employees must be provided with all necessary safety information in an understandable format. Similar appropriate health and safety information also needs to be provided to temporary and non-employees (e.g., contractors).
Adequate health and safety training must be received by every employee. In addition, workers should not be given tasks beyond their competence or physical capabilities.

Shared Premises
Where employers are sharing premises with another employer, it is necessary for the employers to co-operate and co-ordinate health and safety activities. Information from risk assessments — and the resulting preventative measures — must be exchanged between employers.

Governance and Compliance

The Six Pack

The 'six-pack' is the name given to the most widely quoted sets of health and safety regulations. These can cover heating, lighting and ventilation at work, the safe use of computer screens and keyboards, handling heavy or awkward loads, rest breaks, and personal protective equipment.

The six pack of regulations include:

- The Workplace (Health, Safety and Welfare) Regulations 1992
- The Health and Safety (Display Screen Equipment) Regulations 1992
- The Personal Protective Equipment at Work Regulations 1992
- The Manual Handling Operations Regulations 1992
- The Provision and Use of Work Equipment Regulations 1998
- The Reporting of Injuries, Diseases and Dangerous Occurrences Regulations 1995

The Workplace (Health, Safety and Welfare) Regulations 1992

The main provisions of these Regulations require employers to provide:

- *adequate lighting, heating, ventilation and workspace* (and keep them in a clean condition).
- *staff facilities, including toilets, washing facilities and refreshment*
- *safe passageways, i.e., to prevent slipping and tripping hazards.*

Toilets and handwashing facilities along with a rest area where staff can eat their meals is a minimum requirement, but the requirement may be more far reaching. Some tasks are known to cause problems for some people and steps must be taken to minimise this or make provision to limit the exposure to the problem.

The Health and Safety (Display Screen Equipment) Regulations 1992

The main provisions here apply to display screen equipment (DSE) 'users', defined as workers who 'habitually' use a computer as a significant part of their normal work. This includes people who are regular users of DSE equipment or rely on it as part of their job. This covers you if you use DSE for an hour or more continuously, and/or you are making daily use of DSE.

Employers are required to:

- *make a risk assessment of workstation use by DSE users, and reduce the risks identified.*

Governance and Compliance

- *ensure DSE users take 'adequate breaks'.*
- *provide regular eyesight tests.*
- *provide health and safety information.*
- *provide adjustable furniture (e.g., desk, chair, etc.)*
- *demonstrate that they have adequate procedures designed to reduce risks associated with DSE work, such as repetitive strain injury (RSI).*

The Personal Protective Equipment at Work Regulations 1992

The main provisions require employers to:

- **ensure that suitable personal protective equipment (PPE) is provided free of charge "wherever there are risks to health and safety that cannot be adequately controlled in other ways."** *The PPE must be 'suitable' for the risk in question, and include protective face masks and goggles, safety helmets, gloves, air filters, ear defenders, overalls and protective footwear*
- **provide information, training and instruction on the use of this equipment.**

The Manual Handling Operations Regulations 1992

The main provisions of these Regulations require employers to:

- *avoid (so far as is reasonably practicable) the need for employees to undertake any manual handling activities involving risk of injury*
- **make assessments of manual handling risks and try to reduce the risk of injury.** *The assessment should consider the task, the load and the individual's personal characteristics (physical strength, etc.)*
- *provide workers with information on the weight of each load.*

The Provision and Use of Work Equipment Regulations 1998

This requires that equipment provided for use by employees in the workplace is safe.

The main provisions require employers to:

- *ensure the safety and suitability of work equipment for the purpose for which it is provided.*
- *properly maintain the equipment, irrespective of how old it is.*
- *provide information, instruction and training on the use of equipment*
- *protect employees from dangerous parts of machinery.*

Governance and Compliance

The Reporting of Injuries, Diseases and Dangerous Occurrences Regulations 1995 (RIDDOR)

Under these Regulations, employers are required to report a wide range of work-related incidents, injuries and diseases to the Health and Safety Executive (HSE), or to the nearest local authority environmental health department.

The Regulations require an employer to record in an accident book the date and time of the incident, details of the person(s) affected, the nature of their injury or condition, their occupation, the place where the event occurred and a brief note on what happened.

The following injuries or ill health must be reported:

- *the death of any person.*
- *specified injuries including fractures, amputations, eye injuries, injuries from electric shock, and acute illness requiring removal to hospital or immediate medical attention.*
- *'over-seven-day' injuries, which involve relieving someone of their normal work for more than seven days as a result of injury caused by an accident at work.*
- *reportable occupational diseases, including:*
    - *cramp of the hand or forearm due to repetitive movement.*
    - *carpal tunnel syndrome, involving hand-held vibrating tools.*
    - *occupational asthma.*
    - *tendonitis or tenosynovitis (types of tendon injury).*
    - *hand-arm vibration syndrome (HAVS), including where the person's work involves regular use of percussive or vibrating tools*
    - *occupational dermatitis.*
- *near misses (described in the Regulations as 'dangerous occurrences')*

Governance and Compliance

Health and Safety Policy Statements

All employers are required by law to have a Health and Safety Policy. If there are five or more employees, including any owners who work in the business, this policy must be in written form.

Health and Safety Policies are very important documents. They set out the aims and objectives of the company in terms of how it intends to provide and maintain safe and healthy working conditions, safe systems of work, equipment and plant for all its employees and how it will provide information, instruction, training and supervision for all its employees. It will also set out how it will ensure that all its legal requirements are met, how the policy shall be made known to its employees and how it will be monitored and regularly reviewed to make sure that its aims and objectives are achieved.

Health and Safety Policies also contain valuable information about the nature of the business. It also describes who in the company is responsible for what aspects of Health and Safety as well as stating any company specific Health and Safety Rules that apply to all employees.

Although it is your employer's legal responsibility to make you aware of its Health and Safety Policy, it is equally your responsibility to make sure you fully understand it!

You are strongly urged to adopt a positive approach to working safely, to be aware of hazards, correct anything that might cause an accident (unless this would involve risk) and report it to your manager or Supervisor.

Any employee who contravenes or fails to observe relevant health and safety rules could normally expect to be subjected to disciplinary action by their employer.

What you should know poster

A Health and Safety Law Poster is a brief guide to health and safety law and provides a list of the key point's employees and employers have to know.

Every business in the UK must display a copy of this poster, regardless of the number of staff they employ.

Governance and Compliance

Employment Legislation

Employment law, while designed to protect the rights of the employee, covers most of the aspects regarding the relationship between the employer and the employee. The business must comply with all aspects of employment law to avoid the negative impact of not doing so, including costly fines, employment tribunal's, adverse publicity and loss of their brand reputation, for example.

There are several pieces of legislation that can be connected with the delivery of work including:

- *Employment Rights Act 1996*
- *Human Rights Act 1998*
- *Equality Act 2010*
- *Working Time Regulations*

It is not uncommon to hear some people dismissing employment legislation as "red tape" or "health and safety gone mad". However, employment law is aimed at protecting and supporting everyone in the workplace – without it, there would be no guarantee of sickness or holiday pay, for example, and workers might not be able to challenge discrimination, bullying or wrongful dismissal.

Employment law is constantly under review and revision, with additions and changes happening every year, so it is important for managers and their organisations to keep up to date with the latest legislation and regulations.

Employment Rights Act 1996

The main employment legislation in the UK is the Employment Rights Act 1996. This law is very detailed and deals with a huge number of aspects about employment.

Some of the main points covered by the Act are:

- *the employee's right to have a statement or contract of employment*
- *the employee's right to have an itemised pay statement*
- *protection of wages*
- *protection from suffering detriment in employment from taking time off work* – e.g., taking time off for jury service, family reasons or antenatal care
- *sickness*
- *maternity, paternity and adoption payments and leave*
- *suspension from work*
- *procedures for discipline, grievance, dismissal and redundancy*
- *Sunday working and time off*

Governance and Compliance

Statutory rights ensure all workers are treated fairly by their employers under law. These rights apply to most, though not all, workers. The self-employed or those working for an agency may not have the same rights.

The only universal rights for every worker are the right to minimum wage and to not be discriminated against.

UK workers have 8 key legal rights

The right to maximum working hours
Employees cannot be forced to work more than 48 hours in one week so must agree to put in additional hours in writing. Workers also have a legal right to paid holiday every year. Full-time employees can get up to 5.6 weeks (depending on the company) and part-time workers get pro rata holiday.

Workers can also legally take unpaid time off for reasons such as additional training, taking part in trade union activities, and for emergencies, like looking after dependants.

What people often do not realise is if you have been working somewhere for six months you have the right to submit a request for flexible working. The business does not have to accept your request but must give a compelling reason why not if so.

The right to equal pay & minimum wage
UK workers must be paid at least National Minimum Wage. All employees should receive a payslip breaking down their pay and deductions soon after starting, and employers cannot make any illegal wage deductions.

Under the Equal Pay Act 1970, unequal treatment between men and women over pay and employment conditions became completely prohibited. It was repealed but then many of its provisions were replicated in the Equality Act 2010. It is important to distinguish between unequal pay – which is illegal – and the issues surrounding the gender pay gap, where one sex is earning more than the other within a company because one dominates the higher up positions, which is not illegal but is an issue many businesses are tackling.

The right to health and safety at work
Health and safety laws state every worker has a legal right to daily and weekly time off. This means anyone working more than six hours must have a break of at least 20 minutes and everyone must get at least one day off in every seven days.

All workers also have a right to work in an environment where any risks to their health and safety are properly dealt with and controlled. This is the duty of the employer, who must also ensure they communicate with employees on all health and safety matters. The responsibility includes, for example, ensuring staff have a clean environment to work in, any necessary protective clothing, water for drinking, and first aid equipment.

Governance and Compliance

The right to parental leave
Every woman who has a baby is entitled to up to a year of maternity leave, no matter how long they have worked for the company. Statutory leave for fathers is currently only two weeks and the fathers must have worked for the company for at least 26 consecutive weeks by the end of the 15th week of the pregnancy.

Leave is very different to pay, which can be more complex and varies depending on how long you have worked for a company.

Fathers qualifying for paternity pay must earn at least £113 a week before tax and the rate is either £140.98 a week or 90% of your weekly earnings, whichever is lower.

Mothers are only entitled to pay for 39 weeks of their leave, and this changes over time. They get 90% of their pre-tax weekly earnings for the first six weeks, £145.18 a week or 90% of their earnings if it is less for the next 33 weeks and nothing after that.

Shared Parental Leave is a recent ruling which allows both parents to share up to 50 weeks of leave and 37 weeks of pay between you. (*Please check the accuracy of these details before using them as they change frequently*)

The right to trade union membership
Trade unions are organisations of workers who join together to achieve a common goal, like improving wages and working conditions and protecting their trade's integrity.

Employees have the right to belong to a trade union, join or not join a trade union, and leave or remain a member of one at any time during their employment. Employers are not allowed to treat you unfairly or dismiss you because you do any of these things.

Workers decide to join trade unions because they give you the power to negotiate a better deal through collective bargaining.

The right to not be discriminated against
Under no circumstances can anyone be discriminated against at work for gender, sexuality, age, background, race, religious beliefs, marriage and partnership, pregnancy, or disability. Examples of how this could happen include not choosing someone for a job or promotion, not paying them the same, and it could even occur indirectly through rules which put certain employees at a disadvantage.

Employers can actively prevent discrimination from occurring by ensuring they recruit inclusively, have an equal opportunities policy, and ensuring all staff follow these practices, by providing training on this topic, encouraging universal respect, and dealing with any complaints quickly. There is no situation when it is legally acceptable to harass or victimise anyone at work if they complain or expose a wrongdoing.

Governance and Compliance

The right to fair dismissal
Employees must usually give employees at least the notice stated in their employment contract or the legal minimum notice period, whichever is longer.

An employer can only dismiss a worker without notice if it considers someone to have done something which constitutes gross misconduct, for example committing fraud or being violent.

Dismissals related to the following are considered automatically unfair:

- *health and safety concerns*
- *assertion of statutory rights*
- *request for flexible working*

Employers must always pursue the fair procedure when considering dismissal.

If you are threatened with or receive what you consider to be unfair dismissal, you can get help from a third party to solve the issue by mediation, conciliation, and arbitration. Trade union members can speak to their unions. You must have worked for the company for a minimum period before you have the right to claim unfair dismissal, and this completely varies depending on when you started working for the company and how long you have worked there, due to changes in the law.

The right to reasonable adjustments
Under the Equality Act 2010 employers must also ensure there are reasonable adjustments so that workers with disabilities are not disadvantaged, neither in the job application process or in the job itself. A person is classed as disabled under this law if they have a mental or physical impairment which has a substantially adverse and long-term impact on whether they can do day-to-day activities.

Reasonable adjustments remove or minimise disadvantages disabled people face and, while some businesses will spend a lot on expensive equipment, this does not have to happen. Examples of reasonable adjustments include a keyboard for someone with arthritis, a wheelchair ramp, changing performance targets, and a phased return to work after a period off sick.

Governance and Compliance

The Human Rights Act 1998

This Act is designed to provide legal protection to all human beings. It embraces all other Equality & Diversity Acts and ensures human rights are protected in areas not covered by them.

Human Rights Act 1998

The Human Rights Act was set out and agreed in 1948. It was reaffirmed by all nations on its 50th anniversary in 1998 and led to the introduction of the European Convention on Human Rights.

It came into force as law in the UK on 2nd October 2000.

The Human Rights Act declares that:

> *'All human beings are born free and equal in dignity and rights. They are endowed with reason and conscience and should act towards one another in a spirit of brotherhood.'*

It also states that 'Everyone is entitled to all the rights and freedoms set forth in the declaration, without distinction of any kind such as race, colour, sex, language, religion, political or other opinion, national or social origin, property, birth or other status'.

In an equal and fair society all people have rights and these are protected by legislation

For example:

- *The right to be treated as equal as human beings regardless of sex or race*
- *The right to be treated properly at work*
- *The right to be free from discrimination*
- *The right not to be bullied or harassed*
- *The right to be healthy and safe at work*

Harassment

No one should be deliberately harassed at work. Neither should they be bullied or made to feel bad. Employees do not have to put up with it!

Harassment can take many forms such as:

- *Threatening or abusive language*
- *Insulting language or behaviour*
- *Disorderly behaviour*
- *Displaying any writing, sign or other visible representation that alarms or distresses and was intended to do so*

Governance and Compliance

Sexual Harassment
It is perfectly acceptable to court and pay attention to someone if it is wanted or invited, but it is illegal to pester people.

If you are told once 'No, I don't like it', but you do it again, you are in danger of breaking the law, both Civil and Criminal. No one has to put up with sexual harassment at work. Be careful and think. Even a thoughtless comment may cause offence.

> *It might be OK for a man to say to a woman, 'You look smart today'*
> *But it might not be so good to say, 'I like that top you are wearing'*

Bullying
Bullying at work can also take many forms such as:

- *Aggressive or violent behaviour*
- *Threatening postures*
- *Putting you in a position where if you do not do something a threat of some kind hangs over you*
- *Excluding you from a group by intimidation*

If you feel that you are being harassed or bullied at work, you should inform your supervisor

Remember, there are laws that exist to protect you, such as:

- *Sex Discrimination Act 1975*
- *Race Relations Act 1976*
- *Protection from Harassment Act 1997*
- *Gender Reassignment Regulations 1999*
- *The Human Rights Acts of 1948 and 1998*

Equality Act 2010

The Equality Act 2010 is the current legislation that deals with equality and discrimination in the UK.

The term equality and diversity has become a watch word in both the workplace and society. It is vital that everyone is aware of the implications on the workplace.

Equality
Equality in the workplace means equal job opportunities and fairness for employees and job applicants.

Governance and Compliance

In the wider world, you must not treat people unfairly because of reasons protected by discrimination law ('protected characteristics'). For example, because of a person's sex, age or race.

Diversity
Diversity is the range of people in the workforce. For example, this might mean people with different ages, religions, ethnicities, people with disabilities, and both men and women. It also means valuing those differences. Managing equality and diversity involves creating and maintaining a positive environment where the differences of all employees are recognised, understood and valued so that they can reach their full potential and maximise their contributions.

It has also been described as:

> *"promoting equality of opportunity for all, through diversity, giving each individual the chance to achieve their potential, free from prejudice and discrimination."*

Inclusion
An inclusive workplace means everyone feels valued at work. It lets all employees feel safe to:

- *come up with different ideas*
- *raise issues and suggestions to managers, knowing this is encouraged*
- *try doing things differently to how they have been done before, with management approval*

An inclusive workplace can help lower the risk of bullying, harassment and discrimination.

The Act gives individuals rights as it is unlawful to discriminate against anyone because of a protected characteristic. The protected characteristics include:

- **age** – *all people over 18 are protected at work or in work training*
- **disability or impairment** – *organisations must make 'reasonable adjustments' to accommodate staff, customers and visitors with disabilities*
- **gender** – *equal pay, training and opportunity for males and females*
- **gender reassignment** – *people changing from male to female, or female to male*
- **marriage or civil partnership** – *preventing discrimination on the grounds of being married or in a civil partnership, at work or in work training*
- **pregnancy or maternity (including breastfeeding)** – *only reasons of safety are not covered – e.g., equality may not be possible for pregnant women in some circumstances if the activity could harm them or the baby*

Governance and Compliance

- **race** – *wherever they were born, their parents' and their own race, colour, ethnicity are protected*
- **religion or beliefs** – *any religion, lack of religion or personal belief is protected*
- **sexual orientation** – *heterosexual, gay, lesbian and bisexual people are covered*

Genuine Occupational Requirements

There are limited exemptions from liability in all the discrimination legislation. Thus, where the sex, race, age, sexual orientation or religion or belief of an employee is required for the specific job he or she is required to do, that characteristic may amount to a genuine occupational requirement (GOR).

There must be a clear connection between the duties of the post in question and the characteristics required. An example might be the need to recruit a person from a particular racial group to act in a role written for a character from that racial group.

It is permissible to specify gender when:

- *A man or woman is needed to act in a particular role in a play*
- *The job is one of two to be held by a married couple*
- *The work is in a single sex prison or hospital ward*
- *Carers for the mentally ill must be of the same sex*

Discrimination can occur in several different ways, as follows:

Direct discrimination
This is where one individual is treated less favourably than another, and the less favourable treatment is because of a protected characteristic they have, or are thought to have (see perception discrimination), or because they associate with someone who has a protected characteristic.

Indirect discrimination
This is where a provision, criterion or practice applies equally to everyone but has, or would have, a disproportionate impact on those people who share a protected characteristic (e.g. it is more difficult for someone to comply with a requirement because of their religion or belief).

Discrimination by association
This is direct discrimination against an individual because they associate with another person who possesses a protected characteristic.

Perception discrimination
This is direct discrimination against an individual where the person is treated less favourably than another, and the less favourable treatment is because others think they possess a protected characteristic. It applies even if the person does not actually possess that characteristic.

Governance and Compliance

Harassment
This is defined as unwanted conduct related to a relevant protected characteristic which has the purpose or effect of either: (a) violating another person's dignity; or (b) creating an intimidating, hostile, degrading, humiliating or offensive environment for that other person.

Victimisation
This occurs where an individual is subjected to less favourable treatment by reason of the fact that they have done a 'protected act' under the discrimination legislation – e.g., someone has made a complaint about discrimination on grounds of their age or sex, or helped somebody else to do so, and they are now being treated less favourably by their manager.

Employees also have a responsibility to make sure that they do not breach their employer's equality and diversity policies, codes of conduct or guidelines. The law requires each individual to take responsibility and avoid discrimination, and the employer needs to give clear guidelines in contracts of employment, equality and diversity policies, training sessions and so on.

If an individual fails to follow the guidelines, the organisation can implement disciplinary action or claim breach of contract (the employment contract).

Governance and Compliance

Employee Responsibilities

The principles of legislation have to be applied at work and in all dealings with other people. This means that everyone must be treated fairly and equally by you. It is important that you are clear about your personal responsibilities and liabilities under equality legislation and any relevant codes of practice.

Failure to comply with equality legislation could lead to legal action against you or the organisation. If you are unsure of any of your responsibilities it is important that you clarify them with your manager or equality and diversity representative.

Working successfully as a team with your colleagues depends upon all parties involved behaving in a fair and equal manner towards one another.

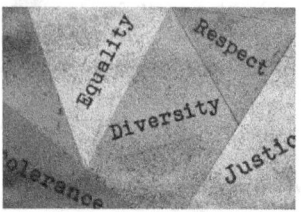

This does not mean you have to like everyone, but you must respect others and not treat people differently because of their individual characteristics and preferences. No matter what your personal views are, your behaviour at work should not be based upon them. A good employee always behaves professionally.

Professional behaviour requires that you are:

- *Respectful towards others in your dealings with them*
- *Consistent in your treatment of others at all times*
- *Honest in your communications with others*

Some organisations may choose to have a written equality and diversity policy. It is important that this policy is communicated quickly and clearly to the relevant people in your area of responsibility e.g., all employees, visitors and contractors.

Treat others as you would expect them to treat you!

Working Time Regulations 1998

The Working Time Regulations generally provide rights for employees to have:

- *a limit of an average 48-hour working week, although individuals may choose to work longer by 'opting out'*
- *5.6 weeks of paid leave a year*
- *11 consecutive hours' rest in any 24-hour period*
- *a 20-minute rest break if the working day is longer than 6 hours*
- *1 day off each week*

Governance and Compliance

- a limit on the normal working hours of night workers to an average 8 hours in any 24-hour period, and an entitlement for night workers to receive regular health assessments

Extra protection is available to young workers (workers aged 15 to 18). In particular, young workers:

- are entitled to a daily uninterrupted rest break of 30 minutes after working more than 4.5 hours.
- are entitled to an uninterrupted 12-hour break in each 24-hour period of work.
- are entitled to weekly rest of at least 48 hours in each seven-day period (and unlike adult workers, they cannot be made to take this rest over two days averaged over two weeks); and
- cannot normally work more than eight hours a day or 40 hours a week. These hours cannot be averaged out. There is no 'opt-out' for young workers.

All full-time workers are entitled to 5.6 weeks' paid holiday each year, reduced pro-rata for part-time workers.

These basic limits on the working week make a vital contribution to health and safety at work.

Employers have the right to ask their staff to enter into a written agreement to opt out of the 48-hour limit, for a specific period or indefinitely. However, if such an agreement is opted into, a worker is entitled to bring the agreement to an end without the employer's consent.

Governance and Compliance

Other Employment legislation and regulations

There are numerous other regulations and pieces of legislation that apply to certain industries or circumstances. Employees and management need to check the organisation's policies and procedures to find out which ones affect them, and what their responsibilities might be. These might include, for instance:

- *Trade Union and Labour Relations (Consolidation) Act 1992* – the ACAS code is issued under this Act
- *National Minimum Wage Act 1998* – dealing with the minimum wage for different age groups
- *Pensions Act 2014* – dealing with contributions to occupational pension schemes and state pensions
- *Modern Slavery Act 2015* – dealing with people trafficking and slavery
- *Part-Time Workers (Prevention of Less Favourable Treatment) Regulations 2000*
- *Fixed-term employees (Prevention of Less Favourable Treatment) Regulations 2002*
- *Statutory Paternity Pay and Statutory Adoption Pay (General) Regulations 2002* – and later amendments
- *Work and Families Act 2006*
- *Enterprise and Regulatory Reform Act 2013*

Governance and Compliance

Operational Legislation

The Data Protection Act 2018

The Data Protection Act 2018 controls how your personal information is used by organisations, businesses or the government.

Data Protection Act 2018

The Data Protection Act 2018 is the UK's implementation of the General Data Protection Regulation (GDPR).

Everyone responsible for using personal data has to follow strict rules called data protection principles. They must make sure the information is:

- *used fairly, lawfully and transparently*
- *used for specified, explicit purposes*
- *used in a way that is adequate, relevant and limited to only what is necessary*
- *accurate and, where necessary, kept up to date*
- *kept for no longer than is necessary*
- *handled in a way that ensures appropriate security, including protection against unlawful or unauthorised processing, access, loss, destruction or damage*

There is stronger legal protection for more sensitive information, such as:

- *race*
- *ethnic background*
- *political opinions*
- *religious beliefs*
- *trade union membership*
- *genetics*
- *biometrics (where used for identification)*
- *health*
- *sex life or orientation*

There are separate safeguards for personal data relating to criminal convictions and offences.

Governance and Compliance

Rights

Under the Data Protection Act 2018, you have the right to find out what information the government and other organisations store about you. These include the right to:

- *be informed about how your data is being used*
- *access personal data*
- *have incorrect data updated*
- *have data erased*
- *stop or restrict the processing of your data*
- *data portability* (allowing you to get and reuse your data for different services)
- *object to how your data is processed in certain circumstances*

You also have rights when an organisation is using your personal data for:

- *automated decision-making processes (without human involvement)*
- *profiling, for example to predict your behaviour or interests*

The General Data Protection Regulation 2016

GDPR stands for General Data Protection Regulation. This was a Europe wide initiative.

The GDPR is a regulation from the Data Protection Act and covers any information related to a person or data subject that can be used to directly or indirectly identify them. It can be anything from a name, a photo and an email address to bank details, social media posts, biometric data and medical information. It also introduces digital rights for individuals.

When it came into effect on May 25, 2018, the GDPR set new standards for data protection, and kickstarted a wave of global privacy laws that forever changed how we use the internet.

The Purpose of GDPR

Personal data is highly valuable — in fact, it supports a trillion-dollar industry. Companies like Facebook and Google make their profits by selling personal information to advertisers. With this much money at stake, do you trust them to have your best interests at heart?

The GDPR defines what companies of all sizes can and cannot do with customer information.

Governance and Compliance

What Is Classified as Personal Data Under GDPR?

Personal data is information that can be used to identify you. Put simply, it is any private details that you would not want to fall into the wrong hands.

These are some examples of personal data:

- **Name**
- **phone number**
- **address**
- **date of birth**
- **bank account**
- **passport number**
- **social media posts**
- **geotagging**
- **health records**
- **race**
- **religious and political opinions**

Think of personal data like a jigsaw. One piece alone might not say much but connected together they reveal a vivid picture of your life.

What Is a 'Breach' under GDPR?

Any incident that leads to personal data being lost, stolen, destroyed, or changed is considered a data breach. Unfortunately, breaches happen all the time.

Here are some newsworthy examples from before the GDPR started cracking down:

- *Almost half the population of the US had their name, date of birth, and social security number stolen from credit reporting agency Equifax as the result of a data breach.*
- *Political consulting firm Cambridge Analytica secretly took information from 50 million Facebook profiles and gave it to the 2016 Trump campaign.*

Both of these incidents illustrate how data breaches have serious real-world consequences. This is exactly what GDPR and similar laws hope to regulate.

What are the penalties for violating the GDPR?

The GDPR threatens would-be violators with some severe penalties. To make sure companies handle your personal data in a legal, ethical way, the fines for noncompliance are:

Up to £18 million or 4% of annual global turnover.

Some big names have already been hit with these noncompliance fines:

Governance and Compliance

British Airways — £165 million. *The UK airline set the record for fines when the booking details of 500,000 customers were stolen in a cyberattack.*
Marriott — £90 million. *After buying the Starwood Hotels group, Marriott failed to update an old system belonging to the group. This system was hacked, revealing information about 339 million guests.*
Google — £40 million. *Important information was hidden when users set up new Android phones, meaning they did not know what data collection practices they were agreeing to. The Google GDPR fine shows even tech giants are not immune to GDPR enforcement.*

Although smaller businesses would not be hit for such high amounts, they are held to the same standards.

A business owner now has to make sure their operations comply with the GDPR.

The only thing most people will need to do is read the cookie consent banners that now appear on websites and click agree (or not). The GDPR affects everything people do online, but it is mostly working behind the scenes.

Freedom of Information Act 2000

The Freedom of Information Act 2000 provides public access to information recorded and held by public authorities. Recorded information includes printed documents, computer files, letters, emails, photographs, and sound or video recordings.

Freedom of Information Act 2000

It does this in two ways:

> *public authorities are obliged to publish certain information about their activities*
> *and*
> *members of the public are entitled to request information from public authorities.*

The Act covers any recorded information that is held by a public authority in England, Wales and Northern Ireland, and by UK-wide public authorities based in Scotland. Information held by Scottish public authorities is covered by Scotland's own Freedom of Information (Scotland) Act 2002.

These organisations include:

> *schools*   *health trusts and hospitals*
> *councils*   *libraries*
> *government departments*   *museums*

Governance and Compliance

Anyone is able to request information, regardless of age, location or nationality. The Act does not necessarily cover every organisation that receives public money. For example, it does not cover some charities that receive grants and certain private sector organisations that perform public functions.

Requests must be made in writing, either by letter or by email. The organisation then has 20 working days to provide the information.

Public bodies do not always have to give requested information if:

The information required is regarded as sensitive - the Data Protection Act 2018 overrules in this instance. For example, a request to find out how much an employee earned would be rejected as that information is sensitive to the employee.

The information will be too costly or time consuming to produce. For a public organisation, such as a school, or a council, the cost limit is £450. Organisations determine costs based on £25 per hour per person. Therefore, if the information requested would take longer than 18 hours (18 x £25 = £450) to produce, the request would be rejected. For the government and armed forces, this limit is raised to £600 (24 hours).

The Act does not give people access to their own personal data (information about themselves) such as their health records or credit reference file. If a member of the public wants to see information that a public authority holds about them, they should make a data protection subject access request.

Digital Economy Act (2017)

The Digital Economy Act 2017 (the Act) makes provision about electronic communications infrastructure and services, including the creation of a broadband Universal Service Order (USO), to give all premises in the UK a legal right to request a minimum standard of broadband connectivity, expected to be 10 megabits per second (Mbps). The Act also introduces reform of the Electronic Communications Code and provides greater clarification on data sharing between public bodies.

Digital Economy Act 2010

The Digital Economy Bill was introduced in the House of Commons on 5 July 2016, completed its parliamentary stages and received Royal Assent, becoming law, on 27 April 2017.

The Bill followed an announcement made in the Queen's Speech to introduce legislation seeking to make the United Kingdom a world leader in the digital economy.

The Act is made up of six parts as follows:

Governance and Compliance

1. Access to digital services
2. Digital infrastructure
3. Online pornography
4. Intellectual property
5. Digital government
6. Miscellaneous.

Copyright, Designs and Patents Act (1988)

The Copyright, Designs and Patents Act 1988 exists to protect peoples' creations.

When a person creates something, they own it. What they create might include:

Copyright, Designs and Patents Act 1988

- a picture, drawing or photograph
- a video, television programme or film
- text, such as a book, article or report
- a game

Copyright is a legal means of protecting the work produced by authors, artists, designers, etc. It applies to certain types of creative work, including artwork, books and computer programs.

Copyright does not apply to ideas.

Copyright is applied automatically as long as certain criteria are met. There is no requirement to formally register the work or use the © symbol.

Work is automatically protected by copyright unless the copyright holder chooses to surrender that right.

Copyright gives the copyright holder exclusive rights to publish, copy, distribute and sell their work as they see fit. No one else can use the work without permission.

Copyright on a piece of work lasts for a long time. In the UK, copyright on artistic work, literature, music and films lasts for 70 years after the death of the creator.

When you buy someone's work, such as a book, film or music CD, the copyright holder grants permission to use it as part of the sale. This is called a licence. The licence is generally only for the purchaser to use.

It is illegal to:

Governance and Compliance

- *make copies of copywritten material*
- *publish it and sell it without permission*
- *share it with other people*
- *sell copies to other people*

This applies to any copywritten material, such as music, films, games and television programmes.

The internet has made it easy to access copyrighted material illegally. If you download a music track, film, game or programme without the copyright holder's permission, you are breaking the law.

For example, shops earn their money by selling goods. If someone takes them without paying, the shop does not make any money. In the same way, musicians, photographers, filmmakers and artists earn their money by selling the material they produce. If someone takes their work without paying, the person who created the work does not make any money.

There are, however, some situations where it is legal to copy, publish, distribute or sell copyrighted material. These are:

- *when you own the copyright*
- *when the copyright holder has given permission*
- *when the copyright holder has surrendered their copyright*

Governance and Compliance

The Computer Misuse Act (1990)

The extensive use of computers in business has led to new types of crime. The Act strives to discourage people from using computers for illegal purposes. There are three separate parts to the Act:

Computer Misuse Act 1990

- *It is illegal to access data stored on a computer unless you have permission to do so. Unauthorised access is often referred to as hacking.*
- *It is illegal to access data on a computer when that material will be used to commit further illegal activity, such as fraud or blackmail.*
- *It is illegal to make changes to any data stored on a computer when the user does not have permission to do so. If you access and change the contents of someone's files without their permission, you are breaking the law. This includes installing a virus or other malware which damages or changes the way the computer works.*

The maximum punishment for breaking this law is a £5,000 fine or several years' imprisonment.

However, one key part of the law is that intent must be proved. If a computer is not well protected, someone could accidentally access its data without meaning to. They might also accidentally change a document without realising it. For anyone to be found guilty, it has to be shown that they intentionally accessed and changed data.

Other employment related legislation and regulations

There are numerous other regulations and pieces of legislation that apply to certain industries or circumstances. Organisations need to review their policies and procedures against all legislation to establish which ones affect them, what their responsibilities might be and whether they are compliant.

These might include, for instance:

- **Trade Union and Labour Relations (Consolidation) Act 1992** – *the ACAS code is issued under this Act*
- **National Minimum Wage Act 1998** – *dealing with the minimum wage for different age groups*
- **Pensions Act 2014** – *dealing with contributions to occupational pension schemes and state pensions*
- **Modern Slavery Act 2015** – *dealing with people trafficking and slavery*
- **Part-Time Workers (Prevention of Less Favourable Treatment) Regulations 2000**

Governance and Compliance

- *Fixed-term employees (Prevention of Less Favourable Treatment) Regulations 2002*
- *Statutory Paternity Pay and Statutory Adoption Pay (General) Regulations 2002* – and later amendments
- *Work and Families Act 2006*
- *Enterprise and Regulatory Reform Act 2013*

Governance and Compliance

Consumer-Related Legislation

Whenever goods or services are provided to customers there are expectations from both the supplier and the customer of the goods and/or services being provided.

There is a minimum expectation that the goods or services will be fit for purpose.

A window cleaner that does not leave clean windows will not have many happy customers nor will they be in business for long. The customer, however, will have paid to have their windows cleaned and if they are not clean, they have a right to demand a refund of the monies paid.

Similarly, promises made by suppliers must be met in full – A new sofa in your home before Christmas is a common message on TV advertising, they are making a promise that they will achieve the delivery deadline – if they do not, they will be in breach of contract and the purchaser can make a claim against them for failing to fulfil the contract.

All these rights are defined and covered by The Consumer Rights Act which came into force on 1 October 2015 and replaced a number of old laws which had become outdated.

The law is now clearer and easier to understand, meaning that consumers can buy with confidence and businesses can sell to them with similar confidence.

On the rare occasions when problems arise, disputes can now be sorted out more quickly and cheaply.

Alternative Dispute Resolution, for example through an Ombudsman, offers a quicker and cheaper way of resolving disputes than going through the courts. The changes are relevant to all consumers and every business which sells directly to them.

UK consumers spend £90 billion a month across all sectors. This new, clear, statement of consumer rights helps them to make better choices when they buy and save both time and money.

The Consumer Rights Act

The Consumer Rights Act came into force on 1 October 2015 which meant from that date new consumer rights became law covering:

Consumer Rights Act 2015

- *what should happen when goods are faulty*
- *what should happen when digital content is faulty*

Governance and Compliance

- *how services should match up to what has been agreed, and what should happen when they do not, or when they are not provided with reasonable care and skill*
- *unfair terms in a contract*
- *what happens when a business is acting in a way which is not competitive?*
- *written notice for routine inspections by public enforcers, such as Trading Standards*
- *greater flexibility for public enforcers, such as Trading Standards, to respond to breaches of consumer law, such as seeking redress for consumers who have suffered harm.*

Most of these changes were important updates to existing laws. But two new areas of law were also introduced.

For the first time, rights on digital content has been set out in legislation. The Act gives consumers a clear right to the repair or replacement of faulty digital content, such as online film and games, music downloads and e-books. The law here has been unclear, and this change has brought us up to date with how digital products have evolved.

There are now also new, clear rules for what should happen if a service is not provided with reasonable care and skill, or as agreed. For example, the business that provided the service must bring it into line with what was agreed with the customer or, if this is not practical, must give some money back.
In terms of what is covered by the new Act, the old standards remain, and these are as follows:

- **Claims about goods** - *It is an offence for the business or any member of staff to issue false statements about services, accommodation and facilities, or to give misleading information about prices, discounts or special offers.*
- **Description of goods** – *Examples are labels such as 'home-made', 'made In France', 'fresh vegetables', etc. There is still a sale by description even where the customer selects the goods, for example, in a self-service restaurant, if he or she relied in some way on the description.*
- **Satisfactory Quality** – *Goods must be fit for the purpose for which they are usually bought*
- **Fitness for a particular purpose** – *Reasonable fitness for a purpose known to the seller*
- **Samples** – *Ensuring that goods when sold correspond with samples*

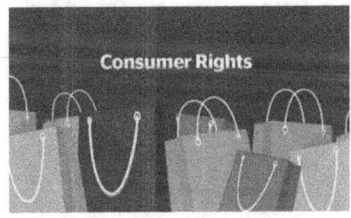

Governance and Compliance

Governance

The term Governance refers to the actions taken by those who run the organisation to ensure legal compliance and uphold the company's integrity.

Governance should promote good relations with stakeholders, including shareholders and employees.

Governance is the exclusive responsibility of the person, or group of people accountable for the performance and conformance of the organisation. In a commercial organisation, this is the Board of Directors or the management team which operate on their behalf.

There is a formal code of governance which is enshrined in company law for organisations listed on the London Stock Exchange. This sets a code of practice for the governance of financial matters; however, governance is required in all organisations and is also across the spectrum of activities.

The most tangible form of governance in an organisation is it policies, practices and procedures. These are put in place not only to ensure legal compliance, but also to ensure the business is operated in a way which maximises the benefit for the owners and employees.

Governance along with compliance aims to avoid and mitigate against:

- *fraud* – e.g., procedures to shred documents to prevent identity theft
- *theft* – e.g., using CCTV to monitor staff using a cash till
- *tax evasion* – e.g., procedures to make sure that cash payments are declared
- *criminal activity* – e.g., taking bribes or trafficking workers
- *misuse of funds and resources* – e.g., monitoring budgets closely to reduce waste and unnecessary spending
- *inefficiency* – e.g., from not monitoring waste or opportunities to steal cash or goods
- *money laundering* – e.g., Disposal of large sums of money which have been derived from illegal activity

Accountability

An organisation is not just accountable to HMRC and Companies House, it is also accountable to its Shareholders, Stakeholders, Investors, Suppliers, Customers and the staff within the organisation.

Internal stakeholders will need to be satisfied that the organisation looks after its financial affairs properly and could include:

Governance and Compliance

- **business owners** – e.g., sole proprietors or partners who need to know the levels of profit and cash flow
- **shareholders** – e.g., employees or others who own shares in a company who need to keep an eye on their investment
- **employees** – e.g., who rely on the organisation to operate payroll and bonus systems

External stakeholders could include, for example:

- **banks and other lenders** – e.g., who provide business loans to the organisation
- **national and local government agencies** – e.g., who collect taxes and provide grants
- **external customers** – e.g., individuals and companies who buy and use the organisation's products and services
- **charity commission** – e.g., who examine accounts and regulate registered charities

The actions taken by some people are deliberate and have a criminal intent – these may include knowingly employing people who are illegal immigrants or stealing products or cash. Some actions are due to negligence and ignorance such as someone not realising that they need to provide workplace pensions for their employees or under-declaring VAT due to lack of knowledge about the rules.

By ensuring an organisation is compliant with legislation and is governed fastidiously and fairly, everyone involved with the business will have confidence in the way the business is being operated and satisfied that the business is being managed equitably and legally.

Systems of Governance

A system of governance needs to be created for every organisation and this can be achieved through the design, implementation and ensuring compliance with the five functions of governance.

These are:

Determining the objectives of the organisation
These are expressed through the vision and mission statements and implemented through its strategic plan. The objectives define the purpose of the organisation and describe how the purpose will be fulfilled.

Determining the ethics of the organisation
It is important to define what aspects of behaviour are really important. The question needs to be asked; how much importance is to be given to factors such a sustainability, corporate social responsibility and stakeholder engagement over profits?

Governance and Compliance

Ethics are based on morals and values and define the rules or standards governing the conduct of people within the organisation. The ethical standards of any organisation are set by the behaviours of people at the top and cascade down the hierarchy.

Creating the culture of the organisation
This is a more subtle process and deals with the way people interact with each other. The governing body decides on the culture it wants and influences the operating culture of the organisation through the people it appoints to executive positions.

'Governmentality', the willingness of people to 'be governed' and to support the governance system is at the centre of an effective culture. Other aspects include how supportive the organisation is, how innovative, how risk seeking or risk averse, how open and transparent, how mature and professional, and how tolerant it is.
It is impossible to have a culture of innovation and sensible risk taking if the organisation is intolerant of failure.

Ensuring compliance by the organisation
Governance is implemented to ensure the organisation meets its regulatory, statutory and legal obligations, as well as ensuring its management and staff work towards achieving the organisation's objectives, while working within the ethical and cultural framework which has been defined by the governing body.

Designing and implementing the governance framework for the organisation.
The governing body is accountable for the performance of the organisation and retains overall responsibility for the organisation it governs; however, in most organisations the governing body cannot undertake all of the work of governance itself.

To ensure the efficient governance of the organisation, various responsibilities need to be delegated to people within the organisation's management. The appropriate levels of authority and responsibility will be delegated to managers and other entities to ensure accountability.

In summary, the governing body appoints, provides direction to and oversees the functioning of the organisation's management and makes the 'rules' the organisation's management and staff are expected to conform to.

Management's job is to achieve the objectives of the organisation; working within its ethical and cultural framework, while complying with the 'rules' and providing assurance back to the governing body that this is being accomplished.

The governance system and the management system are derived from each other. The management system is dependent on the governance framework and the governance system is driven by the management.

Governance and Compliance

A well-governed organisation allows these two systems to work together to the benefit of the organisation's overall stakeholder community.

A good system of corporate governance will strive to:

- *Ensure that the management of an organisation considers the best interests of everyone*
- *Help organisations deliver long-term corporate success and economic growth*
- *Maintain the confidence of investors and as consequence organisations raise capital efficiently and effectively*
- *Has a positive impact on the price of shares as it improves the trust in the market*
- *Improves control over management and information systems* (such as security or risk management)
- *Gives guidance to the owners and managers the strategy of the company*
- *Minimises wastages, corruption, fraud, risks, and mismanagement*
- *Helps to create a strong brand reputation*
- *Most importantly – it makes organisations more resilient.*

Creating a framework for the governance of an organisation can be immensely challenging. You need to spend only a few moments thinking about the number of policies and procedures which are followed each day within one department to realise scale of the task of producing a framework for the governance of a whole organisation. In order to begin to make sense of the process it can be broken down into four elements often known as the four Ps'

These are:

- *People*
- *Purpose*
- *Process*
- *Performance*

People
People come first in the Four Ps because people exist on every side of the business equation. They are the founders, the board, the stakeholder and consumer and impartial observer.

People are the organisers who determine a purpose to work towards, develop a consistent process to achieve it, evaluate their performance outcomes, and use those outcomes to grow themselves and others as people.
This is a cyclical process, but it has to start with people.

Governance and Compliance

Purpose

Purpose is the next step. Every piece of governance exists **for** a purpose and to **achieve** a purpose.

The **'for'** is the guiding principles of the organisation. Their mission statement. Every one of their policies and projects should exist to further this agenda.

The **'achieve'** is the small step on the road to completing that large goal. It might seem pointless to type up minutes for a meeting that felt irrelevant, but those minutes and all the other governance from that meeting contribute to making the business effective at achieving its stated purpose.

Process

Governance is the process by which people achieve their organisation's purpose, and that process is developed by analysing performance. Processes are refined over time in order to consistently achieve their purpose, and it is good practice to constantly review the governance processes.

The questions should be asked of all processes - Can they be streamlined? Are they efficiently achieving their purpose? It takes work and endeavour to make processes function effectively, but once they do, they will quickly allow an organisation to grow.

Performance

Performance analysis is a key skill in any industry. The ability to look at the results of a process and determine whether it was successful (or successful enough), and then apply those findings to the rest of the organisation, is one of the primary functions of the governance process.

The analysis of these performance results should then be used to identify developmental needs in order to refine the process. The question to be asked regularly is: Governance: is it performing?

Examples might include:

- *how sales need to be recorded*
- *how often reports need to be generated*
- *how to use systems that track banking activities*
- *information needed for monthly reports sent to head office*
- *how to prepare quarterly reviews for shareholders*
- *systems to check and monitor compliance*

Governance and Compliance

Developing Governance

The leaders of organisations will not sit around a boardroom table and begin to discuss which policy or procedure of governance they will start with, it is very much more likely to be an organic process.

At day one of the organisation there will probably be only a few people involved and one or two people will be able to manage all four of the elements listed above so the need for detailed, documented governance will be negligible.

As the organisation grows, volumes will increase, more staff will be required and suddenly the business needs far more controls. New policies and procedures will be required and existing ones will need to be reviewed. Organisations will continue on this cycle of designing, developing, documenting and implementing new policies and procedures as the needs of the business require.

The key word here is documenting. If an organisation relies on word of mouth to implement new standards, governance is immediately under threat as it is open to interpretation or omission and people will not follow the prescribed processes.

It may seem that the number of policies an organisation has is excessive, however, it should be remembered that many policies and processes will not apply to all departments.

The key policies will be those that are directly linked to ensuring compliance with legislation. There will then be a number of policies and procedures which relate specifically to a department or team. These will be developed to ensure consistency in behaviour and performance and it is essential that those people affected by the policy adhere to it.

An example might be an escalation policy.

> A problem which cannot be dealt with by a junior team member will need to be escalated to someone in a more senior role, but who is the appropriate person?
>
> This will be defined in the process. If it is a supply issue, it may be directed to an identified member of a sales team. If it involves a quality issue it may need referring to a defined member of the production team. If the issue relates to a refund, it may need a certain level of authority to authorise the refund.
> If the staff member knows this policy or has immediate access to it, they can explain to the stakeholder how they will deal with the problem and pass the query on quickly, to the right person, to ensure a speedy resolution.

It is important that all staff are conversant with the policies which relate to their job role to ensure problems are resolved in a standardised manner to protect all stakeholders involved.

Governance and Compliance

Typical Framework

A framework for governance will necessitate the creation of policies and procedures or processes. These reflect – how a process should be performed in practice – and can be a separate document or a section of the same. It is often worth trying to be clear, as a policy change may or may not alter the procedure, while a necessary change in procedure should not be allowed to change the policy by default. It should be clear in a procedure which policy or policies it relates to.

Basic requirements

Health and Safety Policy and Procedure. *Could include:*
Workstation assessment procedure.
Fire safety.

Equal Opportunities Statement of Intent. *Could include:*
Harassment.
Reference to recruitment procedure.
Confidentiality Policy (including Data Protection).

Staff

Basic terms of employment
Expenses policy (with due regard to Inland Revenue rules)
Staff disciplinary procedure.
Staff grievance procedure.
Staff appraisal procedure.
Supervision.
Staff loans (travel, cycle, car).
Union recognition policy.
Sick leave policy and procedure.

Leave policy and procedure.
Time off in lieu policy and procedure.
Public duties.
Recruitment procedure.
Redundancy policy.
Induction procedure and checklist.
Exit interviews.
Job evaluation.
Retirement policy.

Office Management

Green office policy/Environmental impact.
E-mail/internet use policy.
Personal, or associated group, use of office facilities.
Security.

Governance and Compliance

External

> *Partnership working.*
> *Media handling* – who is authorised to say what
> *Supplier selection*

Ethics, Empowerment, Improvement

> **Complaints procedure** *(for members, service users, public).*
> *Service user/member involvement.*
> *Training policy.*
> *Quality/monitoring policy*
> *Staff involvement policy.*
> *Ethical investment policy.*
> *Whistleblowing.*
> *Child/vulnerable adult protection – 'safeguarding'.*

Finance

> *Insurances*
> *Other accounting policies often part of audit process* (e.g., valuation of assets).
> *Financial policies and procedures.*

Governance

> **AGM procedures.**
> **Committee procedures** *(standing orders).*
> *Management committee/board (and sub-committee) terms of reference.*
> *Job descriptions for directors / board members – chair, secretary and any others.*
> *Conflicts of interest*

Implications of unresolved governance and compliance issues

There can be serious implications if governance and compliance issues are unresolved. Failure to address governance and compliance can cause internal issues that, for example:

- **result in theft and loss of income** – e.g., if sales and transactions are not monitored correctly
- **cause longer-term financial problems for the organisation** – e.g., from paying compensation and having to repay money that has been taken; from a drop in share value as investors lose confidence

Governance and Compliance

- **lead to a breach of contract** – e.g., being sued for releasing information
- **cause a security problem** – e.g., a personal attack or terrorist threat if security arrangements are leaked; passwords and access codes being used by unauthorised people
- **cause embarrassment** – e.g., if personal details or financial records are made public
- **give competitors an advantage** – e.g., from gaining access to confidential operational data
- **increased compliance costs** – e.g., restructuring costs as a consequence of prosecution or loss of reputation
- **increased staff turnover and related costs** – e.g., from staff not wanting to work for an employer with a poor reputation

There can also be serious implications if an organisation's external stakeholders act in response to governance and compliance failures – e.g., government agencies or customers who take enforcement or legal action. Actions could result in:

- **fines and penalties** – e.g., from paying insufficient tax
- **compensation payments** – e.g., to customers when financial data has been mishandled
- **the organisation losing customers** – e.g., from having a bad and unprofessional reputation
- **financial problems for customers** – e.g., if their bank accounts are hacked as a result
- **prosecution of the employer and/or employees** – e.g., under the Data Protection Act, Bribery Act or Money Laundering regulations

The consequences of failure can seriously affect an organisation's ability to survive and thrive due to additional costs and loss of reputation.

Governance and Compliance

Policies

The policies used within an organisation fall into two categories. There are those which are formed out of compliance and are the key business policies for an organisation and those which are formed to maintain governance which can be considered internal policies as they do not affect any external stakeholders directly.

Policies are used to establish high levels of standards and behaviour

Internal policies will include:

- *Dress code*
- *Use of equipment*
- *Social media activity*
- *Annual leave*
- *Data protection*
- *Hours of work*
- *Equal opportunities*
- *Health and safety*

Dress code policy
Dress codes are used to maintain a positive and professional image of the organisation to both internal and external stakeholders. A dress code will include the use of PPE at all appropriate times. Any dress code which is used should be inclusive toward members of staff, not discriminatory in anyway and not put financial strains on any employee or hinder their productivity.

Use of equipment
The use of equipment policy will define how and when employees can use corporate assets such as computer equipment, mobile telephones, a company car, office supplies and stationery, printers and any other equipment that they may require to carry out their job role. The misuse of equipment is widely regarded to be a major cost against many businesses

Social media policy
A social media policy will define what is acceptable and unacceptable behaviour when using the internet and social media at work. A social media policy will define what is acceptable as far as profile updates and photograph updates. It is normal for such a policy to prevent the uploading of any organisational data or images from being uploaded to personal or the organisations social media accounts. It will also state when and how to reply to customers comments. Such responses to customers will normally be restricted to those who have received specific training on what information it is appropriate to post on social media due to the very public nature of the information posted. The abuse of social media platforms is becoming an increasing concern for organisations.

Governance and Compliance

Annual leave policy
An annual leave policy is used to outline employee leave entitlements. The policy will explain the process for requesting leave and to provide a fair policy for all. The policy will normally highlight the notice period an employee may need to give their employer when they are requesting time off for holidays or other purposes. They may also be limits set on the total number of consecutive days which may be taken and also restrictions at particularly busy times of the year.

Data protection
There are many reasons why an organisation needs a data protection policy. The most important being legal compliance with GDPR. The policy should highlight the company's commitment and approach to the collection and handling of data. It should also advise employees how their own personal data will be handled.

Hours of work
Most organisations have set operating hours; however, these hours may be flexible at times and therefore some organisations will allow flexible start and end times for employees. It is important that an organisation provides their employees with clear guidance on the number of hours per day or week that they are expected to work. An hours of work policy should state:

- *the number of hours full time and/or part time you are expected to work per week*
- *the length of lunch breaks*
- *the length of other breaks if provided*

Equal opportunities policy
An equal opportunities policy is simply a written policy that allows the organisation to set out how it intends to ensure it will not discriminate against minority or disadvantaged groups.
The policy is usually separated into sections, section one will include a statement of intent and section 2 a code of practice. The statement of intent tells employees why the organisation is adopting the policy and what it intends to do, Section 2 will provide more detail about how intends to implement the statement of intent.

The code of practice must be realistic and practical.

Many organisations also add a third section, called the code of conduct. This is very clear statement that can be displayed and circulated within the organisation, making it clear that everybody will be treated equally and with respect. It will also highlight the steps that will be taken to ensure this happens.

Health and safety
All organisations must have a health and safety policy however, if a business has fewer than five employees, it does not need to be written down

Governance and Compliance

Health and safety policies are often set out in three sections:

- *General policy*
- *Responsibilities*
- *Arrangements*

The statement of general policy on health and Safety at Work sets out the organisations commitment to manage health and safety, stating what the organisation wants to achieve

The responsibilities section explains the responsibility of managers, team leaders, employees and visitors. It will also define responsibility for specific areas including fire safety, first aid, first workplace safety and safety training, highlighting those who are responsible for these areas.

The arrangement section contains details on what the organisation is going to do in practise to achieve the aims that have been set out in the statement of general policy on health and Safety at Work.

All sectors are different and will have different policies in place and these have been covered in more detail in the earlier part of this document. Some policies will be found in all businesses and include:

- *Health and safety*
- *Equal opportunities*
- *Data protection*

Some will be bespoke to individual organisations and sectors such as:

- *Annual leave*
- *Social media*
- *Dress code*

You have a responsibility to the organisation that you work for to follow the organisation's policies and procedures and promote these to other team members.

This can be done by:

- *discussing the policies at team meetings*
- *making employees aware of any changes to the policies*

If policies are not being followed it could cause a health and safety issue and put other people at risk. You should report all examples of noncompliance to your supervisor or line manager

Chapter 6: Fundamentals of Business Practice

Business Practice

Fundamentals of Business Practice

Business Fundamentals are the basic skills and understanding needed to deal with the different aspects of running an organisation. This includes understanding of broad and generic business practices and functions that apply to every organisation. These skills include:

- *People management*
- *Organisational structure*
- *Human Resources*
- *Financial Management*
- *Economics*
- *Industry trends*
- *Marketing and Sales Strategy*
- *Research and development*
- *Production*
- *Quality*

A basic understanding of business fundamentals is key to success in business administration and career progression to senior roles.

Having a passion for the business you work in is very important for your success. But passion alone is not enough. You also need core business skills to allow the organisation to survive over the longer term.

An understanding of business planning, strategy, finance, and marketing are all necessary for success. If you plan to hire people to help run things, you need communication skills, leadership skills and an understanding of how to motivate and reward employees.

You need to share the strategic vision for the company and an ability to make informed management decisions based on research and analysis of the market, the competition and any other internal or external forces that can impact the organisation.

Developing these skills and knowledge will allow opportunities to be identified to streamline processes, reorganise organisational structures, identify new opportunities, improve quality standards, develop working practices, improve stakeholders' relationships, increase turnover and profits and the list goes on.

The big problem, however, that every single one of these opportunities require change to become effective and change is perhaps the single most resisted factor in business. It is disliked by employees, by customers, by suppliers, by competitors, by almost everyone, except you! As a result, before any of your skills and knowledge can be developed to bring about improvements to the organisation, you must learn the skills of change management.

Business Practice

Business Sectors

There are three principal sectors within business. These are:

- *Private Sector*
- *Public Sector*
- *Voluntary / Third Sector*

The private sectors include all the businesses who are in Private ownership and exist to generate a profit. At its most simple, we have the self-employed which could be a one-man band, to a partnership of two or more individuals who work together to make money. Such organisations are usually privately owned and the people who operate it keep all the profits and divide it between themselves in a previously agreed manner.

The next type of organisation is a Private Company. A company is essentially a legal entity in its own right. It may or may not be limited. The term limited refers to whether or not the liability of the company is limited to the value of its shares and assets or whether the directors have absolute liability for all debts. There are tax benefits depending on the structure of the company.

The next type of company is a Public Limited Company. This indicates the company is owned by shareholders and those shares are available for purchase by anyone on the stock market. People will buy the shares in order to receive a dividend. The divided is paid once or twice a year and the amount paid will depend on the success or otherwise of the company.

Organisations are legally required to take care of their financial obligations. They need to keep records that can be used to show relevant stakeholders that operations are being run properly and in accordance with legislation, regulations and rules.

Depending on the type of organisation, the internal and external stakeholders that need to be satisfied about financial issues will vary.

Internal stakeholders who need to be satisfied about how an organisation looks after its financial procedures could include, for example:

- **business owners** – e.g., sole proprietors or partners who need to know the levels of profit and cash flow
- **shareholders** – e.g., employees or others who own shares in a company who need to keep an eye on their investment
- **employees** – e.g., who rely on the organisation to operate payroll and bonus systems

Business Practice

External stakeholders could include, for example:

- **banks and other lenders** – *e.g., who provide business loans to the organisation*
- **national and local government agencies** – *e.g., who collect taxes and provide grants*
- **external customers** – *e.g., individuals and companies who buy and use the organisation's products and services*
- **charity commission** – *e.g., who examine accounts and regulate registered charities*

Government departments and agencies are also external stakeholders and are responsible for applying finance-related legislation and regulations and the collection of duties and taxes. For example:

- *HM Revenue and Customs (HMRC)* – *e.g., for VAT, tax and national insurance; money laundering regulations*
- *Companies House* – *where accounts and reports are held for limited companies as public records*
- *the Financial Conduct Authority (FCA)* – *for the financial services industry*
- *the Prudential Regulation Authority (PRA)* – *for banks and other financial institutions*
- *the Pensions Regulator* – *for workplace pensions*

Some finance-related legislation is covered by criminal law, such as the Bribery Act 2010.

It is important to consider finance-related governance and compliance that organisations need to follow in order to carry out their activities legally and correctly. These include:

- *the purpose of governance and compliance in finance*
- *governance and compliance processes*
- *implications of unresolved governance and compliance issues*

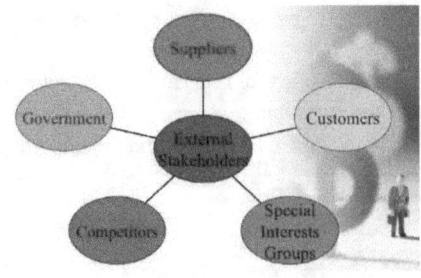

Business Practice

Business Principles

Business Principles are often referred to as the values of the organisation or its guiding ethics. A better explanation is that they are the foundation statements which are adopted by an organisation, department or team, to guide future decisions.

An organisation may publish its principles to the public and a team may publish its principles to its organisation. At the organisational level principles may address things such as professional conduct, sustainability and fairness to people. At a team level, principles become more specific to the types of decision faced by the team.

Three levels of Business Principles.

The first level is actually a set of fundamental benchmarks or tenets for business. These tenets are applicable to every business, every transaction and every decision made by the management team.

Tenets are universal and unbreakable.

The second level reflects fundamentals of business. These rules, guidance and thoughts are not necessarily true and applicable to every business sector and every organisation within that sector. In effect, common business fundamentals are not universal, whereas tenets are.

The third level are the standards set by the organisation and are typically driven by legislation, industry regulation and practice and the historical culture of the industry. Standards exist for systems, production, sales and financial results. Around two thirds of all business rules are really standards.

The entire spectrum of business principle starts with a few universally acceptable tenets, hundreds of fundamentals and tens of thousands of standards. Irrespective of the nature of the business, the sector in which it operates or its structure or size, there are basic principles upon which every organisation must be built. These include:

Integrity
Every organisation must conduct its business with integrity. This means doing the right thing all the time.

Skill, care and diligence
An organisation must conduct its business with all stakeholders with due skill, care and diligence.

Management and control
An organisation must take reasonable care to organise and control its affairs responsibly and effectively, with risk management systems which are adequate, appropriate and effective.

Business Practice

Financial prudence
An organisation must maintain adequate financial resources.

Market conduct
An organisation must observe proper standards of market conduct and behaviour.

Customers' interests
An organisation must pay due regard to the interests of its customers and treat them fairly.

Communications with clients
An organisation must satisfy the information needs of its clients and communicate information to them in a manner which is clear, fair and not misleading.

Conflicts of interest
An organisation must manage conflicts of interest fairly, both between itself and its customers and between other stakeholders.

Relationships of trust
An organisation must take reasonable care to ensure the suitability and accuracy of its advice and discretionary decisions for any customer who is entitled to rely upon its judgment.

Relations with regulators
An organisation must deal with its regulators in an open and cooperative way and disclose anything relating to the organisation of which a regulator would reasonably expect notice.

Business Practice

Business Change Management and Project Management

Project Management and Change Management are often confused.

Although they both involve managing people and processes (and often work together to meet organisational goals), they are quite different disciplines.

Understanding what those differences are and how both practices can (and should) work together to manage projects and their resulting change, is crucial for the success of an organisation.

Whereas project management focuses on the processes and activities needed to complete a project (such as a new software application), change management focuses on the people affected by those projects (or other changes within the organisation).

Project management is about the process required to bring a team or product from point A to point B.

To do this, project managers and their teams manage processes within five main project stages:

- *Initiating*
- *Planning*
- *Executing*
- *Monitoring and Controlling*
- *Closing*

These stages help project managers organise the, often overwhelming, number of tasks and requirements of a project and strategically drive the project forward.

Project management teams focus primarily on fulfilling the strategic objectives of a project.

A project team is often made up of stakeholders from various departments and backgrounds. However, the stakeholders on the team are not always able to address the impact the project may have on stakeholders outside of that isolated team.

This uncertainty can lead to anxiety, confusion, and resistance from the people on the ground who may not fully understand the need for the changes or how to adopt and adapt to new processes. Without buy-in from the rest of the organisation, a project's outcomes can be limited.

Change management is the solution to this employee resistance problem

Business Practice

Change managers help the people affected by a project to transition smoothly. They fulfil this goal through three process stages:

- *Planning for change*
- *Managing change*
- *Reinforcing change*

In many ways, change managers are the cheerleaders for a project. They must craft and deliver the messaging around the project and communicate the reason for the changes with employees and other stakeholders. Additionally, they will work with stakeholders to help them understand how those changes may impact different departments and roles and how to move forward effectively and efficiently.

Because projects can have a significant and lasting impact on the business and its stakeholders, project and change management often work hand in hand to ensure a project's long-term success.

Project Management

The technical element - *the processes and activities needed to design, develop and deliver a solution effectively*

| Initiate | Plan | Execute | Monitor | Close |

| Current state | Transition state | Future state |

| Plan | Manage | Reinforce |

The people element - *the processes needed to help employees embrace, adopt and use the solution effectively*

Change Management

Because each discipline focuses on different aspects of a project (and ultimately its success), both project management and change management should work in tandem to ensure a project's intended outcomes and overall organisational success.

Business Practice

Change Management

When people talk about business change, what they mean is change management, which is the process used to ensure that changes to a business are smoothly implemented, with as little resistance as possible to achieve lasting benefits.

Definition of change management

Change management is the overarching approach taken in an organisation to move from the current to a future desirable state using a coordinated and structured approach in collaboration with stakeholders.

This type of change is not the organic evolution which happens, inevitably, over time in every organisation, but the planned and considered change an organisation will undertake to significantly change the way it operates. The important term here being the word planned.

Business change should never be considered without extensive planning having taken place before hand and every effort made to identify potential problems which could arise and undermine or prevent the change from taking place or being successful.

The net effect of a failed program of business change can devastate an organisation and lead to the loss of substantial amounts of money.

When is Change needed

With all the changes happening in the business world today, change management has become one of the most important business functions an organisation undertakes.

Change management will be necessary to successfully implement changes including:

- *Implementation of a new technology*
- *Mergers & acquisitions*
- *Change in leadership*
- *Change in organisational culture*
- *Time of crisis*

Business Practice

Resistance to Change

People do not like change – they enjoy routine as it allows them to operate within their comfort zone. The moment change is proposed, the status quo is under threat and people automatically react negatively to the prospect of change. A major part of the change process is making sure the change is accepted and adopted by the people who are affected by it. Without proper buy-in, there is a risk that employees will reject or even sabotage the change project, resulting in wasted time and money.

Managing the people-side of the change can help to reduce fear and anxiety and ensure the new goals you are setting are embraced.

A research shows that only 38% of people actually like to leave their comfort zone. When these people are presented with a change, they think, "This is exciting!" Those positive interpretations of change result in positive emotional reactions, such as happiness and satisfaction, which result in greater employee productivity.

The other 62%, however, look at the same statement and immediately feel fear and discomfort. They may think, "Oh great, this change will slow my career development." or "I will not enjoy my job anymore." or "Will they keep me on?".

The acceptance and adoption of change by employees at all levels is the biggest problem to overcome when managing change.

Types of Change

The change undertaken can be relatively small, such as improving the organisation's invoicing procedures, to a complete transformation, such as changing the entire product and service offerings in response to unexpected competition. In most instances though, it will cause major disruption to daily operations.

There are three principal types of change in a business context: developmental, transitional and transformational change.

Developmental Change

A developmental change occurs when an organisation wishes to improve a process or procedure, such as updating the payroll system or refocusing its marketing strategy. These changes are small and incremental – you are not redesigning the entire workflow but are simply refining it to make it better.

Developmental change usually occurs in response to technology upgrades or efforts to reduce costs that aim to improve the efficiency of a work process. As long as you give

Business Practice

staff the training, they need to implement the changes, there should be minimal upheaval associated with this type of change.

Transitional Change
A transitional change is an act of replacing major processes with new ones, such as automating a manual production line or adopting a new IT system. It also includes mergers and acquisitions and other such courses of action. Transitional changes are usually caused by a desire to remain competitive in the marketplace. The organisation is not moving into the unknown when executing a transitional change, but it may have to reconsider its job functions, processes, culture and relationships to manage the change effectively. If handled badly this can cause doubt and insecurity in staff.

Transformational Change
Transformational change is the most disruptive since it requires a fundamental shift in the way an organisation operates. An organisation might decide to completely change direction or restructure the whole organisation using new, proprietary operating systems. Because of the upheaval caused, these types of changes happen only rarely. Managing a transformational change is complex, requiring significant skill from the management team and outside help from change specialists. When the change process is complete, the organisation is unrecognisable from what it was before.

The Impact of Change Management

Change management is needed whenever an organisation undertakes a program or event that interrupts day-to-day operations. Such an undertaking will impact on:

The work content of individual jobs.
Many jobs require individuals or groups to perform tasks repeatedly. An accounts department has daily, weekly, monthly, and annual activities. Over time, most people become comfortable with the tools provided and the rhythm of the work calendar. Even simple changes may disrupt the workflow and be disconcerting for the staff.

The roles of individual employees.
Many people view their value to the organisation as being a good technician, administrator, or data entry clerk. When asked to take on a different role, they may become very uncomfortable. People with excellent technical skills often struggle when asked to become managers. Rather than performing all of the tasks, they have to learn to work through other people. Once they are no longer rewarded for the skills that made them successful, employees may question their purpose.

The organisation itself.
Management teams debate major changes for months before making final decisions, enabling each member of the team to gain a deeper understanding of the effects the change will have on the organisation. Even if they do not agree with the final decision, they have time to determine whether to accept the new direction or to depart gracefully. Individuals lower in the hierarchy rarely have time to process major

Business Practice

changes. Managers do not want employees to worry about events that may never happen until it is clear the change will take place. If the change involves a merger, acquisition, or divestiture there will also be strict controls on sharing information to prevent the possibility of insider dealing. As a result, individuals who are not part of the management team have much less time to prepare for the planned change and may decide to leave while the change is undertaken, making change management even more difficult.

Business Change Manager

The responsibility for delivering the change is usually assigned to an individual who will take on the responsibility for all aspects of the process.

Some tasks a business change manager is responsible for include:

- *Making sure the benefits are achievable.*
- *Preparing affected business areas for transition to new ways of working.*
- *Establishing and implementing mechanisms to measure and deliver benefits.*
- *Optimising the timing of the release of project deliverables into business operations.*
- *Liaising with managers to ensure operational benefits.*
- *Communicating with people and senior leaders about the business vision.*
- *Defining and tracking the benefits and outcomes required from the programme.*
- *Managing the activities effectively that are associated with the desired benefits.*
- *Leading the transition, ensuring that changes are integrated into the business.*
- *Measuring the benefits after the work is complete.*

To achieve all of this the change manager will require a number of competences including

- *Detailed knowledge of the business environment.*
- *An understanding of the management structures, politics, culture and vision of the organisation*
- *Effective marketing and communication skills to sell the vision to all stakeholders.*
- *Knowledge of business change techniques such as business process modelling and gap analysis.*

Business Practice

- *Training in change management, project management or strategic management.*
- *Knowledge in applying best practices in project management.*
- *Knowledge of organisational change models such as Kotter's change model.*

For business change to be successful the process must be underpinned by:

- *A clear vision of the future that is articulated at both an individual and organisational level.*
- *Senior management buy-in and a 'balanced' leadership team.*
- *Business change processes that are embedded in the project delivery lifecycle – they are not an optional extra.*
- *Engagement, communications and 'big' stakeholder relationships.*
- *A team-based culture where the aims of the project are recognised and valued.*
- *Mechanisms to define, measure and monitor success.*

These all need to operate in harmony to maximise the changes of success.

Common challenges in Change Management

Successful business change is all about getting employees' buy-in and embedding new behaviours in the workplace. As noted above, this is not always easy. In addition to the challenges presented by employees, there are additional issues which must be overcome as part of the process.

Defining goals in a timely manner

Most changes get implemented with a goal to improve current processes, products, services or organisational cultures. However, it is critical to identify clear goals and milestones.

Some of the common change management goals and objectives include:

- *Build a culture of innovation*
- *Change or update company's best practices*
- *Implement new technology*
- *Establish milestones and incentives programs*
- *Implement knowledge sharing initiatives*
- *Shift in targeted customer base*

Business Practice

Poor leadership and lack of alignment
Leadership has a big impact on employee engagement. If your leaders are not convinced about the benefits of change, it will be hard to implement it. Poor leadership and lack of alignment among the leaders are some of the main reasons for organisational change fails. On the other hand, great leaders know how to inspire their workforce and embrace the change.

Identifying the resources needed to make change a success
Before starting the change process, identifying the resources and individuals that will facilitate the process and lead the change is crucial for success. However, it can be hard to identify those resources and budgets before the process even starts.

A Lack of agility and slow approval process
Organisations that are not agile struggle to implement changes. Slow approval processes can cause delays in change implementation.
Therefore, it is important to have everyone on the same page in order for the process to get implemented smoothly and on time.

Planning the next steps
Every change management process should have a well-set plan. The plan should consist of a timeline and change milestones should be identified. Without planning, it may be hard to understand the overall success of the change process.

Fear and conflicts
Changes within organisations can develop emotions of uncertainty and fear. This may cause employees take their frustrations out on each other. Here, it is leaders' responsibility to overcome the difficulties and resolve conflicts.

An active leader should always be ready to dive deeper into the problem while working in accordance with their organisational change management.

Resistance to change and lack of commitment
Some employees are resistant to change, do not want to collaborate or commit to new practices. Leaders should be able to address resistance on a psychological level and proactively remove behavioural barriers that restrict change.

Poor communication in the workplace
Communication is crucial for successful change management, and the cost of poor communication can be significant. Every employer that has a successful change management team expresses the need for constant communication during the change experience.

Aligning all the teams with the new strategy
Having everyone on board and informed before and during the implementation process may be a challenge. This is especially true for large organisations with various offices and departments across the world. Therefore, global and interdepartmental communication has to become a priority.

Business Practice

Updating everyone on the new materials, policies and procedures in a timely manner
Changes should be documented and those documents should be easily accessible and shared with the employees.

Every highly effective change management strategy keeps all changes well-documented and transparent.

Best Practice in Change Management

Change management processes can be very complex. Additionally, change in the workplace can cause high levels of stress among employees.

However, there are some rules and best practices every organisation should follow.

Define clear goals
Every change management initiative should be clearly defined. Even though SMART goals are not easy to define for change management, companies should strive towards setting up as clear goals as possible. This way, employees and leaders will have something to reference to when evaluating their change management efforts.

Be honest and transparent
Over 30% of employees say that their employer is not always honest and truthful. In order to implement transitions successfully, employers should be honest and transparent. As most employees do not feel comfortable with changes, being transparent at every step of the change management process helps build trust and connection with employees.

Train and reassure your teams
Support your employees with reassurance, offer new training sessions and give employees time they need to adapt to new practices. Empathy and reassurance help speed up the process and ease future organisational changes. Yet, many line managers do not even understand why the change is happening!

Encourage conversations and communicate regularly
Employee relations have a big impact on encouraging conversations before, during and after the changes are implemented. Start a conversation among your employees in order to find out how they feel about the new initiatives. Understand that true communication is a two-way conversation.

Listen to your employees
When driving engagement and communication, you should not be the only one talking. Listen to what your employees have to say. Allow them to lead the conversation where employees can ask questions, comment and suggest their ideas for improvement.

Business Practice

Bring your leaders on board
The evidence is clear- excellent change management increases the business outcomes of change initiatives. Companies should work on proving the real return on investment derived from change management and communicate that to the business leaders to bring them on board and support the change.

Choose the right communication tool
Millennials in the workplace expect an easier way of communication than through emails. In fact, many emails are never read which causes important information to get lost.

Choose the right employee communication and engagement solution that your employees will actually want to use. Make sure the solution is mobile friendly. Younger generations are used to being able to do everything on their mobile phones. Company tools should, for that reason, be mobile-friendly.

Empower your employees
Empower your change management leaders as well as employees to engage in the change process by giving them freedom to make their own decisions and implement new ideas.

If your employees do not feel empowered, the engagement level will drop and result in resistance to change.

Encourage knowledge sharing
Some employees will learn and adapt to change faster than the others.
However, knowledge sharing among employees can speed up this learning process significantly. Employee collaboration tools enable organisational knowledge sharing in a way that is easy and fun for employees.

Document and make information easily accessible
Documenting everything does not help if this information is not easily accessible to employees. Having a central place where all the important documents and information are kept, makes change management much more efficient.

Recognise and reward
77% of employees say that they would work harder if they were recognised for their work. Therefore, this approach can be a great motivation to comply with and implement the changes faster. Recognise and reward employees for accomplishments and for adopting new behaviours during the transformation process. Celebrate the wins and milestones.

Make it social
If you are implementing a new technology solution you are proud of, share it publicly! Modern employee communication tools allow you and your employees to easily share information both within and outside your organisation. Having employee advocates can also be a huge help for your recruitment and talent acquisition efforts.

Business Practice

Change Management Models

There are many change management models but the most common ones are as follows:

Kotter's Change Management Theory

This change management theory is one of the most popular and most adopted ones in the world. It is divided into eight stages where each one of them focuses on a key principle that is associated with the response of people to change.

- **Increase urgency** – Create a sense of urgency among the people so as to motivate them to move forward towards objectives.
- **Build the team** – Get the right people on the team by selecting a mix of skills, knowledge and commitment.
- **Get the vision correct** – Consider not just the strategy but also creativity, emotional connect and objectives.
- **Communicate** – Openly and frequently communicate with people regarding the change.
- **Get things moving** – Get support, remove the roadblocks and implement feedback in a constructive way.
- **Focus on short term goals** – Set small goals and achievable parts is a good way to achieve success without too much pressure.
- **Do not give up** – Be persistent while the process of change management is going on, no matter how tough things may seem.
- **Incorporate change** – Reinforce and make it a part of the workplace culture.

Kotter's change management model is pretty easy to follow and incorporate. It focuses on preparing employees for change rather than change implementation itself. The focus on employee experience and proper workplace communication is one of the reasons why this is one of the most commonly used change management models.

McKinsey 7-S Change Management Model

McKinsey 7-S framework or model is one of the longest lasting change management models out there.

This model consists of 7 crucial categories that companies should be aware of when implementing change:

- **Strategy** – Strategy is the change management plan that should consist of a step-by-step procedure or future plan.
- **Structure** – This factor is related to the structure in which the organisation is divided or the structure it follows.

Business Practice

- **Systems** – This stage focuses on the systems that will be used to complete day-to-day tasks and activities.
- **Shared values** – Shared values refer to the core or main values of an organisation according to which it runs or works.
- **Style** – The manner in which change is adopted or implemented is known as 'style'.
- **Staff** – The staff refers to the workforce or employees and their working capabilities.
- **Skills** – The competencies as well as other skills possessed by the employees working in the organisation.

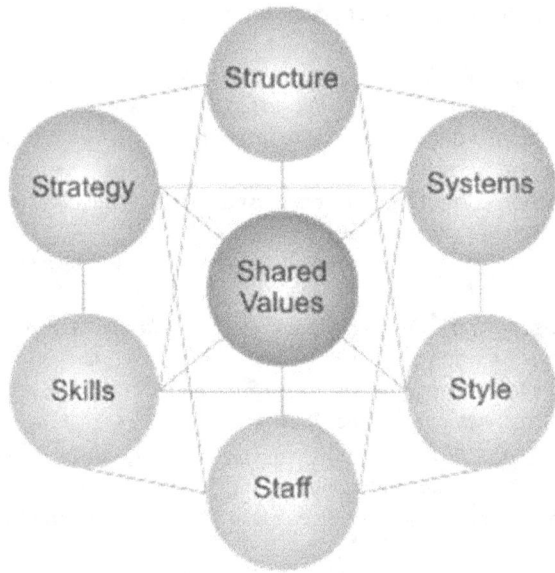

Unlike most other models, this model focuses on all the important factors that change may impact.

While most other models represent some kind of a process or workflow, McKinsey's model simply reminds us of all the business aspects that should be defined before the change strategy is implemented.

Business Practice

ADKAR Model

This powerful model is based on the understanding that organisational change can only happen when individuals change. The ADKAR model or theory of change is goal oriented. This makes it possible for change management teams to focus on activities that are directly related to the goals the company is trying to achieve. It guides individuals through change and addresses any roadblocks or barriers along the way.

The model can be used by change managers to find out the various challenges in the process of change management so that effective training can be offered to the employees.

ADKAR Model stands for:

- **Awareness** – of the need and requirement for change
- **Desire** – to bring about change and be a participant in it
- **Knowledge** – of how to bring about this change
- **Ability** – to incorporate the change on a regular basis
- **Reinforcement** – to keep it implemented and reinforced later on as well.

Pre-contemplation	Contemplation	Preparation	Action	Maintenance
A	**D**	**K**	**A**	**R**
Awareness	Desire	Knowledge	Ability	Reinforcement
Why is change necessary?	How do you motivate people to want to change?	What will be their involvement in the change?	Address issues which may prevent someone from changing	Maintain the change – do not let them slip back top old ways
Make employees aware of the change.	Instil a desire to change	Teach employees how to make the change	Transform knowledge into the ability to make the change.	Make the change permanent by reinforcing new methods

This change management model is a good solution for organisations that are trying to look at both the business and people dimensions of change.

Business Practice

Unlike other change management models, this model focuses on the identification and evaluation of the reasons why change is working or not, and why desired results are not being obtained.

Kübler-Ross Five Stage Change Management Model

This model is different from the others in the sense that is 100% employee oriented. The model can also be applied to other life situations such as loss of job, changes in work and other less serious health conditions.

This model helps employers understand better their employees and empathise with them. This model consists of five stages through which your employees may be going during organisational changes.

- **Denial** – In this stage, employees are not willing to or unable to accept change. This happens because most people show resistance towards change and may not want to believe what is happening.
- **Anger** – This model assumes that when the news first gets absorbed, anger follows. Denial converts into anger when employees realise that the change is actually happening.
- **Bargaining** – During the bargaining stage, employees try to get to the best possible solution out of the situation or circumstance. Bargaining is a way for people to avoid ending up with the worst-case scenario.
- **Depression** – When employees realise that bargaining is not working, they may end up getting depressed and may lose faith. Some of the symptoms include low energy, non-commitment, low motivation and lack of any kind of excitement or happiness.
- **Acceptance** – When employees realise that there is no point in fighting change any more, they may finally accept what is happening and may begin to resign to it.

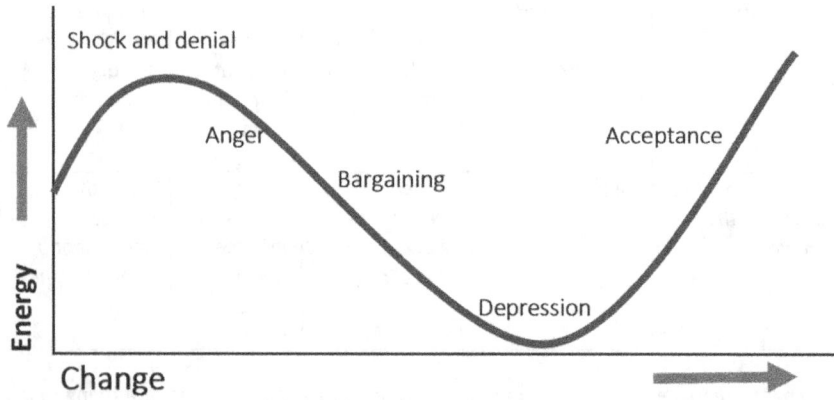

Business Practice

This is a good change management model because of its focus on employees, their feelings, concerns and needs. Organisations that manage to understand their employees are much more likely to eliminate some of the biggest barriers towards successful change management. Because most employees go through the above-mentioned feelings, it is extremely important to keep employees informed and to have an effective business communication strategy.

Lewin's Change Management Model

Lewin's Change Management Model is one of the most popular, most accepted and most effective models that make it possible for companies to understand organisational and structured change.

This model consists of three main stages which are: **unfreeze, change and refreeze**.

- **Unfreeze:** *The first stage of the change process is the preparation for change. Here, employers must get prepared for the change and explain to people why the change is necessary. As most people are resistant to change, this step helps to break this status quo.*
- **Change:** *In this stage, the change process takes place. Good leadership and effective employee communications are crucial for this step.*
- **Refreeze:** *In this stage, the change has been accepted. This is the time when the employees start going back to their normal pace and routine. This last step requires leaders to make sure that the changes are adopted and used even after the change management objectives have been achieved.*

Unfreeze	Change	Refreeze
Recognise the need for change	*Plan the changes*	*Changes are reinforced in stabilising*
Determine what needs to change	*Implement the changes*	*Integrate changes into the normal way of doing things*
Encourage the replacement of old behaviours and attitudes	*Help employees to learn the new concept or points of view*	*Develop ways to sustain the change*
Ensure there is strong support from management		*Celebrate success*
Manage and understand the doubts and concerns		

Lewin's change management model describes in a very simple way the main 3 stages that every change management process has to go through: pre-change, during change and post-change. Because of its simplicity, many organisations choose to follow this model when implementing change.

Business Practice

Communication Strategy

Communicating change is not a one-off effort. Be prepared to communicate not just once, but again and again throughout the change process. Restate the vision, retell the story, enable employees to act as heroes, and chart and re-chart the path when struggles arise. The organisation will be more motivated and equipped to make that change effort with continued communication.

> *Change is possible. Individuals make real changes every day.*

Organisations shift gears and become increasingly successful as a result. The communication strategy can play an important role in enabling transformation and lasting impact.

Businesses have to find effective ways to communicate the abrupt changes they are implementing so that employees can understand the new strategies and adjust their work accordingly.

Broadly speaking, when driving change, you need to:

- *Explain to employees the changes being implemented as well as the different steps the organisational change plan includes.*
- *Tell them the reasons why change is being implemented, the specific changes and the impacts they may have on their work*
- *There is no organisational change plan without objectives and goals. Clearly explain to employees the objectives set and help them identify the impacts their work will have on the team's ability to reach these goals.*
- *Encourage employees to ask any questions they may have in mind and most importantly, make sure they are all answered in full.*

This is also one of the best ways to connect and build trust with remote teams. If needed, appoint a spokesperson that will be able to keep the dialogue with employees open.

Some common examples of best practices for communicating change are as follows:

- *Share the new company policies and procedures with teams in a timely manner*
- *Share safety tips with employees on a daily basis. Sharing with them informative and educational materials such as short videos is a great way to help them.*
- *Monitor updates from management and other stakeholders and instantly share them with employees*
- *Inform employees about urgent matters as soon as possible*

Business Practice

- *Know the employees and then care about the things they are interested in*
- *Make it easy for teams to keep up with the latest news related to the change*
- *Track the effectiveness of the change plan*
- *Use a mobile app so you can reach all employees, no matter where they are, and they can update themselves*
- *Align communication efforts so messages are consistent, no matter who they are shared with. It is all about building trust!*

Employee communication is the keystone of every change management model and the key to successful change.

Within organisations, change initiatives mostly come from the top down. However, *it is* ultimately the employees of the organisation who have to change how they do their jobs. If these individuals are unsuccessful in their personal transitions, if they do not embrace change and learn a new way of working, the initiative will fail.

Aligning employees with business goals is not an easy task. Communication is the central part of every change management model meaning; if employees are not on board, implementing change will be extremely challenging and failure must be considered a realistic possibility.

A recent survey has revealed that 70% of change management projects fail!

Only 14% of business change managers said that change failures can be attributed to a company's inability to cope with technology.

The other 86% of failures are related to:

- *Improperly defined objectives (17%),*
- *Unfamiliar scope (17%),*
- *Lack of effective communication (20%)*
- *Poor project management skills (32%)*

How to Communicate Organisational Change

When it comes to change management, internal communication plays an even more critical role today. Effective communication, in particular, plays a vital role in making organisational change possible. There are two questions which ned to be asked when communicating change:

Business Practice

- *Do the employees have the motivation to change?*
- *Are the employees equipped with the ability to change?*

Both of these responses are incredibly important. One without the other can jeopardise attempts at organisational change.

When communicating change, focus should be on increasing motivation and the company's ability to adapt.

Four steps to communicate organisational change

1. Share a Vision
One of the best things to do when communicating change is share a vision of how the organisation can benefit from the transition. Individuals need to know the change is both good for them and the organisation overall. The vision can be created by answering these questions:

- *How will the organisation operate once the change is made?*
- *What will employees experience as a result of making the necessary transitions?*
- *Will there be tangible results? What will those results look like?*
- *Will there be a sense of accomplishment? What will that feel like?*
- *What will the rewards be, both for the individuals and your organisation as a whole?*

By answering these questions, employees will have a better understanding of why organisational change is imminent, which is critical to success. Clarifying the motivations behind organisational change helps team members reach a mutual understanding, allowing everyone to work toward one shared vision.

Today, businesses around the world are coping with challenges brought on by the COVID-19 and a temporarily stalled economy. To survive this sudden disruption to business as usual, many organisations have been forced to undergo rapid organisational change initiatives, such as embracing remote work.

Those which have successfully adapted have been transparent in their efforts and communicated a clear vision for employees to rally around.

2. Tell a Story
Telling a story enables everyone to understand where the company needs to be, but also where it currently is and how to transition.

Take the example of Scandinavian Airlines.

Business Practice

Scandinavian Airlines needed to make an organisational shift in the early 1980s. The airline industry was struggling. The company was losing money at the tune of £17 million a year. The market was stagnant.

Through its change efforts, the company not only met its goal of increasing earnings by £20 million in the first year; Scandinavian Airlines increased them by £70 million! Within a couple of years, it was named the best airline for business travellers. Employees were on board with the change, which was making a difference. How did Scandinavian Airlines do it?

All 20,000 of its employees received a short handbook communicating the change, which centred around focusing on a subset of customers—the business flyer—to turn the company around. This was not a typical corporate communication. Titled "Let's Get in There and Fight," the booklet included characterisations of airplanes, complete with cartoons and large typeface fonts that highlighted where the company was and the vision for where it wanted to be. It told how "storm clouds" and "bad weather" had struck the business and how it faced challenges in being profitable. It described its competition and how employees could help it stay competitive.

Your strategy may not involve cartoons and large text like Scandinavian Airlines but communicating the story of the change initiative can have a powerful effect on illuminating the vision.

Communicating change in this manner can allay some of the fear and uncertainty employees may be feeling, while simultaneously rallying them around common goals.

We are going to be much more punctual. Everyone can help.
"Operation Punctuality" is starting soon. It's going to give everyone a chance to help us one of Europe most punctual airlines.

Business Practice

3. Make those in the Organisation the Heroes
The change communication strategy should focus on telling the members of the organisation what to do and what they need to change. Does it inspire and enable them to be change agents as well?

In the book **"Winning 'Em Over"**, author Jay Conger shares Scandinavian Airlines' message to employees, which was:

> "We have to fight in a stagnating market. We have to fight competitors who are more efficient than we are and who are at least as good as we are in figuring out the best deals. We can do it, but only if we are prepared to fight. side by side. We are all in this together."

Every employee received Scandinavian Airlines' handbook. Everyone was able to understand where the company wanted to go and what role they played. Telling a story where the employees were not only part of that change, but could be heroes in the story, provided a rallying cry that allowed them to stand side-by-side as active players in the change initiative.

How can the individuals in the organisation be made active participants in the change efforts? How can they be made to feel that changing with the organisation will make them the hero and not the victim?

By making the employees the heroes of the change story and explaining the specific roles each person plays, they will be empowered to exercise agency in helping the organisation meet its goals.

4. Chart the Path
Equip those in the organisation to become leaders in the change communication. Once the vision is shared - one that your employees believe is good for the company – they must be shown the path that will get them there.

> Japan's largest online retailer, Rakuten, wanted to change the working language of the organisation. Instead of the majority of the company speaking their native Japanese, the CEO wanted his 7,100 Tokyo employees to transition to conducting business in English.
>
> This change was to support the company's effort to become number one in internet services across the globe. In two years, the CEO expected his employees to be proficient in English. With just a few months left to go in his change initiative, however, surveys found that a large percentage of employees, especially native Japanese speakers, felt afraid, frustrated, nervous, and even oppressed by the initiative.
>
> The employees of Rakuten were not experiencing the change as something positive for them, personally. They may have believed it was good for the

Business Practice

company, and possibly good for them, but they were finding themselves challenged and discouraged.

A leader should not need the change to be good for employees every step of the way. Some change will be gruellingly difficult. It will involve scaling steep inclines and, for some, working harder than they have before. The solution is to identify what can be done to increase their ability to keep going on this path.

While the initial change initiative shared by the CEO was clear, there needed to be additional communication that would help employees chart the path. Rakuten provided funding for language learning programs, communicating to employees that the company was there for them. They would not have to make the change alone. Action, as well as words, were powerful tools.

Business Practice

Project Management

The term "project management" can seem both obvious and yet vague.

While most people intuitively understand what project management is, it is useful to refer to the official definition.

> *Project management is the application of knowledge, skills, tools, and techniques to meet the requirements of a project.*

Project management is a formalised and well documented. There is a defined start end date for each project that includes tasks, milestones and final deliverables as well as formally identified processes and agreed to requirements and goals.

Project management typically involves the implementation of a product or service.

The Need for a Project

A project usually begins when an idea is put forward and is accepted as being a good idea, after discussion and the decision to implement this is taken. This is the start of the project after which, plans and decisions will be made as to how the project should be implemented and planning will take place. This is the beginning of the project. The next step is the middle of the project which is the plan being implemented. The project does not end when the implementation finishes, this is only the end of the middle. The project will end when the organisation has taken feedback and evaluated the whole of the project from start to finish.

A project therefore has a:

Beginning
Middle
End

A working example

A small project which may be assigned to a staff member could be the event outlined below.

A company wishes to hold a charity dinner for its stakeholders to support a local charitable organisation.

Tasks for the planning team might team could include:

Business Practice

- **researching and planning the project** – finding a venue, booking caterers
- **working out timescales** – planning when things need to be delivered
- **finding and organising resources** – hiring service staff on the day; seating and tables; ordering portable toilets
- **sending out invitations the event** – publicity materials to news agencies and media; putting up posters; arranging TV, radio and press advertisements
- **contacting people coming to the event** – sending invitations and tickets; dealing with telephone and email queries
- **preparing the venue** – decorating the venue and dealing with queries from suppliers
- **host guests and performers** – arranging transport or giving directions
- **supporting staff after the concert** – taking care of lost property; taking unused programmes back to the office; dealing with queries
- **evaluating the success of the concert** – reviewing sales; responding to feedback, complaints and comments; helping to sort receipts and analyse the costs; assess monies generated

The tasks undertaken are focused on the project and follow the plans and objectives of the project. They are not part of the regular, routine work of the organisation. Once the project is over, the tasks cease.

Working to strict timescales is critical. Things must be done on time as delays can have a knock-on effect on other people and tasks connected with the project.

Key stages in the Project Lifecycle

The lifecycle of a project follows the natural sequence of the project itself. The project will need to be started, comprehensive planning will then be required before the project is delivered and subsequently it will need to be monitored and controlled before being concluded, evaluated and reviewed.

The key stages in a project are therefore:

- *initiation*
- *comprehensive planning*
- *project delivery*
- *monitoring and control*
- *closure and review*

Initiation
At the initiation stage the purpose of the project needs to be clarified before planning and preparation can take place.

Business Practice

Working to an agreed purpose helps to focus everyone involved with the project. It helps to stop them being distracted, especially if the project becomes very intense and they are working under pressure.

In the working example, the agreed purpose of the charity dinner is to raise funds for the charity.

Before the planning gets fully underway, the decision-makers also need to agree the scope of the project.

The scope is defined as the broad outline of what is needed to achieve a satisfactory result. It is good practice to include details about what is not included within the scope of the project, so that people can see the parameters clearly.

In the working example, the organisers need to agree, for example:

- **the size of the venue they think they can fill** – *the factory canteen can seat 75 people; a village hall can seat 125 whilst a local conference centre can accommodate 250.*
- **the catering services available** – *inhouse, outside caterers, contract caterers*
- **the type of entertainment they can afford and are able to organise** – *discos, local bands and entertainers or well-known bands*
- **what they can achieve with the resources they have available**

Project team members, especially the main decision-makers, need to agree the scope of their particular role in the project – e.g., how much time and expertise they can contribute.

They will look carefully at the reason for the project – the planned outcomes, costs and benefits to the organisation – and how the project fits into the activities, culture and objectives of the organisation as a whole.

The aims and objectives of the project all need to be agreed so that everyone understands where they will be going with the project, and what they will have to do to make it a success at every stage.

In the example, the *purpose* of the charity dinner is to raise money for the charity.

The *aim* is to run a concert that makes a decent profit that can be given to the charity.

The *objectives* along the way could include, for example:

- *raising the profile of the charity*
- *bringing public attention to the charity's work*
- *increasing the number of supporters*
- *giving the guests a really good and memorable night*

Business Practice

- *career development for staff, by increasing their skills, knowledge and experience*

All of this information will then be put into a brief, along with terms of reference to provide the basic structure for the planning stage.

Comprehensive planning
When planning and preparing for a project, there are several things that need to be agreed to make sure that:

- *the project is planned appropriately*
- *people understand what is expected of them and the project team*
- *sufficient resources are put in place*
- *sufficient budgets are put in place*
- *stakeholders' expectations are met*

In the planning stages, consideration needs to be given to:

- *timescales*
- *resources*
- *budgets*
- *risk assessments*
- *contingency plans*

When planning and preparing for a project, the timescales need to be agreed so that all of the different elements can be brought together on time. Very often, different parts of the project are interdependent meaning one part of the project cannot go ahead until the previous stage has been completed, so a delay at any stage can delay the whole project or lead to Its failure.

For the working example agreed timescales could include:

- *starting the planning and preparation in February*
- *booking caterers, bands, resources, etc. and a venue for a date in August*
- *having the invitations and tickets ready for April*
- *launching the publicity for the concert in March*
- *sending out tickets from June onwards*
- *recruiting and training staff and volunteers to help at the concert between July and August*

Once the timescales are agreed they will usually be mapped onto a Gannt chart along with the key milestones of the project where reviews of targets being met will be conducted and mitigation used to correct any anomalies.

Business Practice

Resources will also need to be planned:

- ***human resources*** – *staff, volunteers and agency workers*
- ***physical resources*** – *accommodation, transport, seating, lighting, stationery, telephones and communication equipment*

These must be agreed at the beginning of a project as resources need to be planned in line with budgets and timescales. There will need to be a total overview of resources and costs, and anyone working on the project team needs to be aware of any limits or deadlines.

In the working example, when planning the resources for volunteers who will help at the concert, the organisers will agree things like:

- *the number of volunteers that they are going to need*
- *the budget that is allocated for their uniforms, training, welfare, travel and other costs*
- *the locations to be used for training sessions*

When planning or preparing a project, the overall budget may already be set. The organisers might have already allocated funds and the people running the project will have to deliver it within the budget they have been given. Early in the process, they need to check the budget to make sure that they can achieve what is expected. Alternatively, the event may need to be self-financing where there is upfront funding to support the planning, but the whole costs of the event must be deducted from the money generated by the event. As a consequence, an event such as the working example will only generate a charitable contribution if there is money left over after all the costs of the event have been paid.

For other projects, part of the planning process might be to research the likely costs and to forecast the budget that will be needed to deliver the project. Budgets will then be negotiated and agreed with the organisation before starting on the main planning, preparation and delivery of the project.

Most projects have a contingency budget that is also agreed at the beginning. This is a separate budget to cover unexpected problems – such as last-minute change to entertainment due to illness.

Once agreed budgets need to be allocated to different elements of the project – e.g., staff costs, stationery costs, catering and hospitality.

Part of project planning is to make contingency plans to cover unforeseen costs, last-minute problems and unforeseen events or issues that have an impact on the project. For the working example, the organisers would have contingency plans for extreme weather around the time of the dinner, for example: to provide dry access to the venue, provide sufficient umbrellas, lighting for photography, etc.

Business Practice

There must be a contingency budget set aside to cover their contingency plans. This makes it easier to make quick decisions to get the project back on track if funds, and limits of authority to use them, have been agreed in advance.

Project Delivery
After a great deal of planning and many meetings, the time comes to deliver the project. This is when everything is put into practice. The better the planning, the smoother and easier this step will be. If everyone has been briefed and knows their role, responsibilities, duties and timescales the project should commence without problems or issues arising.

Decision-making and problem-solving skills will be needed to deal with queries and problems that could threaten to alter the progress of the project.

Progress needs to be monitored and measured so that any potential problems are identified as soon as possible, maybe against SMART targets, planners, flow-charts budgets and risk assessments.

Monitoring and Controlling a Project
Monitoring and control can involve performing both internal and external audits.

Regular progress reviews and team meetings during a project will help to identify actual and potential problems as they arise. By reviewing flow-charts, task lists, planners, project plans, objectives and so on, the team can see the problems, reprioritise and allocate resources to deal with the issues.

Closure and Review
As the project moves into its final phase, it is time to evaluate what has been achieved against the agreed scope, aims and objectives set at the start of the project to see how it met and / or exceeded expectations.

Projects need to be closed down with care and lessons need to be learned and recorded for future research and development.

The review stage is extremely important as it gives people the chance to make notes, give and receive feedback and record information for future projects whilst issues, problems and successes are still fresh in the memory.
Closure needs to be managed well so that:

- *people who worked on the project feel valued and appreciated*
- *the clients or other decision-makers who authorised the project appreciate its value, see what has been achieved and feel confident about commissioning further projects*
- *contacts made within the supply chain feel valued and are kept up to date*

Business Practice

- all stakeholders can see the benefits and positive results of the project before they move onto the next activity

Business Practice

The Project Manager

Responsibility for all aspects of the project lie with the Project Manager. The project manager will have total autonomy for the project and its overall success is dependent upon their performance.

A project manager leads projects from initiation to close, to ensure stakeholder objectives are met with success, and facilitates meetings between team members, company leadership, stakeholders, vendors, and other relevant parties.

The project manager maintains communication relating to project activities with all stakeholders and is responsible for ensuring projects remain within scope. Their project management knowledge and experience is used to help sponsors, team members and other stakeholders to effectively collaborate and make more informed decisions. They work with the company leadership to ensure projects are aligned with overall business strategies and to ensure project risks are mitigated and negative impact to project stakeholders are minimised.

Ultimately, project managers play the role of facilitator and leader for project activities.

Roles and responsibilities within the project team

Project teams can have many different members. They might work on the project full time, they might only be involved in one particular stage, or their role may only require their involvement from time to time. People on a project team can include, for example:

- *board members*
- *sponsors*
- *managers*
- *team leaders*
- *team members*
- *subject specialists*
- *administrators*

Board Members
There may be board members who have direct or indirect functions on a project team. In the charity dinner example, input from board members might have included:

- **the managing director** – *providing initial ideas and overall strategy; weekly progress meetings to monitor and evaluate progress and plans; main contact to agree budgets at organisational level*
- **charity trustees** – *on the board to oversee operations from a distance and ensure compliance with regulatory requirements of the Charities Commission and the charity's own constitution*

Business Practice

- **shareholder representative** – to monitor shareholders' interests and funds
- **sales director** – with an interest in sales revenue

Sponsors
Some projects have sponsors who make contributions of finance and/or expertise. In national sports clubs, for example, sponsors pay for advertising their own businesses around the pitch, on shirts and other merchandise, and in marketing materials. They also use the venue for entertaining their own guests and customers and enjoy special privileges.

If a football club's project is to rebuild one of the stands, for example, a major sponsor may agree to cover the costs and be closely involved with the whole project, form initiation to closure and review.

Managers
Direction may come from the board, but the main planning, delivery and controlling of project plans will be the responsibilities of various managers. There may be:

- **a senior project coordinator** – with overall authority over budgets and important decisions for several projects
- **the project manager** – the main manager for the project; the main point of contact for most decisions and problems; has overall control of everyday activities for the whole project
- **department managers** – such as an HR or health and safety manager who are only involved with certain aspects of the project

In organisations whose core business is project management, and in some other large organisations, there may be several full-time managers. Managers will deal with the different business functions and coordinate their activities with the project managers who have the overall view and control.

Team Leaders
As the project is broken down into different components, there may be team leaders in charge of each section. They will answer to the project manager and be responsible for their sub-teams and special areas only, which could include, for example:

- **induction and training** – new team members and volunteers
- **a catering team** – looks after one of the food court areas in a large venue
- **running one of the bars** – one of ten bars in the large venue
- **a customer service team** – dealing with customer queries at information points
- **a media team** – that looks after press, TV and radio coverage

Business Practice

Team Members

Team members can be, for example, employees, agency workers, freelance workers or volunteers. They might be allocated to, for example:

- **the project full time** –*working in the planning office for the whole project*
- **the project part time** –*spending a regular two days a week on the accounts and budgets*
- **short-term roles** –*directing cars in a car park for a two-day event*

They will all work within the limits of their authority and refer to the team leader for everyday queries and problems.

Subject Specialists

Subject specialists can be called in from time to time when the project manager needs specific skills, usually during the planning and delivery stages. Specialist could be called in to deal with:

- **health and safety assessments** – *e.g., in unusual work areas or environments*
- **fireworks display for an event**
- **designers for stationery, posters and other marketing materials**
- **branding** – *e.g., for sponsorship coverage*
- **specialist equipment that is not normally used or owned by the organisation** – *e.g., staging, marquees, lighting or sound systems*
- **accounts and audits**

Such subject specialists might:

- **work for other departments within the organisation** – *and be asked to assist with specific parts of the project only*
- **work as freelancers** – *and be engaged for particular roles on a consultancy basis*
- **be part of specialist organisations** – *working as part of an independent external team that is tasked to do specific activities*
- **be a full team member for the duration of the project**

Subject specialists are often separate from the main team, so the lines of communication and responsibility need to be clearly defined. They are likely to be answerable to the project manager, who acts as a line manager, and have access to more senior decision-makers when required.

Business Practice

Administrators

Administrators perform a wide range of tasks in project management, such as:

- *processing receipts and invoices*
- *keeping accounts records up to date*
- *processing sales records and enquiries*
- *archiving information*
- *keeping Gantt charts and other monitoring systems up to date*

Administrators might work for other departments within the organisation, such as the accounts department, and be asked to assist with specific parts of the project only. Others may be part of the project team full time, performing administrative tasks for the project only.

As for other project management roles, administrators can be, for example:

- **freelancers** – *engaged for particular roles on a consultancy basis*
- **employed by specialist external organisations** – *working as part of an independent team that is tasked to do specific activities*
- **employed by the organisation on a temporary basis** – *for the duration of the project*
- **employed by the organisation on a permanent basis** – *working on the project team part or full time*

Delivering the Project

It is true to say that no two projects are the same and everyone will have different objectives, parameters, budgets, constraints, outcomes, etc.

As a consequence, every project will need to be managed differently with different emphasis on different elements. There cannot therefore be a definitive guide as to how a project should be delivered and everyone should be assessed and planned on its own merits before a delivery plan is drawn up.

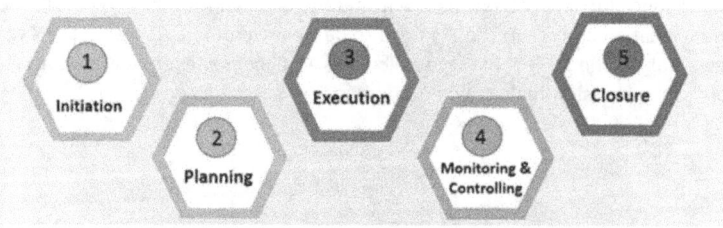

Business Practice

Key Project Documentation

As noted above, no two projects are the same and therefore a standard set of documentation cannot be prescribed to a project. The documentation will be unique to each project. Key pieces that may be used to deliver a project can include:

- *a brief and terms of reference*
- *project plans*
- *definitions of project roles*
- *a risk log (RAID) or register*
- *project monitoring records* – e.g., Gantt charts or progress reports

Brief and Terms of Reference

During the initiation stage, a brief and terms of reference to provide a framework for the project must be produced. By agreeing these early in the process, everyone can agree their role and commitment to it, and the project managers can check whether or not the project is viable. This needs to be agreed before the organisation commits to planning and using its resources, finances and stakeholders' time.

It is important to show what is not covered by the project too. This is key in large organisations in particular, where people may look at a project and assume that it covers their area when it does not.

Project Plans

The project plans will include all aspects of the project, including:

- *timescales, deadlines and critical review points*
- *human and physical resources*
- *the budgets that relate to the project*
- *contingency plans*

The plan needs to go into detail about how the different timescales and tasks will overlap and affect each other.

Definitions of Project Roles

The various people involved with the project need to have their job descriptions in definitions of project roles. Having these together helps the project manager to have an overall view of who is tasked to do what, so that they can make sure that all aspects and tasks have been covered.

A Risk Log or Register

An important element of the planning stage is to prepare a risk log or register and put in measures to minimise risk. A risk assessment needs to be performed for each aspect of the project, and these are kept together in a risk log.

Business Practice

For example, organisations can use a RAID log for their projects:

Risks – events that will have an adverse effect on the project

Assumptions – factors that are assumed to be in place

Issues – something that is going wrong on the project and needs managing

Dependencies – events or work that are dependent on the result of the project, or things on which the project will be dependent

Risks can be defined in many ways – e.g., financial risk when investing or borrowing money; reputation when making decisions that affect the organisation's image and good name; weather or other external influences; health and safety.

According to the Health and Safety Executive, there are five main steps to risk assessment. Many organisations use these as guidelines when designing and implementing their own risk assessments:

- *Identify the hazards*
- *Decide who might be harmed, and how*
- *Evaluate the risks and decide on precautions*
- *Record findings and implement them*
- *Review the assessment and update as necessary*

These risk assessment guidelines can be modified to apply to any type of risk as they help everyone to see and understand the potential hazards, and to take steps to reduce the chance of harm by having control measures in place.

A risk management log could include columns such as:

- **risk impact** – high, medium or low
- **probability of occurrence** – high, medium or low
- **risk descriptions**
- **project impact** – timescales or resources that may be affected
- **risk area** – budget, resources or schedule
- **symptoms** – human resources are not fully decided when a project is about to start
- **triggers** – 24 hours before bad weather is inevitable, contingency plans to cancel will come into effect
- **risk response** – mitigation
- **response strategy** – allocate extra resources, reschedule or cancel
- **contingency plan** – bring in qualified agency staff to cover short term

Business Practice

Project Monitoring Records
Once the project is underway, documents are needed for monitoring the project's progress against plans and objectives. These could include, for example, Gantt charts or progress reports.

Business Practice

Project Management Tools

A variety of project management tools can be used at appropriate phases of the project. They might be used, for example:

- **during the planning phase** – to provide a clear structure for the project
- **when monitoring progress** – using plans, progress charts, actions plans and risk logs when communicating with stakeholders
- **when reviewing a project** – to illustrate and explain progress and plans during review meetings

Tools can include, for example:

- *SWOT analyses*
- *Work Breakdown Structures (WBS)*
- *PERT Diagrams*
- *SMART objectives*
- *Gantt charts*
- *Plan on a Page*
- *RACI matrix*
- *Time management techniques*
- *Kotter's 8-stage change model*

SWOT Analyses
In the workplace, a SWOT analysis can be used in many different situations to identify and measure:

- **Strengths of a project** – e.g., well supported; well financed
- **Weaknesses of a project** – e.g., very short on time; not enough trained staff to do all the tasks effectively
- **Opportunities to improve** – e.g., recruitment drive to bring in the staff needed
- **Threats to progress** – e.g., competition from other employers who need to recruit staff with the same skills

The SWOT analysis can be applied at any scale and can be simple or more detailed. It acts as a snapshot and does not track progress or interdependency of tasks, goals or resources. It can be used in any part of the project that needs a simple, focused analysis on where we are now, where we need to be and how we are going to get there.

Work Breakdown Structures (WBS)
A WBS is a useful project management tool that breaks down a project into smaller components.

The tasks and responsibilities are broken down into manageable sections that align to ensure that overall objectives can be met.

Business Practice

A WBS is useful in the earlier stages of planning so that:

- tasks can be broken down into small pieces
- an overall picture of how elements will work together can be seen at a glance
- different people can see how the tasks may overlap and work together

Below is a small sample of a simple WBS planner for the Charity Dinner working example. It could be developed to go into more detail about the actual days of the month, and names and contact details for all of the internal and external team members.

	February	March	April	May	June	July	August
Tickets	Print tickets by 1st April				Launch sales 5th June	Last boost for tickets	
Caterers	Identify potential candidates	Meet shortlisted companies	Appoint caterers			Finalise menu	
Volunteers			Publicise and start recruitment	Recruit & do phone interviews	Recruit & do interviews Provisional order of uniforms by 16 Jun	In-house training Final order for uniforms by 22 Jul	Training at venue Give out uniforms
Performers		Confirm bookings and contracts		Make contact to stay in touch	Check rehearsal dates are OK	Contact about special requests – food, drink etc. Book transport	Venue rehearsals 20, 21, 22 Aug Event 23rd Aug
Transport			Research taxi & limo companies	Reserve transport for performers, guest speakers		Confirm transport bookings OK	3 limos, 6 taxis, 1 minibus needed 22, 23 Aug

PERT Diagram

Another project management tool is a PERT diagram, which stands for *Programme Evaluation Review Technique*. This chart is a graphic representation of the project's schedule and it is used to schedule, organise and coordinate tasks within the project. It was developed in the 1950s by the US Navy to manage the Polaris submarine, an extremely complex project.

A PERT diagram usually shows:

- the sequence of tasks and milestones
- how these are prioritised

Business Practice

- a three-point estimation technique that shows the duration of each task as being 'optimistic', 'pessimistic' or 'most likely'

The main feature of a PERT diagram that is made using software is the instant calculation of timelines with every change in the workflow. The project manager can instantly see how one changed timescale affects other parts of the project. Its main benefit is to have an overall view of the whole project, rather than individual details, showing how parts of the project can move and impact each other.

Below is a simple PERT diagram about making and packing a teddy bear that has a customised T-shirt:

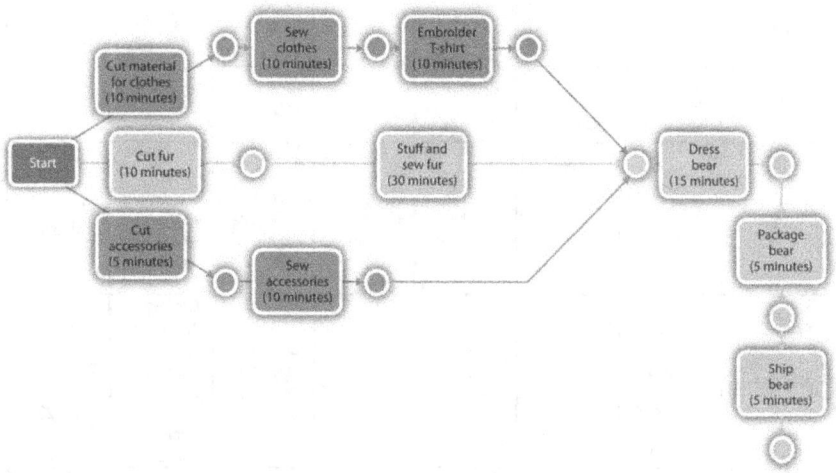

SMART Targets or Objectives

Another tool to use is the familiar SMART targets or objectives. As we see in many aspects of management, SMART targets are:

> *Specific*
> *Measurable*
> *Achievable*
> *Realistic*
> *Time-bound*

As with SWOT analyses, they can be used for the project as a whole or for small tasks within the project.

Business Practice

Gantt Charts

Another planning tool is a Gantt chart, which is a useful and flexible device for illustrating a project's progress. It makes the timeline very clear and can be simple or complicated and can be adapted to match the complexity of the project. A Gantt chart illustrates the breakdown structure of the project in terms of cascading horizontal bars that show, for example:

- *start and finish dates*
- *various relationships between project activities*
- *how tasks track and influence each other*

The Gantt chart was developed by Henry Gantt, who was an American engineer and management consultant in the 1910s and can be set up using specialist software or in Excel.

As with PERT diagrams, the Gantt chart gives an overall view of the project with very clear references to timelines and how elements of the project impact each other.

Here is a simple example of a Gantt chart which reflects the data in the Pert chart above:

Activity/Day	1	2	3	4	5	6	7	8	9	10	11	12	13
Cut fur	■	■											
Stuff and sew fur		■	■	■	■	■							
Cut material	■	■											
Sew clothes		■	■	■									
Embroider T-shirt					■								
Cut accessories	■												
Sew accessories		■	■										
Dress bears								■	■				
Package bears											■	■	
Ship bears													■

Lot size: 100 bears

All activities are scheduled to begin at their earliest start time.

■ Completed work
□ Work to be completed

Business Practice

Plan on a Page
This is a simple tool that condenses the whole project down to one page of information. It is particularly useful to, for example:

- help the project manager focus on the main points of a project
- when making presentations to people outside the project show stakeholders a very quick overview of the entire project
- when applying for extra funding or resources from new sources
- show the media the main points of the project
- when launching a new product use as a leaflet
- when distributing information to the local community about a project that will affect or involve them

Long and detailed reports and explanations are not always required, so a one-page version of the project can be an accessible and effective device for sharing the main points.

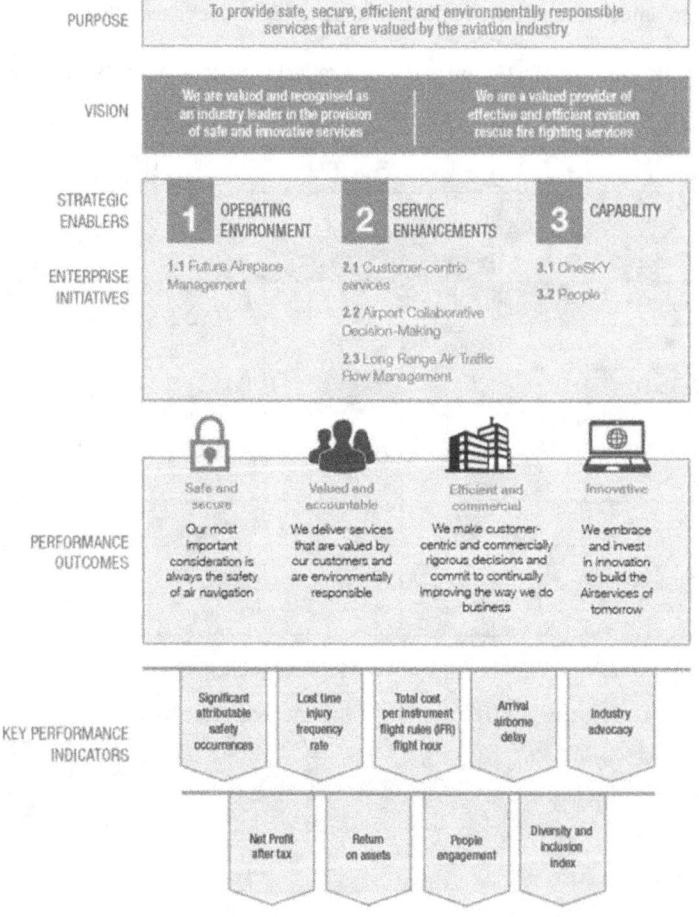

Business Practice

RACI Matrix
The RACI model is a straightforward tool that is used in project management to identify roles and responsibilities. It stands for:

- **Responsible** – *the person who does the work to achieve the task*
- **Accountable** – *the person who is accountable for the correct completion of the task – e.g., the project manager who approves the Responsible person's work*
- **Consulted** – *the people who provide information for the project in two-way communication – e.g., subject specialists*
- **Informed** – *the people who are affected by the outcomes of tasks and need to be kept informed about progress in one-way communication – shareholders, directors or senior managers who are not involved with the day-to-day running of the project*

This helps to avoid confusion about the decision-making process by providing a clear illustration for all relevant stakeholders to see who is responsible for tasks, and who needs to be informed along the way. A RACI model can help the project manager to manage expectations and identify roles and responsibilities early in the project.

Time Management Techniques

The tools used for project management help managers to:

- *plan ahead for each element and stage*
- *keep elements of the project on time*
- *predict busy and quiet times*
- *prioritise human and physical resources to meet deadlines*

Time management techniques can be extremely valuable for the project manager and their team members. For example:

- *allow time each day to plan activities*
- *prioritise communications* – *e.g., deal with urgent messages and accept that some emails and telephone calls do not have to be answered immediately*
- **factor in some time for interruptions and unplanned activities**
- *plan meetings and be firm about time spent*
- *remove distractions when focus is needed*

Business Practice

Eisenhower Grid
An Eisenhower grid or matrix can be designed to give an overview for personal time management, for example:

	Urgent	Not Urgent
Important	**1) DO NOW** emergencies complaints planned tasks and projects due now staff needs problem-solving	**2) PLAN TO DO** planning preparation research networking system development strategy planning
Not Important	**3) REJECT AND EXPLAIN** trivial requests from others ad hoc interruptions distractions pointless routines or activities	**4) RESIST AND CEASE** 'comfort' activities – computer games, excessive breaks chat, gossip daydreaming and doodling reading irrelevant material unnecessary travel

Kotter's 8-stage Change Model
Developed in 1996, the stages of Kotter's change model can be used as a tool as an overall change management framework when managing a project. The eight stages are:

- **Establish a sense of urgency** – when initiating the project and presenting the project plans.
- **Create a guiding coalition** – convince people that the project has value and benefits; bring together a strong coalition or team of people from different departments to guide the team.
- **Develop a shared vision** – create a strategy to deliver the objectives of the project.
- **Communicate the vision** – communicate the purpose, aims and objectives of the project efficiently, address concerns openly.
- **Empower people to act on the vision** – remove obstacles that may stop progress.
- **Create short-term wins to motivate with success** – set smaller objectives that can be achieved, praised and rewarded.
- **Consolidate and build on the changes made by the project** – analyse each 'win' for success and areas for improvement; set goals to continue the momentum.

Business Practice

- *Institutionalise the change* – talk about progress; include relevant lessons learned during the project within the organisation's training and recruitment practices.

Managing Resources Effectively

When managing the project's resources, a range of the tools above can be used. They can help to provide an up-to-date, three-dimensional view of the project at all stages, which helps the project manager to, for example:

- *make sure that resources are available on time for each stage of the project*
- *identify problems and potential risks as soon as possible*
- *find solutions to address problems, issues and risks*
- *make decisions about how to reallocate resources*
- *provide evidence to support requests for increased resources and timescales*
- *show more senior decision-makers how they are managing the project*

When managing resources, the purpose, scope, aims and objectives for the whole project need to be very clear. This gives a focus so that time, human and physical resources can be geared up to achieve goals without unnecessary waste.

Human Resources

When managing human resources for a project, managers perform the usual functions associated with people management, for example:

- *planning and allocating work to match the skills, experience and knowledge of team members*
- *developing and maintaining a common sense of purpose and a positive working environment*
- *working to retain team members*
- *recruiting and training team members*
- *making sure everyone understands aims and objectives*
- *supporting team members in career and skills development*
- *ensuring compliance with legislation* – e.g., health and safety, data protection and equality and diversity
- *monitoring work and taking action to improve performance*

In addition to these management tasks, the project manager's main focus is to make sure that people with the right skills are available when required for each stage of the project. During the planning stage, they can:

- *identify exactly which human resources are going to be needed for specific parts of the project*

Business Practice

- *work out the lead times for preparing and recruiting staff*
- *ensure that existing team members have the right skills*
- *recruit new team members, from inside or outside the organisation*
- *train and brief all team members in time*
- *emphasise the importance of timescales and quality* – and how these can affect other areas of the project
- *ensure that team members have the equipment they need to perform their duties* – e.g., Hi-Viz jackets, stationery, laptops, tablets, travel tickets, radios or mobile phones

During the delivery and control stage, these points need to be monitored, supported and reinforced, as necessary.

Physical Resources

Projects are very focused and visible, which often means that the resources are under more scrutiny than in other business activities. As projects are usually stand-alone activities, every physical resource needs to be planned and allocated to them – e.g., venues, desks and stationery.

The project team is accountable and responsible for managing resources effectively and may have to answer to, for example:

- **senior managers and directors** – who need the project to make a profit for the organisation
- **clients** – customers who have commissioned and paid for the project
- **sponsors** – companies who have associated their brand with the project
- **government agencies** – enforcing regulations on the environment or health and safety

Due to the temporary nature of a project, with its beginning, middle and end, resources need to be flexible. This means that everything needs to be planned in great detail, which requires a considerable amount of management to keep things on track. For example, the project manager for our charity dinner example will have to manage:

- **the venue for the dinner** – checking its capacity and suitability; booking it; setting up kitchens for the dinner; dismantling everything afterwards
- **resources needed at the venue** – sound and lighting systems; hiring toilets and changing rooms for the artists; parking facilities for staff and artists; rest areas, training rooms and catering facilities for volunteers

Business Practice

- **office space for staff** – at the venue and within the organisation's premises
- **office equipment** – integrated IT and telephone equipment at the venue and head office
- **vehicles** – hiring cars and vans for volunteers, artists and full-time staff to use
- **catering and other resources for the artists** – extra portable toilets; catering outlets; smoking areas
- **sales, marketing and ticketing** – printing and distributing tickets, leaflets and posters
- **insurance and inspections of resources** – insurance for the venue, public liability, vehicles and rented equipment; dealing with the health and safety representatives from the local council who inspect the venue

Every item has a cost and a lead time, so careful management is required to make sure that:

- **each item is fit for purpose and satisfies regulatory requirements**
- **it is available on time**
- **the quality is as agreed and expected** – as set out in a service level agreement
- **waste is kept to a minimum**
- **there is a plan for all resources at the end of the project** – handing rented venues, equipment and machinery back in good condition; selling purchased items that are no longer required; returning equipment and supplies to head office

Financial Resources

Budgets are usually strictly controlled for projects and the project manager is accountable and responsible for agreeing, controlling and managing budgets. They need to consider, for example:

- **timescales** – to show when money is due to come in and out – when money from ticket sales and sponsors is likely to be available
- **priorities** – to target resources correctly to support the efficiency and effectiveness of the organisation – prioritising workforce costs, assessing and arranging payments for urgent, planned and essential purchases
- **financial resources** – to match funding with anticipated income and expenditure – helping to arrange business loans to finance long-term projects; dealing with increases and decreases in revenue and expenses
- **contingencies** – negotiating and setting aside budgets and resources for unpredictable and unforeseen circumstances

Business Practice

Management Tools for Monitoring Progress

By using management tools, the project manager can monitor progress and see when it is time to implement the next stage of delivery of the project. The example of the volunteers working example at the charity dinner, the sequence might include:

- *establishing the uniform sizes needed for the new recruits*
- *giving a provisional order to the supplier* – so that they can start to prepare
- *finishing recruitment of volunteers*
- *confirming the uniform sizes that are needed and making the final order a month before the dinner* – the company needs two weeks to print and deliver the uniforms

Until the volunteer recruitment has been finalised, it is not possible to make the final uniform order. As a contingency, a few extras of the standard sizes will be ordered. By tracking all of this information using, for example, a PERT diagram or a Gantt chart, the project manager can identify critical points and make sure that everything is on track.

Using the project management tools we mentioned before, here are some suggestions about how they might be used to monitor progress in the recruitment and training of team members in the charity dinner example:

Business Practice

Management tool/method	Suggestions of how this could be applied to monitoring progress
SWOT analysis	To track the strengths and weaknesses of recruitment policies compared to expected targets; to review the opportunities for finding the right people if there are issues; to review the threats to progress to make sure that they are still relevant
Work Breakdown Structures (WBS)	To monitor the job descriptions set out in the initial WBS to make sure that the right people are being selected; to monitor training programmes set out in the WBS to make sure that they are relevant and suitable
PERT diagrams	To have a visual record about how a delay in advertising vacancies has a knock-on effect on applications, interviews and training
SMART objectives	To review levels of recruitment and training against the SMART targets on a regular basis
Gantt charts	To see how the recruitment and training elements of the project are progressing in relation to all other aspects of the project, such as physical resources and finance
Plan on a Page	To prepare a quick overview for progress meetings and interim management reports
RACI matrix	To use as a guide to make sure that communication is as expected and agreed between different stakeholders – to ensure that the relevant directors and external stakeholders are being informed of progress

RAG Rating

Another useful tool to use when monitoring a project's progress is to show the RAG status – red, amber, green. During the planning stage, the planning team can set parameters about what the colours mean, for example:

Red – *major problems that will affect the viability of the whole project and cannot be resolved by the project manager – the matter should be escalated to the project board member*

Amber – *problems that have a negative effect on one or more aspects of the project's viability and performance – problems can be dealt with by the project manager and their team, who then notify the board about progress*

Green – *the project is performing to plan – all problems are within tolerances and expectations and can be dealt with within normal limits of authority*

There can be drawbacks to the traffic-light system; it can oversimplify a project's progress and it is very dependent on the integrity of the information that can turn an element from red to amber or green. As a visual aid, it is effective as it draws attention to the problem areas and shows when everything is on track.

Business Practice

It can really help to keep everyone involved and motivated by letting them know how things are going. If the news is not very good, it can help to reassure everyone, so that they work harder to get back on track and understand the problems behind problems and potential issues. If things are going well, the team and other stakeholders benefit from knowing and getting some positive praise and feedback. This lifts morale and helps to keep people motivated and focused.

Evaluating Project Performance

The project manager needs to evaluate a project and look at all of the data that has been collected, so that the team can, for example:

- **compare the outcomes with the original objectives** – *to see if the project has achieved its intended aims and the correct quality standards*
- **understand how the project has achieved its purpose** – *or why it has failed*
- **identify how the project used human resources** *–to analyse the skills used and identify career development opportunities*
- **identify how efficiently the project used physical resources** *–comparing budget forecasts with actual costs, reviewing the levels of waste*
- **identify problems and potential improvements**
- **advise stakeholders and decision-makers** – *about how to repeat, develop or improve actions and plans for future projects*
- **identify needs for further project work** *–to set up a new project to solve major issues that were discovered when working on the first project*

When evaluating a project, the data needs to be reliable and relevant to be of use. We need to consider what we want to know, and what we want to measure, to be able to identify what data we need and how we will collect it.

Organisations will have their own ways of evaluating a project, which could include, for example:

- **comparing estimated costs with actual costs** – *to evaluate the budget allocations and identify the causes of variance*
- **collecting and reviewing feedback from customers and other users of the services and products covered in the project** – *e.g., independent surveys, feedback forms, forum comments, focus groups or satisfaction surveys*
- **analysing operational data** – *e.g., looking at patient records in a hospital to evaluate changes in services*
- **reviewing progress reports** – *e.g., final 'wash-up' reports from staff and other stakeholders about their experiences and recommendations*
- **analysing sales patterns** – *e.g., to see when tickets were purchased and by whom; to see if business changes have affected sales as expected*

Business Practice

- *analysing changes in activity and comments on websites and social media* – e.g., to illustrate a change towards Internet shopping following a project on online sales

The methods selected will depend upon who needs and wants to see the evaluation of project performance. The media, for example, might only be interested in the initial financial impact of changes made by the project, whereas the organisation's HR department will be more interested in evaluating the impact on staff skills, experience, training and career development.

Reviews of project performance need to be presented in ways that satisfy the needs of stakeholders.

In general, the project team's review needs to:

- *show the successes of the project*
- *praise everyone who contributed to the success*
- *identify areas of weakness and lessons that can be learned for future projects*
- *illustrate the project team's value to support bids for future projects*

Managing Project Risks and Issues

Difference between project risks and issues

Preparing a risk log or register is part of planning a project and as part of this process, it is important to be able to identify differences between risks and issues.

A **risk** is the probability of harm happening. It is only a 'what if' and the harm may not happen at all, especially if measures are put in place to minimise the risk of harm to the project. For example, there can be a physical risk of harm from:

- **slips, trips and falls** – due to unsafe flooring, obstructions, wires, badly-positioned equipment or other trip hazards
- **working at height** – up ladders or on scaffolds
- **cross-contamination when handling food and drink** – when staff do not wash their hands and pass on germs to customers
- **illness and injury** – from poor crowd control, excessive alcohol or excessive noise, if loose wires on machinery are not dealt with correctly

Projects are also at risk due to, for example:

- **failure of an event or task** – from insufficient planning
- **financial failure** – if revenue is too low or costs are too high
- **equipment failure** – due to inadequate maintenance

Business Practice

- ***changes in external factors*** – *planning rules or employment laws; world prices; national or international political influence; weather; local community action*
- ***changes in internal factors*** – *reorganisation of premises, workforce or management structures; organisational culture*

An issue that affects a project, has actually happened. It is something that is real and actually has an impact on the project. Despite every effort to minimise risk, there are some things that cannot be mitigated and they do cause issues for the project team.

If any one of the identified potential risks becomes a reality, it becomes an issue that the project management team needs to address. Examples of issues that affect projects include, for example:

- ***weather*** – *leading to cancellation or reorganisation of an event; leading to increased costs from having to use extra resources to deal with the consequences*
- ***inability to recruit sufficient, good-quality team members*** – *due to insufficient local supply or competition from other organisations*
- ***illness or injury to team members or others*** – *following an accident in the workplace*
- ***increased prices of supplies*** – *due to a change in world prices of raw materials*
- ***decreased revenue*** – *as a result of bad weather*
- ***political change*** – *the UK deciding to leave the European Union*

As risks and issues can both affect how a project is run, they need to be managed and tracked. The project team need to do all that they can to minimise the risks of harm to the project, and to make plans and forecasts about how they will deal with issues that do arise.

The implications of failing to mitigate risks and plan how to deal with issues can be extremely serious – from physical harm to people to the failure of the whole project or the organisation.

Business Practice

Identifying and Mitigating Risks

When identifying and mitigating risks, the project manager needs to:

- identify potential hazards and risks during the planning stage
- create a risk log or register – and use it to mitigate risk
- maintain awareness of potential risks
- consult stakeholders to agree approaches to risk management
- use leadership skills to manage risks that materialise
- amend plans when risks have an impact on the critical path or other timelines

The following table shows some suggestions about how the risks mentioned above could be identified and mitigated:

Area of risk	How to identify the potential risks	Suggestions about how to mitigate the risks
Slips, trips and falls	Risk assessment of hazards – e.g., wires, wet floors, obstructions Observation Accident records	Have good health and safety working practices – e.g., keep wires out of the way; put yellow hazard warning signs up; inform people about hazard; improve general hazard awareness of staff; have procedures for reporting potential hazards quickly
Working at height	Identify times and tasks where working at height will be necessary	Provide regular 'working at height' training for relevant team members and contractors Provide correct personal protective equipment (PPE) – e.g., harness, hard hat, safety boots
Cross-contamination when handling food and drink	Identify critical control points – e.g., when catering staff handle customers' food	Provide food handling training to relevant staff Insist on good hygiene – e.g., hand washing Monitor temperature control Provide equipment needed – e.g., well-maintained fridges and other storage; heat lamps; PPE; thermometers Ensure that catering contractors are properly equipped and trained

Business Practice

Area of risk	How to identify the potential risks	Suggestions about how to mitigate the risks
Illness and injury	Risk assessments of all areas Accident records Industry experience	Health and safety training for all team members Ensure the environment is safe Deal with potential hazards immediately Enforce noise limits Restrict access to alcohol Arrange support from security and medical specialists – e.g., door staff to keep an eye on alcohol consumption; first-aiders and ambulance crews on standby
Failure of an event	During progress checks or reviews	Improve planning and communication between project team members and other stakeholders
Financial failure	Changes in sales or costs against forecast amounts	Review finances regularly – e.g., to identify problems and act quickly Have a contingency plan and budget – e.g., to use as agreed in the planning stage Stick to budgets and escalate problems as soon as possible
Equipment failure	Intermittent or complete breakdowns of equipment or machinery	Follow regular maintenance routines Train staff to report potential problems early – e.g., when they see a frayed wire or a crack Establish contacts who can fix and maintain equipment, especially in an emergency – e.g., IT or lighting specialists who can attend critical breakdowns that will affect delivery of the project
Changes in external factors	Changes that affect the resources used in the project – e.g., an increase in fuel costs	Review factors that may affect the project regularly – e.g., to identify potential problems and act quickly Have a contingency plan and budget – e.g., to use as agreed in the planning stage Escalate problems that are outside the limits of authority as soon as possible
Changes in internal factors	Organisational meetings or communications about changes that could affect the project	Stay in touch with the whole organisation, not just the project team Check internal factors before committing to the project – e.g., to see if assumptions about resources and future plans are reliable and correct

Business Practice

Managing Issues

When managing issues, the project manager needs to:

- **understand the nature of the issue** – *the reasons why recruitment of new team members is so difficult, maybe using a PESTLE analysis (to look at political, economic, social, technological, legal and environmental impacts)*
- **evaluate the scope of the issue** – *how big a problem this could be and how the recruitment problem could either ease or get worse*
- **evaluate the impact on the project** – *how the recruitment problems could cause extra work for current team members or complete failure of the whole project*

Doing a SWOT analysis as soon as an issue has been identified could be an effective activity to focus attention and aid the decision-making process. By looking at the strengths, weaknesses, opportunities and threats to progress of each possible solution, the project manager can evaluate the issue and work out how to limit or eliminate the impact of the issue.

> For example, a project manager still needs another 50 stewards to run an event.
>
> They normally have trained volunteer stewards. However, with only one month to go, they do not have enough people to steward the event, and there is a legal requirement to have sufficient stewards on duty whenever the public are in the venue.
>
> All stewards need to have a full day's training if they do not hold a current Spectator Security qualification.
>
> The project manager does a SWOT analysis to help them identify the pros and cons of each option:

Business Practice

	Option A Increase publicity to attract new applications from new volunteers – e.g., advertise, make public appeals, approach organisations that place volunteers	**Option B** Approach another organisation that has large numbers of trained volunteers who might help for this one event	**Option C** Employ an event company who use qualified, paid staff
Strengths	New team members add to the pool of talent for future events and projects Control over type of person selected Control over training and monitoring Low cost	Volunteers already used to working at large events Good to have relationship between organisations that can help each other out from time to time	Staff can be provided in time Identifiable costs The company's service history should indicate reliability Staff will be qualified and will know how to operate without further training Less input required from the project team as the event company will manage the 50 staff and associated resources
Weaknesses	Time taken to deal with advertising, applications, interviews and recruitment of new volunteers No guarantee that enough people can be found, recruited and trained in time Unknown numbers for uniforms and other resources until the last-minute Cost of advertising	Volunteers might not be available or willing to work with a new project team The other organisation might not want to lose its volunteers Restricted choice in the actual individuals who join the team Staff training time required	Need to rely on the event company to choose suitable individuals High costs Volunteers might resent paid staff doing the same job as them
Opportunities	Local radio is running a volunteer campaign next week One week to advertise, then two weeks to interview and recruit Training sessions for all volunteers booked in 4 weeks' time	Three or four well-known groups in the local area that could be approached Three weeks to sort out before training is due	Plenty of event companies and staff available if researched online and using trade networks Could be arranged quickly
Threats to success	Lack of time – leading to a high chance of failure, which would put the whole event at risk Other events might be competing to recruit volunteers	Lack of cooperation from others Other events might be competing to recruit volunteers	High costs might not be covered by contingency budget Other events might be competing to recruit staff for the same day

Business Practice

Following the PDCA cycle devised by J Edwards Deming can also help the project manager to focus on how to manage issues:

- **Plan** – *identify the problem and root causes; collect data; set objectives; allocate resources and training*
- **Do** – *implement the plan and take action*
- **Check** – *review and measure progress against objectives; analyse strengths and weaknesses of the plan*
- **Act/Adjust** – *praise success; identify further improvements; communicate any changes to the people involved*

The most important thing to do, though, is to act promptly when a potential or actual hazard, risk or issue is identified, and to take steps to minimise or eliminate the causes before the effects become even more serious. A combination of actions may be required that might include, for example:

- **reallocating human resources** – *e.g., to cover emergencies or sickness*
- **reallocating physical resources** – *e.g., moving equipment to where it will be used more efficiently*
- **negotiating extra funds or time** – *e.g., a contingency budget or an extension on a deadline*
- **asking people for help and advice** – *e.g., team members, colleagues or industry contacts due to an emergency*
- **escalating issues** – *e.g., when decisions are outside the limits of authority, or the project is in danger of failing*

Business Practice

Differences between Project Management and Change Management

Change Management	Project Management
Definitions	
applying processes and tools to manage the people side of change from a current state to a new future state such that you achieve the desired results of the change (and expected return on investment)	applying knowledge, skills, tools and techniques to project activities to meet project requirements
Intent	
to ensure that impacted employees embrace, adopt and use the solution associated with the change	to ensure that the solution is designed, developed and delivered effectively
Focus	
employees impacted by a project or initiative (those who must adopt and use the change)	tasks and activities required to create and implement the technical solution associated with a change
Scaling Factors	
characteristics of the change, attributes of impacted organisations, and degree of "people change" required	complexity and degree of technical change associated with the particular project or initiative
Process	
Phase 1 – Preparing for Change Phase 2 – Managing Change Phase 3 – Reinforcing Change	Initiating Planning Executing Monitoring and controlling Closing
Tools	
Individual change model Readiness assessments Communication plans Sponsor roadmaps Coaching plans Training plans Resistance management Reinforcement mechanisms	Statement of work Project charter Business case Work breakdown structure Gantt chart Budget estimations Resource allocation Schedule and tracking
Success Measurement	
measurement focuses on the people side of change elements, including: Speed of adoption by impacted employees Ultimate utilisation by impacted employees Proficiency of impacted employees Achievement of results and outcomes*	measurement focuses on the technical side of change elements, primarily: On time On budget Meets technical requirements Achievement of results and outcomes*
*Because results and outcomes depend on individuals adopting the change, this is a primary focus.	*In some cases, intended results and outcomes take a secondary role behind time and budget targets.

When projects are initiated, they create a significant amount of undue stress on stakeholders and employees in general. While project managers maintain complete focus on overall project objectives with the goal of ensuring stakeholder value, change

Business Practice

management professionals should not only attend project meetings, but also be an integral part of the project team.

Collaborating provides a holistic approach to strategy and ensures the impact to people within the organisation can be sufficiently addressed, to reduce unnecessary stress and anxiety, and also create a smooth transition in terms of processes and acceptance levels not only during the project phases, but long after the project is complete.

Overall, organisations should encourage change management professionals and project managers to work closely together to ensure project efforts and the resulting change are sufficiently addressed to reduce the impact on its people and level of product and service delivery.

Benefits of an Integrated Approach

Increased Efficiency: Working independently of each other can lead to redundancies, miscommunication, and inefficiency. All of these factors result in messy implementation and subpar outcomes. When change and project management processes and teams integrate and work together, they can manage a project (and its impact) holistically and strategically.

Greater Alignment: Integrating project management and change management in a project allows the teams to align their processes in the most effective and logical sequence. In other words, aligning the technical and people activities helps teams take the right action at the right time.

Risk Mitigation: If both teams work in silos (or if change management is applied at the end of a project rather than from the beginning), they might miss significant risks and opportunities to manage and mitigate those issues.

For instance, change managers can identify areas where they expect greater pushback and resistance from stakeholders. When the two processes are integrated, managers can more effectively plan milestones and delivery.

Communication: In a similar vein, integrated project and change management improves communication and knowledge within the project. Change managers can ensure project management teams understand how people are reacting to the changes, and project managers can use that feedback to adapt their strategies and improve outcomes.

There are different ways to incorporate change management into project management practice.

- *Project Management is about installation* ... *it focuses on a plan built around events and timelines with the aim of getting from a current state (no installation) to a future state (installation achieved).*

Business Practice

- *Change Management is about adoption* ... *it focuses on the people aspects of the change with the aim of getting a critical mass of people to be committed to the change involved, to learn new behaviours and to sustain them willingly.*

Whatever your approach, keep these ideas in mind for greater success.

Align goals and outcome objectives
Change management and project management naturally have complementary processes with the same basic underlying goal: to ensure the long-term success of a project (and its impact).
However, that shared goal can sometimes get lost if the two sides struggle to come together. Because change management is newer and follows a different pattern, it can be easy for the two groups to feel disconnected.

To prevent an "us vs. them" mentality, it is important for both teams to collaborate and clearly define and align their goals.

Consider: What exactly are you trying to achieve? What are the desired outcomes?
By answering these questions, you can then get to work planning a strategic and dual approach to manage the project and its impact.

Establish Structured Change Management Processes
We noted above that the change management discipline does not follow strict guidelines or standard processes. However, for change management integration to be successful, a structured approach is best.

Communicate with the project manager to decide on a practical methodology and process. The more rigorous and structured, the better. Following a defined process with clear objectives and milestones, will more easily align that process with the project management timeline and ensure a more strategic application of activities.

Clearly Define Roles and Responsibilities
Finally, it is crucial to sit down with both teams and hammer out who is responsible for what. Projects often take months to develop and implement. Make sure it is identified who is accountable for each activity or outcome throughout the process. That way, nothing gets lost in the shuffle, and everyone understands what to do and when.

By clearly defining responsibilities, you can not only improve your team effectiveness but also prevent delays from miscommunication and conflict.

Business Practice

Change management:	Project management:
Has no standard guidelines	Has well-documented guidelines and standards
Includes less formal processes	Follows a specific timeline
Has no concrete timeline	Puts focus on technical processes and systems
Puts focus on people	Manages the activities of a project to meet specific goals and requirements
Manages the impact of change resulting from organisational or project developments	Drive solution delivery
Work towards change sustainability and integration.	Communicate progress and impact on solution deliverables and project goals.
Communicate progress and impact on people readiness.	Implementation and technical risk management.
People-side risk management.	Focuses on project time, cost, quality, scope.
Focuses on people-side strategies and planning for change adoption and timely benefits realisation.	Follows project management lifecycle.
Follows change management lifecycle.	Steps and tools for managing the project from start to end.
Steps and tools for managing and motivating people who are experiencing change.	Delivering project solution.
Concerned with the optimal ownership, use and benefit of the delivered solution	

Finance

Financial Management is the third key area of knowledge and understanding needed by those operating in a commercial administrative role.

Financial management is of critical importance to all aspects of business. The income and expenditure of a business is controlled by law and financial accountability is a prerequisite of all stakeholders, regardless of their role.

Business Practice

A Framework of Rules and Practices

The framework an organisation uses will depend on is size, type and activities. In a small company that owns and runs a single high-street shop, the rules and practices could be geared up to a part-time bookkeeper who, for example:

- *counts and banks takings from the shop*
- *deals with electronic payments made on the shop's card machine*
- *deals with payments to suppliers*
- *accounts for VAT on sales and purchases*
- *does a monthly payroll for three employees and two directors, and sends the tax and national insurance to HMRC*
- *makes the company's payment into staff pensions*
- *keeps and balances banking records*
- *sends all bookkeeping records to the accountant to prepare and submit annual accounts and returns for HMRC and Companies House*

In bigger organisations, similar activities will still take place, but will be administered on a bigger scale. For a national chain of stores, for example, there will be an entire department to deal with accounts, payroll, etc. The rules and practices will be laid down in a range of policies and procedures that the staff have to follow to make sure that the organisation is compliant.

Some large organisations may outsource their administrative, payroll and financial record-keeping to specialist companies – e.g., many local councils engage companies who provide a full range of administration support services. These specialist companies' systems are geared up to full compliance, but the organisation still has responsibilities to provide the correct information.

Issues that governance and compliance aim to avoid and mitigate

Broadly speaking, governance and compliance aim to avoid and mitigate issues such as:

- **fraud** – *e.g., procedures to shred documents to prevent identity theft*
- **theft** – *e.g., using CCTV to monitor staff using a cash till*
- **tax evasion** – *e.g., procedures to make sure that cash payments are declared*
- **criminal activity** – *e.g., taking bribes or trafficking workers*
- **misuse of funds and resources** – *e.g., monitoring budgets closely to reduce waste and unnecessary spending*
- **inefficiency** – *e.g., from not monitoring waste or opportunities to steal cash or goods*

Business Practice

Sometimes actions are deliberate and have a criminal intent – e.g., knowingly employing people who are illegal immigrants or those who have been trafficked, stealing products or cash. Some actions are due to negligence and ignorance – e.g., from someone not realising that they need to provide workplace pensions for their employees; under-declaring VAT due to lack of knowledge about the rules.

How governance and compliance relate to financial management

When dealing with financial management, managers need to make sure that the governance and compliance procedures are in place and up to date. They need to make sure that people working for the organisation are:

- *aware of their legal obligations for their specific industry and activities*
- *following policies and procedures*
- *keeping their knowledge up to date*

Procedures need to be tested and monitored to make sure that they are robust enough to identify and deal with any non-compliance.

Business Practice

Governance and Compliance Processes

Organisations have a variety of processes to deal with their financial affairs. They support the organisation's activities, aid efficiency and make sure that activities are compliant with the internal and external requirements for each situation. Processes cover, for example:

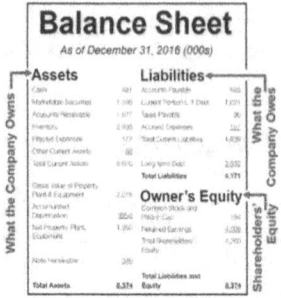

- *financial reporting*
- *dealing with income*
- *record-keeping*
- *audits*

Financial Reporting

Organisations produce a range of financial reports, including:

- **income and expenditure statements** – to show income, expenses and profits over a period of time – enabling the organisation to see how well it is performing.
- **balance sheets** – giving a 'snapshot' of the assets and liabilities at any given time, usually at the end of the financial year.
- **cash flow statements** – to show what cash is available and moving through the organisation, so that managers can see what they can afford to do.
- **annual accounts and statutory returns** – to show a true picture of the organisation's income, expenditure, assets and liabilities at any given time, often after being audited by registered practitioners or chartered accountants.

Financial reports are used by managers when preparing business plans and to monitor progress. Investors and shareholders use the information to make decisions about funding and investment choices. They are also used in the preparation of statutory returns and reports, including:

- *corporation or income tax returns sent to HM Revenue and Customs*
- *VAT returns*
- **PAYE returns** – e.g., to declare tax and national insurance for the workforce
- **audited accounts** – e.g., to be submitted to the Charities Commission, shareholders or lenders
- *company returns to Companies House*

Financial reporting may be provided in paper or computer derived formats, these will be identified in their policies, procedures, training records and accounting manuals.

Business Practice

Dealing with Income

Various methods are used to track income and expenditure to make sure that organisations comply with internal and external requirements. Ways to safeguard income could include:

- **checking cash against till records at the end of each shift**
- **requiring employees to sign for floats when they change shifts**
- **checking income against stock levels** – e.g., to make sure that staff are not giving away stock for nothing
- **requiring supervisors or managers authorising refunds above a certain amount**
- **doing bank reconciliations against sales invoices and ledgers** – e.g., to track income and make sure everything has cleared
- **having automated stock and security systems** – e.g., bar code systems that track each item, using CCTV
- **doing spot checks** – e.g., open checks by managers; covert checks with mystery shoppers observing procedures at the point of sale
- **checking identities of new customers when large amounts of money are being spent or deposited** – e.g., to safeguard against money laundering
- **having robust procedures for international transactions**
- **using and monitoring reliable electronic payment systems** – e.g., PayPal
- **managing debtors** – e.g., chasing outstanding payments that are due from customers

Record-keeping

It is a legal requirement that businesses need to set up and maintain records that meet the requirements of governance and compliance which apply to their situation and activities. When designing ways to keep records, organisations need to consider:

- the type of information
- the people who are going to access the records
- the security and confidentiality of the contents
- how it needs to be circulated and shared

There are many ways of organising electronic and paper-based financial information, for example:

- in sales and purchase ledgers – electronic and paper-based
- in cash books – electronic or manual
- paper forms, reports and files

Business Practice

The guidelines in the General Data Protection Regulations provide a good framework about how records need to be organised as it covers how data is used, stored and deleted. Processes need to be in place for every aspect of recording of financial information:

- **ensuring that only authorised people have access** – e.g., by having passwords and security passes; using encryption for electronic data; vetting staff who handle sensitive information; using information for the correct purposes only
- **storing paper-based and electronic data safely** – e.g., with password access; locking files away in fireproof storage; archiving records safely in a secure warehouse or data management facility
- **destroying records correctly** – e.g., shredding paper; using a secure disposal agency; destroying backed-up information on hard drives and other IT systems securely

In addition, organisations need to comply with requirement to keep records for different lengths of time. Some records need to be kept indefinitely and others can be destroyed securely after a short period of time, so processes need to be in place to monitor and manage this. Organisations need to make sure that they store information for the correct amount of time.

Audits

Some organisations are required to perform audits to provide stakeholders with assurance that financial statements are accurate. An audit is a three-dimensional inspection and review of all aspects of an organisation to make sure that everything balances and complies with relevant regulatory requirements.

In a medium-sized company, for instance, a registered auditor from the firm's accountants will be tasked to check samples of records to make sure that reports are accurate and truly representative. They make look at, for example:

- **sales ledgers** – to check the level of income received
- **cash books** – to see that the income has been banked correctly
- **debtors** – to assess the amount of money owed to the company
- **stock** – to see that the stock records are accurate and to give the remaining stock a value as an asset
- **purchase ledgers** – to check that costs put through the business are correct, legal and compliant
- **bank reconciliations** – to see that payments in and out are all balanced or accounted for
- **creditors** – to see how much the company owes at the end of its financial year
- **payroll records** – to make sure that tax, national insurance and pension contributions have been dealt with and paid correctly
- **VAT returns** – to ensure that the correct amounts have been declared and paid

Business Practice

During the process, the auditor will check that other regulations are complied with – e.g., money laundering or data protection. Processes need to be robust and transparent to enable audits to be performed that can provide an accurate view of the organisation to internal and external stakeholders – e.g., shareholders, lenders and HMRC.

Implications of Unresolved Governance and Compliance Issues

There can be serious implications if governance and compliance issues are unresolved. Failure to address governance and compliance can cause internal issues that, for example:

- **result in theft and loss of income** – *e.g., if sales and transactions are not monitored correctly*
- **cause longer-term financial problems for the organisation** – *e.g., from paying compensation and having to repay money that has been taken; from a drop in share value as investors lose confidence*
- **lead to a breach of contract** – *e.g., being sued for releasing information*
- **cause a security problem** – *e.g., a personal attack or terrorist threat if security arrangements are leaked; passwords and access codes being used by unauthorised people*
- **cause embarrassment** – *e.g., if personal details or financial records are made public*
- **give competitors an advantage** – *e.g., from gaining access to confidential operational data*
- **increased compliance costs** – *e.g., restructuring costs as a consequence of prosecution or loss of reputation*
- **increased staff turnover and related costs** – *e.g., from staff not wanting to work for an employer with a poor reputation*

There can also be serious implications if an organisation's external stakeholders act in response to governance and compliance failures – e.g., government agencies or customers who take enforcement or legal action. Actions could, for example:

- **result in fines and penalties** – *e.g., from paying insufficient tax*
- **result in compensation payments** – *e.g., to customers when financial data has been mishandled*
- **result in the organisation losing customers** – *e.g., from having a bad and unprofessional reputation*
- **cause financial problems for customers** – *e.g., if their bank accounts are hacked as a result*
- **lead to prosecution of the employer and/or employees** – *e.g., under the Data Protection Act, Bribery Act or Money Laundering regulations*

The consequences of failure can seriously affect an organisation's ability to survive and thrive due to additional costs and loss of reputation.

Business Practice

Delivering Value for Money

Responsible financial management includes delivering and receiving good value for money.

The Concept of Value for Money

According to the Oxford dictionary, the phrase value for money is:

> *'used in reference to something that is well worth the money spent on it'.*

The concept of value for money encourages organisations to make the best use of their resources to achieve objectives. Today, "value for money" has changed to become a term for something which is cheap. Value for Money supermarkets are considered to sell cheap lower grade products. A better term to bring this back into context is to think of the term "value for price"

Offering value for money/price helps an organisation to have a good reputation and stand out against competitors. In the workplace, when organisations concentrate on giving value for money, this can refer to:

- **products and services that are provided for external customers** – e.g., supermarket goods, cars or legal services
- **services delivered to internal customers** – e.g., credit control staff who collect money owed to the organisation; maintenance teams who look after the buildings and other facilities

Organisations also work to receive value for money when they manage, for example:

- **operations** – e.g., refining policies and procedures to be as efficient as possible
- **suppliers** – e.g., services provided by specialist contractors and consultants, suppliers of raw materials and other goods
- **human resources** – e.g., employees, HR departments and management costs
- **physical resources** – e.g., equipment and machinery; factories, offices and retail outlets
- **finance** – e.g., finding the best business loans for a business venture
- **waste** – e.g., energy, time, human and physical resources

Achieving value for money/price helps an organisation to operate efficiently and effectively, which is an important element when delivering profits to shareholders and securing jobs for employees.

Business Practice

Many organisations also have a statutory responsibility to achieve value for money – e.g., when using public funds.

Achieving Value for Money

There are many things that organisations can do to give and receive value for money when working with suppliers and customers.

Customers

Customers have expectations and they want:

- **an efficient and polite service before, during and after a transaction (buying or using products or services)**
- **good-quality and value-for-money products and services**
- **any complaints and problems to be dealt with properly**
- **their opinion to matter**

An organisation needs to offer good customer service and value for money at all times so that it can survive and thrive. If the customers are satisfied with the products or services, they return and they recommend the organisation to others. Quite simply, this keeps the organisation alive and means that their employees' jobs are safer.

Organisations offer value for money to customer through, for example:

- **the range of goods and services offered** – e.g., offering budget and luxury ranges
- **pricing** – e.g., offering competitive prices; grouping complementary products together as a bundle
- **discounts** – e.g., buy one get one free
- **Incentives** – e.g., 10% off if customers buy today
- **delivery options** – e.g., free for standard delivery when customers spend above a minimum amount, charges for overnight or weekend delivery
- **installation options** – e.g., charges for installing household appliances like washing machines
- **warranties** – e.g., free or low-cost extended warranties on electrical goods that guarantee repairs or replacement if there are faults after the period covered by the manufacturer
- **returns policies** – e.g., rules about exchanges or refunds on returned items that are not faulty
- **other value-added features** – e.g., loyalty card points; membership and privilege cards

Business Practice

Products and services need to be in line with the standards promised in catalogues, brochures, websites, customer charters, company policies, etc. They may also be covered in a Service Level Agreement (SLA) between two parties.

Suppliers

When working with suppliers, organisations can negotiate the same things because they are now the customers. In smaller organisations, managers and directors will make the decisions about how to obtain value for money when managing human and physical resources. Larger organisations can have procurement specialists and departments – e.g., in national supermarket chains or the Ministry of Defence.

Whatever the size of the organisation, the principles are the same. Physical resources need to be:

- **fit for purpose** – *of sufficient quality for the intended use*
- **sustainable** – *from sources that can maintain the supply chain for future purchases*
- **ethically and legally sourced** – *e.g., to comply with the organisation's own ethical policies*
- **able to be reused, recycled or reconditioned** – *where possible at the end of their useful working lives*

These factors are important when assessing value for money as money is not the only consideration. Even if something is incredibly cheap, if it is not fit for purpose, it will not provide value for money.

In parallel to these factors, organisations will also negotiate with suppliers to get deals – e.g., the best prices and discounts; favourable delivery and installation options; inexpensive and effective warranties and aftercare service; other added-value features that may be available.

How teams or departments can deliver value for money for the organisation

Teams and departments can also make the most of the organisation's resources and energy use to maximise value for money. There can be a mixture of obvious and hidden costs that need to be monitored as they all form part of the running costs that have to be met by the organisation.

Teams or departments can deliver value for money for the organisation by:

- *reviewing costs and operational activities regularly*
- *using resources efficiently*
- *using energy efficiently*

Business Practice

Reviewing costs and operational activities regularly

Managers need to review how their team or department spends its budgets on a regular basis, to make sure that funds are being allocated in the most efficient way to achieve objectives and maintain quality. They need to look at all aspects to make sure that everything is fit for purpose and good value for money, for example:

- **fixed costs** – e.g., machinery and equipment
- **variable costs** – e.g., raw materials or components
- **human resources** – e.g., to make sure that the right people are being employed at the right cost to achieve the team's objectives and quality standards
- **working practices** – e.g., to make sure that procedures are relevant and efficient
- **outsourcing opportunities** – e.g., analysing whether it is better to perform some activities in-house or to outsource them to specialist companies

Organisations need a framework for discussing and reviewing all aspects so that managers and others can:

- *identify areas that need improvement*
- *address potential problems*
- *work collaboratively to make decisions about maximising value for money*

Using resources efficiently

When looking to improve the use of resources in the workplace that are related to external customers, managers need to consider, for example:

- **reducing packaging** – e.g., encouraging customers to buy loose vegetables and fruit; using smaller boxes, aerosol cans or plastic bags; cutting out unnecessary packaging; using refill packs of coffee rather than new jars every time
- **developing packaging that uses fewer resources** – e.g., boxes that stay together with folds rather than glue, reusable bags for customers
- **reducing consumables given out** – e.g., giving out one serviette per customer rather than letting them help themselves to a handful; smaller serviettes or tray liners; small hygienic packets of butter rather than a dish of butter that might be wasted

When keeping down operational costs of the team or department, managers may consider, for example:

- **reusing materials** – e.g., storage boxes and trays that can be used many times, using China mugs rather than disposable cups
- **avoiding scrap or waste** – e.g., managing portion control in a restaurant; training and monitoring production staff in a factory to help cut down on rejects and wasted

Business Practice

  materials; checking cutting patterns to make sure that they are as efficient as possible
- **reviewing, designing or adjusting procedures, products or services** – to maximise the use of resources
- **electronic communication** – rather than printed paper; emails or texts rather than paper memos
- **telephone and videoconferencing** – rather than travelling around the UK or abroad for meetings
- **using technology effectively** – e.g., using smart meters or sophisticated tills to measure consumption and target production efficiently; stock tracking systems to support Just-In-Time supply chain management; computer-based training for staff
- **working to improve staff retention** – e.g., managing the team well to avoid excessive recruitment and training costs that occur when there is a high turnover of staff
- **ensuring work practices support compliance** – e.g., to help avoid unnecessary investigations, legal proceedings, fines, penalties, compensation and loss of reputation

Managers need to be aware of changes to technology, products and processes to see if there are well-researched, better alternatives.

Business Practice

Marketing

The fourth element of Business Fundamentals is Marketing. The Marketing function is critical to the success of the organisation.

The definition of marketing is:

> *"the action or business of promoting and selling products or services, including market research and advertising."*

Marketing is something that every organisation must implement in its growth strategy. Many organisations use marketing techniques to achieve their goals without even realising it. Marketing refers to actions an organisation takes to promote itself and increase sales of their product or service. It is one of the key aspects of business.

People often do not know exactly what marketing is and, when asked, they define it as selling or advertising. While these answers are not wrong, they are only one part of marketing. It involves many other things like product distribution, promotion, designing and creating materials like landing pages and social media content, building customer experience, doing market research and establishing target markets, and much more.

Marketing is very broad and encompasses all strategies that help a company, brand, or individual achieve its objectives.

Marketing can be many different things to many different people so finding an informative and concise definition is almost impossible.

Marketing is basically the process of getting potential clients or customers interested in your products and services. The keyword in this definition is "***process***". Marketing Involves researching, promoting, selling, and distributing your products or services.

Peoples view of marketing has changed. They no longer believe the promotional methods and resources used previously. They now challenge the advertising and promotion they see and it is this which has caused a rethink about what marketing really is.

A far better definition is:

> *"The aim of marketing is to know and understand the customer so well the product or service fits them and sells itself."* Peter F. Drucker

Business Practice

Marketing is simply a conversation

Marketing is essentially the conversation that starts between two people – the organisation and the customer - who do not know each other well. Great conversations lead to a deep understanding of needs. Deep understanding like this leads to the development of amazing products delivered through engaging customer experiences. THIS is marketing.

When we meet someone, we do not know, we ask them questions. We try to get to know them. We try to understand their dreams and problems and needs. We do NOT talk about ourselves unless there is a genuine interest from the other person to learn about us as well. This only comes from true and authentic empathy. We have to actually care about this other person to earn their trust.

This conversation continues as we get to know each other better. In the same way, the brands who continue to develop deeper conversations are the ones who are considered to care more about the other person than they do about themselves.

The brands who win more customers are the ones who put their customers ahead of their desire to sell more stuff.

They show potential customers that they are interested in solving real problems. They do not just act like they care. They actually care and they prove it in the way they act. They genuinely seek to help their customer to improve their lives through their content, their expertise, their passion and, if they are lucky, through the stuff they sell.

Marketing means you have to give much more than you hope to receive. Great marketeers are passionate teachers, giving away their expertise with only the hope that they are helping people. The business benefit is in establishing trust and building an audience of people who believe in you to help them in times of need.

When given a choice, we only buy from brands we know, like and trust!

Marketing is not about who can talk faster or close a deal better. As Peter Drucker explained, it is about developing a deep psychological understanding of customer needs. Steve Jobs had this gift and Apple stand as testament to that today.

Every innovation in the history of the world has combined an uncanny understanding of human needs and the innovative vision to deliver it.

An organisation today is composed of two simple elements - marketing and innovation. Without these two, there would be no business. Furthermore, if marketing is about deep customer insights, then marketing is the job and responsibility of every employee.

Social media has only made this point even more painfully clear: every employee is an extension of the brand. The brand serves to meet the needs of the customer and the business serves to innovate.

Business Practice

- Marketing starts by asking customers who they are, what they want, and what they care about.
- Marketing starts with a question.
- Marketing is not a statement
- Effective marketing simply asks, "How are you?"

Purpose of Marketing

Marketing is the process of getting people interested in the organisation's products or services. This process starts with market research, analysis, and understanding the "ideal" customer's interests and needs.

Marketing pertains to all aspects of a business, including product development, distribution methods, sales, and advertising.

Modern marketing began in the 1950s when people began to have access to more than just print media to promote a product.
As TV - and more recently, the internet - entered households, marketeers could conduct simultaneous campaigns across multiple platforms. Over the last 70 years, marketeers have become increasingly important in fine-tuning how an organisation sells a product to consumers to optimise success.

The distribution and sales channels will impact on who buys the products and services, when they buy them, and how they buy them.

The 4 Ps of Marketing

In the 1960's, F Jerome McCarthy came up with the 4 Ps of marketing: product, price, place, promotion.

Essentially, these 4 Ps explain how marketing interacts with each stage of the business.

Product
Marketing starts when an idea for a product or service is identified and developed. Before launching the product or service, a decision as to what is to be sold, how many options or variations are available and how it will be packaged and presented to consumers.

Price
Before an idea can be revealed to the public, marketing research and testing must be performed. Marketing departments usually test new product concepts with focus groups and surveys to gauge consumer interest, refine product ideas, and determine what price to set. Researching competitors can also help set an optimal price and generate ideas for positioning the brand in an existing market.

Business Practice

Place
The information gathered in research will help define the marketing strategy and create an advertising campaign. Campaigns can include different forms of media, events, direct advertising, paid partnerships, public relations, and more. Before beginning an advertising campaign, benchmarks must be set that can be used to measure how effective the advertising campaign is.

Promotion
Determine where and how the product will be sold to customers. Consumer product companies, for example, sell to wholesalers who then sell to retailers. In the industrial market, the buying process is longer and involves more decision-makers. They may be sold locally, nationally, or even internationally, and some organisations only sell their products or services online.

Marketing Concepts

Marketing professionals seldom study these five concepts before creating their marketing plan, however, it is important to understand how these concepts influence and inform business strategy. These concepts, or 'marketing management philosophies', are helpful in understanding where the company and the potential customer meet.

Since the entire role of the marketeer, is to bring the brand and the customer together, it is helpful to throw these concepts into the marketing mix.

Production Concept
The production-focused marketing concept first began when Capitalism took its hold on developed countries throughout the world. During this time, beginning with the Industrial Revolution, companies were focused primarily on production and manufacturing.

The competitive advantage was to be able to provide as many products as possible for as little cost as possible. Marketing professionals during that time only had to convince the potential customer that they had the cheapest products available. Since product prices went down when production went up, most companies opted for mass production when possible. Modern marketing, on the other hand, does not have it so easy.

National Minimum Wage and Human Rights issues have pushed many organisations into a direction that increases the price per product, forcing them to develop a marketing message that makes the inherent value of the product worth the price tag. Even so, many organisations still have a Production Concept mindset that works well for them.

Product Concept
When companies use the Product Concept to develop their marketing strategy, they focus on quality over quantity. Rather than sacrificing quality for low cost, businesses focus on improving the quality of their products to better meet customer needs.

Business Practice

Understanding the target audience will help identify what the customer's perceived value is in a particular product so that can be clearly articulated in the marketing message.

This is clearly evidenced in well-written product descriptions that highlight the product benefits and features. This is especially relevant in the tech industry, where new features develop faster than the production line can keep up with.

Selling Concept
No competent marketing manager will focus solely on sales, but some quick-and-dirty online shops still abide by the Hard Sell Concept, even in modern marketing.

Why? – Simply because it leads to more money!

Businesses that focus primarily on sales will do whatever it takes to turn a profit. Most of the marketing effort, then, goes into paid ads, cheap discounts, and low-cost production.

Very little attention is paid to the consumer and as a result, often leads to poor satisfaction.

Considering that customer reviews weigh heavily on the decision-making process for consumers, though, the Selling Concept is an unsustainable way to run a marketing campaign.

Marketing Concept
Traditional marketing and modern marketing both follow the Marketing Concept when developing an effective marketing plan. With this concept, the potential customer is the primary focus and everything, from product development to customer service, is focused on the consumer.

Some marketing programs focus on the consumer more than others. Relationship marketing, for example, aims to develop a lifelong relationship with the brand's customer base so that it has customers for the rest of its or their life! Content marketing, on the other hand, seeks to understand the potential customer simply to be able to produce content that they will like.

Societal Marketing Concept
With about 8 billion people on the planet, it makes sense that marketing activity would begin to focus on the wellbeing of people over profit, or at least, alongside profit.

Brands focusing on the Societal Marketing Concept, will direct all marketing activity toward understanding and improving the lives of not only their target market but also of society as a whole. This is most often seen when brands incorporate charity into their marketing campaign.

Business Practice

Marketing Strategies

The choice of marketing strategy depends entirely on where customers spend their time. Market research will determine which types of marketing -- and which mix of tools within each type -- is best for building a particular brand. Here are a number of contemporary marketing strategies that are relevant today, some of which have stood the test of time:

Social Networks and Viral Marketing
Social media marketing focuses on providing users with content they find valuable and want to share across their social networks, resulting in increased visibility and traffic. Social media shares of content, videos, and images also influence search engine optimisation (SEO) efforts in that they often increase relevancy in search results within social media networks like Facebook, twitter, YouTube, and Instagram and search engines like Google and Yahoo.

> *61% of companies use social media to increase conversions, and 50% use it to gain customer or market insights*

Paid Media Advertising
Paid media is a tool that companies use to grow their website traffic through paid advertising. One of the most popular methods is pay-per-click (PPC) links. Essentially, a company buys or "sponsors" a link that appears as an ad in search engine results when keywords related to their product or service are searched (this process is commonly known as search engine marketing, or SEM). Every time the ad is clicked, the company pays the search engine (or other third-party host site) a small fee for the visitor — literally a "pay per click."

> *When customers are close to making their purchase decision, 65% will click on a paid ad*

Internet Marketing
Internet marketing, or online marketing, combines web and email to advertise and drive e-commerce sales. Social media platforms may also be included to emphasise brand presence and promote products and services. In total, these efforts are typically used in conjunction with traditional advertising formats like radio, television, and print.

There is also a lot to be said about online reviews and opinions. Word-of-mouth advertising is unpaid, organic and very powerful, because those having nice things to say about your product or service generally have nothing to gain from it other than sharing good news. A recommendation from a friend, colleague, or family member has built-in credibility and can spur dozens of leads who anticipate positive experiences with your brand.

Business Practice

global e-commerce is anticipated to grow by 14% between now and 2023, with the spike attributed to contactless buying behaviour, resulting from the Covid-19 pandemic

Email Marketing
Email marketing is a highly effective way to nurture and convert leads. However, it is not a game of chance, as to whether your message winds up in spam filters. Instead, email marketing is an automated process that targets specific prospects and customers with the goal of influencing their purchasing decisions. Email marketing success is measured by open rates and click-through rates, so strategy comes into play, particularly when it is used as a component of a larger internet marketing initiative.

the average expected return on email marketing is £30 for every £1 spent

Direct Selling
Direct selling accomplishes exactly what the name suggests — marketing and selling products directly to consumers. In this model, sales agents build face-to-face relationships with individuals by demonstrating and selling products away from retail settings, usually in an individual's home (e.g., Amway, Avon, Herbalife).

the direct selling market is currently valued at £45 billion pounds

Point-of-Purchase Marketing (POP)
Point-of-purchase marketing (or pop marketing) sells to a captive audience — those shoppers already in-store and ready to purchase. Product displays, on-package coupons, shelf talkers that tout product benefits, and other attention-getting "sizzle" often sway buying decisions at the shelf by making an offer simply too good — and too visible — to pass up.

in the UK annual impulse purchases total £21.7 billion

Co-branding, Affinity, and Cause marketing
Co-branding is a marketing methodology in which at least two brands join together to promote and sell a single product or service. The brands lend their collective credibility to increase the perception of the product or service's value, so consumers are willing to pay more. Similarly, affinity marketing is a partnership between a company (supplier) and an organisation that gathers persons sharing the same interests — for instance, a coffee shop that sells goods from a local bakery.

There is no shortage of co-branding partnerships, but several more recent examples demonstrate particularly good natural brand alignment including the adventurous go-pro and red bull, luxurious BMW and Louis Vuitton and Gordons Gin and Schweppes Tonic

Business Practice

Likewise, Cause marketing leverages and enhances brand reputation. Cause marketing is a cooperative effort between a for-profit business and a non-profit organisation to mutually promote and benefit from social and other charitable causes. Cause marketing is not to be confused with corporate giving, which is tied to specific tax-deductible donations made by an organisation. Cause marketing relationships are "feel goods" and assure your customers you share their desire to make the world a better place.

> *customers interpret co-branding as a value endorsement from a brand they already trust, creating a potentially lucrative halo effect*

Conversational Marketing

Conversational marketing is just that — a conversation. Real-time interaction via a chatbot or live chat gets the right information in front of prospects and customers at the right time, allows them to self-service, and get questions answered immediately.

> *messaging is the preferred method of customer communication with businesses — 90% of customers want a chat option*

Personalised, relevant engagement vastly improves the user experience. For B2C businesses, conversational marketing is especially effective because it and scales your customer service, typically cuts the time buyers stay in the sales funnel. Conversions happen quicker because relationships are established quicker.

Conversational marketing is effective because it:

- **Removes layers of impersonal lead capture and creates an authentic, personal customer experience**
- **Fosters clear communication** — buyers can plainly state their needs, and businesses can more readily understand and assist since there is appropriate context around the request
- **Strengthens relationships as bots can also recommend additional content or products relevant to buyers based on their past behaviour**

Earned Media/PR

Earned media (or "free media") is publicity that is created through efforts other than paid advertising. It can take a variety of forms — a social media testimonial, word-of-mouth, a television or radio mention, a newspaper article or editorial — but one thing is constant: earned media is unsolicited and can only be gained organically. It cannot be bought or owned like traditional advertising.

> *92% of customers say they trust earned media, with 51% of millennials being highly influenced by it*

Business Practice

Storytelling

Brand storytelling uses a familiar communication format to engage consumers at an emotional level. Rather than just spout facts and figures, storytelling allows you to weave a memorable tale of who your company is, what you do, how you solve problems, want you value, and how you engage and contribute to your community and the public in general.

> *in a recent survey, 91% of respondents reported having a positive emotional connection with at least one brand*

Marketing and Advertising

> *If we think of marketing as a wheel, advertising is just one spoke of that wheel.*

Marketing entails product development, market research, product distribution, sales strategy, public relations, and customer support. Marketing is necessary in all stages of a business's selling journey, and it can use numerous platforms, social media channels, and teams within their organisation to identify their audience, communicate to it, amplify its voice, and build brand loyalty over time.

Advertising is just one component of marketing. It is a strategic effort, usually paid for, to spread awareness of a product or service as a part of the more holistic goals outlined above.

Advertising is not the only method used by marketeers to sell a product.

> Example:
>
> Let us say a business is rolling out a brand-new product and wants to create a campaign promoting that product to its customer base. This company's channels of choice are Facebook, Instagram, Google, and its company website. It uses all of these spaces to support its various campaigns every quarter and generate leads through those campaigns.
>
> To broadcast its new product launch, it publishes a downloadable product guide to its website, posts a video to Instagram demonstrating its new product, and invests in a series of sponsored search results on Google directing traffic to a new product page on its website.
>
> **Now, which of the above decisions were marketing, and which were advertising?**

The advertising took place on Instagram and Google. Instagram generally is not an advertising channel, but when used for branding, you can develop a base of followers that is primed for a gentle product announcement every now and again. Google was definitely used for advertising in this example; the company paid for space on Google -- a program

Business Practice

known as pay-per-click (PPC) -- on which to drive traffic to a specific page focused on its product. A classic online ad.

Where did the marketing take place? This was a bit of a trick question, as the marketing was the entire process. By aligning Instagram, Google, and its own website around a customer-focused initiative, the company ran a three-part marketing campaign that identified its audience, created a message for that audience, and delivered it across the industry to maximise its impact.

Marketing is more than promotion

Marketing intersects with all areas of a business, so it is important you understand how to use marketing to increase your business's efficiency and success.

Marketing is what you say and how you say it when you want to explain how awesome your product is and why people should buy it.

Marketing gives direction
Marketing provides the businesses with a planned and focused approach regarding the implementation of their future decisions so that they have a clear understanding and idea of how they are to progress, marking their marketing milestones and objectives.

Marketing provides competitive edge
Saturated markets have increased competition among businesses and to survive the cut-throat competition, it is essential that businesses employ tactics to stand out from others. Exclusivity and a distinctive identity, along with the implementation of all the necessary measures to beat your competition is the only way to emerge out as a market leader.

Marketing provides the businesses with perspective and a way to implement effective placement, packaging, pricing and promotional strategies to ensure their long-term success.

Marketing provides insight into market trends and environment
Marketing undertakings and endeavours necessitate the analysis of all the influential factors that may affect your business operations and success in the marketplace. This includes a study of the consumer behaviour, current and future market trends, an analysis of the activities and progress of your competitors and various other political, legal, economic and social aspects.

Ultimately, the derived conclusions do not only help you with the creation of an effective marketing plan, but these may also be relied upon to predict future trends and enhance various other aspects of a business, ensuring its long-term success and survival in the marketplace.

Business Practice

Marketing builds brand
Increased competition and saturated markets highlight the need for the creation of a unique brand identity so that a business can stand out, among others. Marketing is the major directive force that contributes towards brand creation and brand building.

Marketing enables businesses to make correct branding decisions and lay down the foundation for brand values, which eventually serve as a set of major decisive factors behind all branding decisions. Consequently, it may be concluded that marketing provides the business with a foundation of an effective branding plan.

With the emergence of digital or social marketing era, marketing concepts and practices have undergone a considerable change. The internet is the new TV, and mobile devices are considered as new age computers. Technology now follows a steep curve of evolution, laying down the foundation for the path and pace for progress of marketing. Where content marketing has emerged out as a leader in the marketing field, internet and social media are the most dominant platforms used for marketing endeavours.

Global approach
Distances are shrinking, and markets are moving towards globalisation. Resultantly, businesses need to give due consideration to increasing globalisation and hence, realise the growing need to modify their operations and communicative networks in accordance with the modern marketing demands.

There is a need to bring into place a broader marketing vision and increased organisation of the operational machinery to survive and progress in the rapidly changing scenario.

Shifting the focus to older consumers
Conventionally, young adults, corresponding to an age bracket of 25-34 years, formed the primary focus of marketing endeavours for various businesses. Due to their higher percentage, these were considered a consumer segment that was to generate higher revenues.

However, there has been a shift in marketing trends, with older consumers now being considered as a more influential consumer segment. A study of consumer demographics has revealed older consumers as being more capable of spending, and hence, businesses need to modify their marketing preferences and strategies accordingly.

Emphasis on abstraction
Modern marketing trends lay greater emphasis on developing an emotional connect with the consumers, focusing on the explaining the relevance of the products or services to the consumers, rather than focusing on conveying the product or service utility and benefits.

Businesses need to realise that marketing success, in present times, is achieved through convincing the consumers that availing a product or a service they will be able to accomplish their dreams and aspirations.

Business Practice

Online Advertising
Though television has not completely lost its importance as a major advertising platform, it is no more a leading advertising medium. The Internet has a much wider access, and it is the most widely used advertising medium today. The increasing fragmentation of television coupled with the increasing influence of the internet and social media has led to the emergence of online marketing as a more potent promotional dynamic.

Since it is established that marketing serves as a major factor that contributes towards decision making, defines a business' vision and determines a company's success, marketing management has become a multi-disciplinary aspect, which has become more complicated over time.

Resultantly, effective marketing planning, strategizing and applications are faced with various challenges.

Effective communication
Communication plays a major role in determining the success of a marketing strategy and application. However, the definition of communication has changed considerably, in the context of marketing. It is no more limited to the effective conveyance of the utility of a product, but it now also includes the employment of techniques to motivate a consumer towards an implied action.

Consequently, marketing communication today focuses on the establishment of an emotional bond with the consumer, to effectively convey a brand's values, making them more relevant to the target consumers.

Selecting a Medium for Communication
Effective communication has become the key focus of marketing, and in the wake of drastic technological advances, numerous communicative channels have emerged. Consequently, with the increasing need to adopt a more focused approach for all marketing undertakings, businesses need to consider and analyse all the available options for selecting an effective communicative medium to reach out to their target consumers.

Television, print media, social media, internet and mobiles, all serve as effective communicative mediums and can be employed to work as feasible marketing tools. Businesses need to consider their objectives, various consumer metrics and market trends before they select a suitable medium which offers wide and efficient consumer access.

Constant need for data collection and research
Effective marketing thrives on latest data, stats and research conclusions. Consumer preferences and behaviour undergo constant change, and so do market trends. Not only are businesses required to keep track of these evolving marketing dynamics, but they also need to give due consideration to monitoring the activities of their competitors.

Business Practice

Benefits of Marketing

Marketing helps business in countless ways but some of the most impactful ones are listed below:

Raising Brand Awareness
This is important because it gets people acquainted with the brand and the products or services the organisation provides. It also makes the brand memorable to customers who can begin to trust the brand, become loyal clients, and promote it to their network.

Generating Traffic
Growing the number of visitors to a website site means getting more qualified leads and ultimately increasing sales. An effective marketing strategy will help throughout this process.

Increasing Revenue
Every organisation wants to increase sales and marketing can help achieve this goal through a variety of strategies like optimising the website and SEO, creating email campaigns, performing A/B tests to pinpoint the best strategy, and much more.

Building Trust in the Brand
Creating a high level of trust in the brand leads to customer loyalty and repeat purchases. This not only increases revenue but also leads to great reviews both online and by word of mouth, which is still one of the most effective types of promotion.

Tracking Metrics
Metrics are incredibly helpful when it comes to creating marketing strategy. They not only drive the strategy and help track its progress, but also inform what can be adapted or adjusted to continually optimise your campaigns.

The History of Marketing

Not too long ago, marketing mostly consisted of only outbound marketing, which meant chasing potential customers with promotions without really knowing if that person was interested in purchasing. The digital transformation and the rise of new communication channels, means marketing has drastically changed over the years.

Business Practice

Marketing Timeline	
1450-1900	***Printed advertising***
1450	*Gutenberg invents the printing press. The world of books and mass copies is revolutionised.*
1730	*The magazine emerges as a means of communication.*
1839	*Posters become so popular that it becomes prohibited to put them in London properties.*
1920-1949	***New media***
1922	*Radio advertising begins*
1933	*More than half of the population has a radio in their home*
1950-1972	***Marketing is Born and Grows***
1955	*Television advertising begins on ITV on September 22, 1955, advertising Gibbs SR toothpaste.*
1972	*Print media suffers an exhaustion of the outbound marketing formula.*
1973-1994	***The digital era flourishes***
1973	*Martin Cooper, a Motorola researcher, makes the first call through a cell phone*
1981	*IBM launches its first personal computer.*
1984	*Apple introduces the new Macintosh*
1990-1994	*Major advances in 2G technology, lay the foundation for the future explosion of mobile TV.*
1994	*The first case of commercial spam through e-commerce is produced.*
1995-2020	***The Era of Search Engines and social media***
1995	*Yahoo! And Altavista search engines are born.*
1995-1997	*The concept of SEO is born.*
1998	*Google and MSN launch new search engines*
1998	*The concept of blogging arises. By mid-2006, there are already 50 million blogs worldwide.*
2003-2012	*The era of inbound marketing begins.*
2003-2004	*Three social networks are launched: LinkedIn, Myspace and Facebook.*
2005	*The first video is posted on YouTube*
2006	*Twitter is born.*
2009	*Google launches real time searches.*
2010	*Instagram is created in October 2010. Young people between the ages of 13 and 24 spend 13.7 hours on the Internet, compared to 13.6 hours watching television.*
2011	*Snapchat is created, driving even more young users to their phones and fuelling the social media app craze*
2012	*There are already 54.8 million tablet users*

Business Practice

2014	The rise of Influencer marketing begins. Users and brands alike begin to realise the power of social media users with large followings
2014	For the first time ever, mobile usage outweighs desktop usage. More users are checking social media, reading emails, and making purchases on their phones.
2015-2016	Big data and marketing automation are explored and used more robustly to advertise to users.
2018	Video marketing continues to grow, especially with Instagram's launch of IGTV. Video content is no longer just limited to YouTube and Facebook.
2019-2020	Move over millennials! Gen Z is the new focus, and they have a hot new app: Tik-Tok.

It will be interesting to see how and where marketing continues to grow. With new world events, like the COVID-19 crisis of 2020 causing millions of people to stay indoors, social media and marketing trends are sure to change.

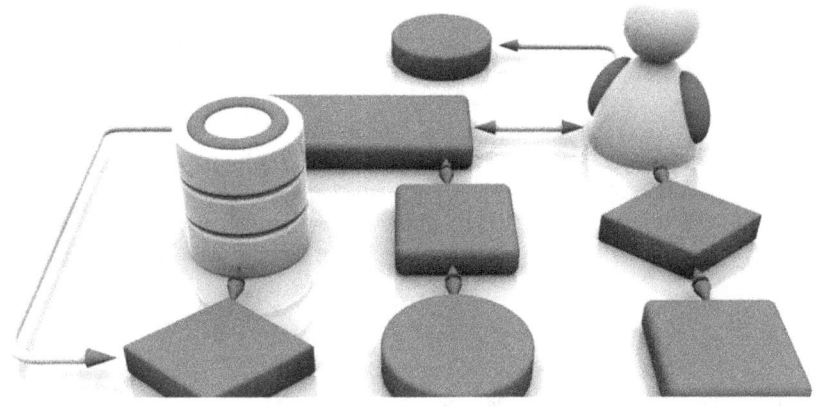

Chapter 7: Processes

Processes

Policy and Process

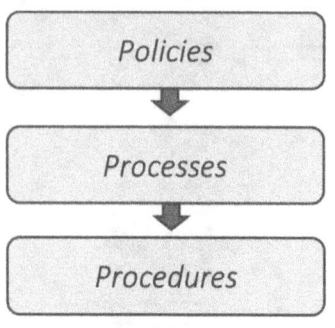

Policies and Processes are two key elements in the delivery of governance and compliance within an organisation.

The organisation's policies define its approach to fulfilling legal compliance and set out operational governance. The policies will explain the organisations approach to this and they are the basis for defining the process of how the policy will be satisfied.

These processes will define the procedures necessary to ensure the processes are completed properly and in a timely manner.

Policies

The Policies of an organisation are set by senior managers and form the basis of the Compliance and Governance of the organisation.

There are two key types of policy:

- *Internal Policies*
- *Business Policies*

All organisational policies should have the following fundamental characteristics, regardless of what they relate to.

- *Must be clear, specific and easily understood*
- *Specify company rules*
- *Explain their purpose*
- *State when policy should be applied*
- *Who it covers*
- *Method of enforcement*
- *Describe consequences of non-compliance*

Well-written policies give employees a way to handle problems and issues without having to constantly involve management every time a decision needs to be made.

Policies define the limits of decision-making and outline the alternatives. A policy ensures an employee fully understands the parameters and constraints of their job.

Processes

Policies communicate the individual and team responsibilities; this allows everyone to work together towards achieving the company's objectives. They help employees understand how to perform their tasks quickly, easily, effectively and safely. As a result, managers are able to control the business by exception rather than micro-managing the employee's activities.

When policies are easily understood by a layperson, the organisation has a better position on legal issues in the case of court challenges.

Business Policies

The business policies are the rules or guidelines which are set down to cover the behaviours and conduct of employees and define what is expected of them. These policies are usually linked to compliance with legislation which directly affects the industry or sector in which the business operates as well as those which are common to all organisations regardless of sector or industry.

The subject of these policies can include:

- *data protection*
- *GDPR*
- *working time*
- *equal opportunities*
- *health and safety*
- *occupational health*

Policies define how the organisation complies with the relevant legislation and how the employees are expected to behave and conduct themselves to satisfy that compliance. Some sectors will have additional requirements such as the financial sector having to comply with legislation aimed at controlling illegal activities such as money laundering, fraud, etc. and the Hospitality industry must comply with food safety legislation and laws controlling the retail sale of alcohol.

Internal Policies

The internal policies are the ones which relate directly to organisational governance.

- *use of corporate resources*
- *use of social media*
- *annual leave*
- *sickness reporting*
- *dress code*
- *smoking*
- *disciplinary*

Processes

This is just a very small sample of the policies which will exist, even in a fairly small organisation. The dress code will outline how employees are expected to present themselves, an acceptable standard of dress and it will also involve the wearing of uniforms, use of PPE, etc. The smoking policy will explain the how, when and where employees are allowed to smoke during their working hours. These policies will often be contained in an employee handbook which may be issued to all employees or signposted on the company's intranet.

There may also be policies on the use of company resources such as the telephone, internet access, etc. along with policies on the use of personal mobile phones in the workplace.
Processes

The processes of a business are the methods it uses to satisfy the requirements of the policies and deliver the goods and services it produces.

> *If you can't describe what you are doing as a process, you don't know what you're doing.* – W. Edwards Deming

Processes

Types of Business Process

There are three types of Process which are in common use across organisations. These are:

Primary Processes: These are the fundamental processes of a business through which a company delivers the end product to the customer. Every step involving in these processes works towards adding value to the final offering.

Support Processes: Support processes don't add value to the final product directly but they make an environment for primary processes to operate efficiently and effectively. These processes support the everyday operations of an organisation.

Management Processes: Management processes govern operations, corporate governance and strategic management. These processes set goals and standards which lead to the efficient and effective working of primary and support processes. Besides planning, these processes also involve monitoring and control of other business processes. Management processes are used to manage a business through strategic planning, tactical and operational planning.

The processes will change depending on the sector or industry in which it operates. When assessing a business there are a number of questions which can be asked to better understand what the business does and therefore begin to understand the processes it uses:

- *When does the business operate*
- *Where does the business operate*
  (Sector/Market, Location)
- *What does the business do?*
- *Who does it do it for?*
- *Why does it do it?*
- *How does the business operate?*

The last question – How does the business operate? Deals with the way it operates and the processes which define how things should be done, from simple step by step processes to deal with a sales order through to complex processes which may be necessary to deal with technical or production failures.

> *The processes are the way the organisations satisfies the policies it has defined*

By using a framework of processes the need for close management and supervision is significantly reduced and employees can work quickly and efficiently by simply following the processes.

Processes

There should be processes in place for every eventuality and they may include:

- *Dealing with enquiries*
- *Processing Customer information*
- *Sales order processing*
- *Sales invoice processes*
- *Payment processing*
- *Staff recruitment processes*

Each process will specify the steps which should be taken to ensure the task is completed satisfactorily not only for the organisation, but also in compliance with legislation and within the governance framework set out by the organisation's policies and procedures.

Reasons to have well-defined business processes

- *Help to identify what tasks are important to the larger business goals*
- *Improve efficiency*
- *Streamline communication between people/functions/teams/departments*
- *Creates accountability to ensure optimum use of resources*
- *Prevents chaos from infecting day-to-day operations*
- *Creates standardised procedures to complete*

Processes

Developing and Writing a Process

It may seem fairly straightforward to write a process for most routine activities, especially when there is little variation in the way things are done on a day-to-day basis. The process, however, is not designed to deal with day-to-day issues, it is designed to address out of the ordinary issues and allow the employees to make decisions in line with the process without the need to request management input.

Think about the recruitment process

- *Management will approve the recruitment of a new member of staff*
- *Multiple candidates apply for the role*
- *Candidates are short listed*
- *Successful candidate is recruited*
- *Salary and T&C negotiations take place*
- *Offer letter sent*
- *New employee is inducted*

This is a relatively straightforward process and simply thinking through the process step by step will result in a process which serves its purpose, however, there is the scope for problems to arise at any point in this sequence.

- **Insufficient candidates may apply** – *what happens then?*
- **Too many candidates are a perfect fit for the role** – *How are they rationalised into the very best candidates?*
- **The candidate demands more money than has been agreed** – *who makes the decision on the money on offer?*
- **The chosen candidates declines the role** – *What happens next?*

These are just a few of the frustrations which could arise during the process and must be considered when designing the process itself.

When planning and writing processes it is important to consider every possible eventuality to avoid the prospect of having to change or redesign a process once it has been implemented.
The best way to develop processes is to follow the simple guide below, ensuring that every step is completed in full before moving on to the next one.

Step 1: Define the goals

- *What is the purpose of the process?*
- *Why is it being created?*
- *How will you know if it is successful?*

Processes

Step 2: Plan and map your process

- What are the strategies needed to achieve the goals?
- This is the broad roadmap for the process.

Step 3: Set actions and assign responsibility to stakeholders

- Identify the individual tasks your teams and other resources need to do in order to execute the plan.

Step 4: Test the process

- Run the process on a small scale to see how it performs.
- Observe any gaps and make adjustments.

Step 5: Implement the process

- Start running the process in a live environment.
- Properly communicate and train all stakeholders.

Step 6: Monitor the results

- Review the process and analyse its patterns.
- Document the process history.

Step 7: Repeat

- If the process is able to achieve the goals set for it, replicate it for future processes.

Processes

Legal Compliance in Processes

When a customer places an order or buys something from the organisation, a great deal of personal and private information is captured as part of that order process. That data falls under the scope of the Data Protection Act and it must be kept secure and safe from anyone who does not have a direct interest or reason for having access to it. The process will define how this information should be captured and how it should be managed.

Example:

A Pop star contacts your organisation and places an order for goods or services. Details of the address, payment details, telephone number, email address, etc are all gathered to say nothing of other personal details – sizes, personal preferences, etc. Sadly, there are those people who crave to know those details whether their intentions are good or bad.

As a result, a process will be created to ensure that the data captured is not only used for its intended purpose of delivering goods or services to the customer, but also to ensure that the information which
has been gathered is kept safe and secure.

Details of the order may have been jotted down on a notepad or scrap of paper in the order office. That piece of paper contains a great deal of information about the person and it is quite reasonable therefore to expect the process to include a step whereby any client details are shredded once they have been entered onto a sale order processing system.

Alternatively, the process may prevent the use of paper and pens and require that all information be entered directly into a computer where it can not only be stored, but access to it can also be controlled.

The consequences of that information becoming widely available can barely be imagined.

> **There are 8 principles regarding the security of information set down by the Data Protection Act which will influence every process involving personal information. Failure to comply will result in the law being broken.**

In order to control the processes more closely, many organisations today will use computer managed process to ensure that processes are complied with. One of the most important operational systems which manage processes is the CRM or Customer Relationship Management System.

Processes

Customer Relationship Management System (CRM)

The CRM system is used to manage the relationship the organisation has with its customers. It is essentially a comprehensive database of information about the customers which will include their personal details along with a great deal of other information which will be accumulated over time and becomes invaluable as a marketing tool for approaching the customer in future.

The list might include, but is not limited to:

CRM data can include any or all of the following customer information:

- *Geographic location*
- *Business name, type, size*
- *Contact information*
- *Online identities (Email, social media, etc.)*
- *Demographic data (Social profile, age, sex, income, etc.)*
- *How they heard of you*
- *Date of first contact*
- *Date of most recent interaction*
- *Reason for contacting the organisation*
- *Customer Service representative responsible*
- *How their needs were met*
- *What products they use now*
- *What they have bought from you in the past*
- *Payment history*
- *Renewal schedule*
- *Which marketing campaigns they have responded to*
- *Comments they have made on social media*
- *Feedback Survey responses#*
- *Etc.*

This is not an exhaustive list of potential data, but the value of a CRM system and database should already be obvious as should the security risk that volume of data presents.

A well-maintained database tells you who your customers are, what they're worth to you, how to engage with them, what their likes and dislikes are, and what they might want from you in the future. All of this information is gathered from processes which work side by side with the CRM. The CRM itself will have processes for gathering data and it will also have processes in place for who can access that data using access security levels, password protection etc.

Processes

The CRM system can then be integrated with other business applications allowing the entire organisation to have access to information about the customers on a need-to-know basis which means only those who need access to data, have access to it.

Transaction Processing System (TPS)

A TPS system is used to automate routine processes which are typically carried out on a regular basis. This could be sending out monthly invoices, statement, or marketing materials and resources.

These systems can be set to operate autonomously with the only human intervention necessary to manage consumable stocks such as paper, ink, envelopes, etc.

Some systems may also allow real-time processing which means that one off orders and non-standard transactions can be entered manually onto the system and processed in a similar manner.

Payment Processing

It is vital that any payments are properly processed and accurately recorded to avoid conflict with customers and to maintain detailed financial records to ensure that the accounts produced at the end of the period are true and accurate.

Once again, this process involves handling financial details which must be held securely and only accessed by those who have a right to do so. All such records must be:

Processes

- *Detailed and accurate*
- *Comply with all relevant legislation*
- *Comply with organisational policies and procedures*
- *Be kept secure from unauthorised access*

Invoices which are raised by the business must also comply with all appropriate legislation and comply with the following requirements:

- *total amount payable*
- *amount of VAT (if applicable)*
- *due date for payment*
- *unique invoice number*
- *date of the invoice*
- *registered name and address of the business*
- *contact details*
- *the name and address of the customer*
- *clear description of the goods or services being paid for*
- *date the goods or service were supplied*

The use of computerised systems today, significantly reduces the problems which used to exist with manual processes which were subject to human error as well as short cuts being taken or processes not being used at all.

Once a process has been embedded into an organisation and is working well, without failures, there is a great deal of reluctance on behalf of those who oversee the process as well those who use it, to change the process from what it has always been.

If it ain't broken – don't try to fix it!!

As a result, changing a process becomes a major upheaval for everyone involved. There is often great resistance to change of any kind and many people will do all they can to prevent the change, some even intentionally sabotaging the new process to prevent the change from happening.

Any change to a process must therefore be very carefully planned and considered before being put forward for approval. Getting management approval for the change is actually only the start of the change. Everyone who is involved in the process must fully understand why the process is being changed and what their role in the new process will be.

All organisational processes are interdependent on each other and operate across teams, departments, divisions, and regions.

Processes

Change is often planned and intended to be of benefit to the organisation, but all too often it has a negative impact on the business simply because all situations and circumstances were not considered.

A process must have a beginning a middle and an end.

The process will start at the beginning, run through the middle section, coming to an end when the process is complete and the desired outcome has been achieved. If the process is interrupted part way through because of a problem, the process simply stops and cannot be completed until that problem is rectified.

A failure to anticipate a problem which subsequently arises could bring the entire organisation to halt until such time as the problem in the process is rectified.

On a small scale, the issues arising from a minor change can probably be overcome quite easily with a few, quick, management decisions and the process can restart. In a major international organisation, this cannot happen. It is not only important to consider the benefits change can bring, but an equal amount of energy and attention must be given to the anticipation of what and where problems may arise which could jeopardise all the planned benefits the change could deliver.

A very small, minor, change can have major repercussions throughout the organisation. Change, therefore, must be planned in detail, implemented in a totally structured manner and managed very carefully. It is here were the unbreakable bond between project management and change management becomes most important because neither will succeed without the other.

SWOT Analysis

A SWOT analysis can be used to assess the potential benefits of a proposed change as well as the potential weaknesses, but more importantly it can help to consider the opportunities and threats it poses to the organisation. Such an assessment should be conducted before any planning for change begins.

Process Diagrams

In order to better understand a process and where change may be needed or necessary, it is best to draw out the change in a process diagram.

A process diagram details step by step how the process works and what happens at each point where problems may arise and how they may be overcome so the process can continue, or what additional steps or authorisations are necessary before the process can be allowed to continue.

Processes

Below is a process diagram which deals with a troubleshooting process for a faulty toaster. When bread is put into the toaster and it is pressed for the machine to toast it – nothing happens. It would be foolhardy and expensive to simply throw the toaster away and buy a new one without fully assessing whether is beyond repair or it is simply a minor fault which is easily corrected.

The process goes through each step to correctly identify the cause of the problem and offers suggestions as to how it might be fixed when a possible cause is identified.

This simple process may oversimplify the actual process for checking a faulty toaster and there may be more steps which could be included depending on the degree of technical knowledge and skill which is held; however, it does serve to illustrate how a process works and how detailed the analysis should be before any change is ever considered, never mind planned

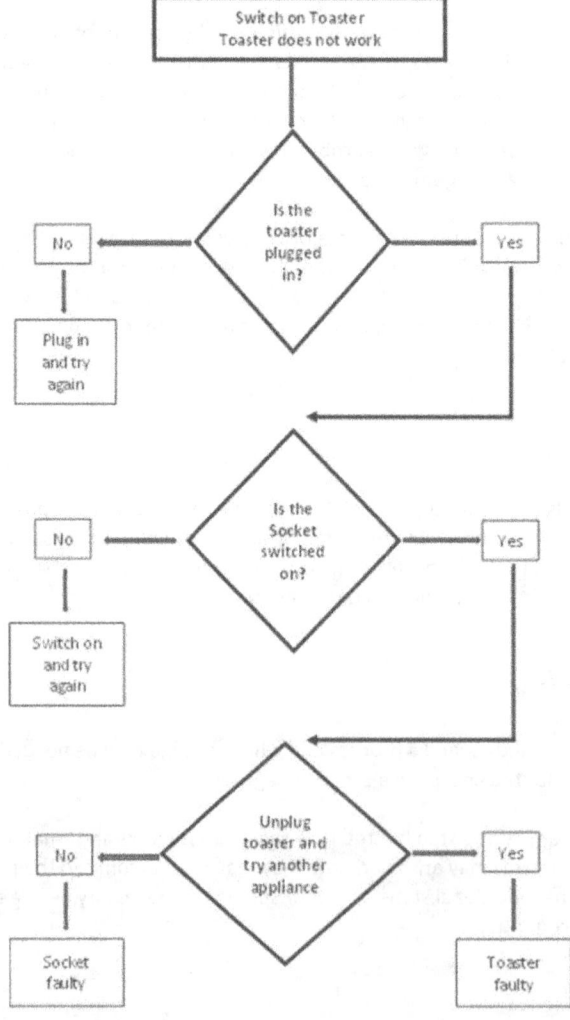

Processes

Adherence to Processes

Processes are not only used to streamline production and the way in which administrative activities are progressed through the business. They are also used to ensure compliance with legislation and will therefore be necessary in all situations where legal compliance is required. This can include all areas which involve:

- Consumer Rights Act
- Food Safety Act
- The Health and Safety at Work Act
- Data Protection Act
- GDPR
- Equality Act
- Employment Rights Act

These are just a few examples of the legislation involved, there are many more and some additional legislation may apply to the specific sector or business in which you are employed.

A great deal of this legislation will be covered by staff inductions, handbooks, etc. and processes such as emergency evacuations, fire procedures, sickness reporting, etc. will be reminded by regular, planned refresher training. Less regularly used processes should be documented and stored with the appropriate departments or on the organisations intranet so they can be accessed by staff at any time when support or guidance is needed.

Changing a Process

It is clear that any change to processes must be fully and very carefully considered before being implemented.

A proposal to make the change must be carefully documented before being presented to management for consideration. You should consider this in the same vein as a sales presentation. You aim is to get the management to buy into your idea for change and fully support the proposal throughout the entire change process. A change process which starts to hit problems will fail if it is not supported by management and the whole endeavour will have been a waste of time.

The proposal should include:

- Existing process diagram and explanation
- Revised process diagram and explanation
- Timeframe for implementation
- Training that will be needed for everyone involved in the process
- The benefits to be anticipated from the change

Processes

- *Cost benefit Analysis for the change*
- *Organisation wide benefits to be derived*

It would also be prudent to include details of any possible problems which might be anticipated as a result of the change and how it is proposed to overcome these. If management are aware of the possibility of problems arising and where they may arise, they are likely to respond more proactively if they do arise.

Monitoring the Process Change

Once the change has been implemented, it is important to closely monitor the new process and observe carefully as the process is followed. This must include across other teams and departments where they are affected to identify where the problem points are and how each one should be dealt with. The revised process diagram can then be updated with the new steps and problem points. Once the process has started to settle, it is important to be aware that problems will still arise. There will always be non-conformances where under exceptional situations the process is halted pending a decision. These should be reported to everyone who is affected by the interruption and their feedback considered when identifying solutions to these less common occurrences

Evaluating the Process Change

Once the process has settled, it is important to assess whether it has achieved its objectives. The change was prompted by a need to adjust, alter, streamline or tighten a process, so it is important to examine whether that need has been fully satisfied by the change and the process is now more effective than it was prior to the change.

The evaluation could include feedback from those employees who are involved in the process along with financial evaluations which might reflect the savings which have been made as a result of the change, or the actual costs being incurred as a result of the change compared to the budgeted costs which were estimated at the start of the process.

A process change does not have to be a money saving exercise – it could actually increase costs.

Benefits of Processes

The benefits of well-planned processes which align with strategies and policies are as follows:

Processes

- **Reduced expenditure and risk:** - *a process will reduce expenditure and risk by laying out the most efficient ways of doing the tasks by considering what could go wrong in advance.*
- **Reduce human error:** - *a process will limit the possibility of human error by assigning tasks to the people who are specialists.*
- **Improving efficiency:** *a process will enhance productivity by mapping out the moves and relevant steps which are most appropriate for the business.*
- **More customer focused:** - *processes are typically customer-oriented and will continuously update the organisation about the customer wants and needs with regard to the product/service it offers.*
- **Bridging communication gaps:** - *processes bridge the communication gap between the organisation and its customers through reviews and market research.*
- **Improved time management:** - *processes improve time efficiency by developing strategies and procedures to minimise the time taken to do certain activities.*
- **Adaption of new technology:** - *processes are often changed and improved over time. The organisation can improve processes by utilising the latest technologies.*

It should also be noted, however, that these benefits can only be achieved if all processes are mapped out and optimised to maximise their effect. A weakness in one will have repercussions across the rest. Failure to do so could result in:

- **Failure to recognise problem:** - *an organisation which doesn't focus on its business processes will fail to recognise the root cause of the problem that prevented it from achieving its goals due to an inability to set standardised processes.*
- **Low motivation:** *the absence of competent processes will demotivated employees due to a lack of involvement and knowledge in the process.*
- **Lack of change:** - *organisations often repeat the same errors over and over again as without a standardised process, the problem will not be recognised so change in the process cannot be implemented*
- **Time-consuming endeavour:** - *without proper flowcharts and workflow plans, work will take more time to complete than normal due to the need to obtain authorisation to progress.*
- **Lower efficiency:** - *without a process, an organisation will not be productive and efficiency will be lower than one with a proper process.*
- **High risk and increased expenditure:** - *organisations without adequate processes fail to see the future risks and are unable to find a cost-effective way to do a task*

Chapter 8: Project Management

Project Management

Project Management

Each day, whether at home or work we perform a wide range of tasks which we often regard as being routine or business as usual. At work, in addition to the routine tasks, some activities are not routine and are therefore called projects.

A project usually begins when an idea is put forward and is accepted as being a good idea. After discussion, the decision whether to implement the project, or not, is taken.

This is the start of the project, after which, plans and decisions will be made as to how the project should be implemented and planning will begin. This is the beginning of the project.

The next step is the middle of the project which is the plan being implemented. The project does not end when the implementation finishes either, this is only the end of the middle!

The project will actually end when the organisation has taken feedback and evaluated the whole of the project from start to finish.

A project therefore has a:

Beginning   *Middle*   *End*

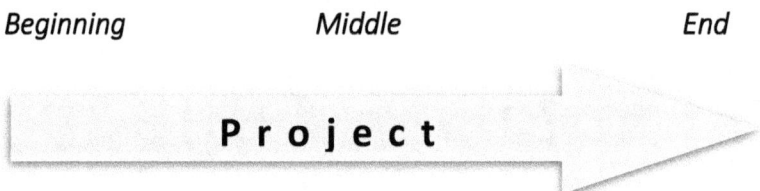

An example of a work-based project

A company wishes to hold a charity dinner for its stakeholders to support a local charitable organisation. Tasks for the planning team might team could include:

- **researching and planning the project** – finding a venue, booking caterers
- **working out timescales** – planning when things need to be delivered
- **finding and organising resources** – hiring service staff on the day; seating and tables; ordering portable toilets
- **sending out invitations the event** – publicity materials to news agencies and media; putting up posters; arranging TV, radio and press advertisements
- **contacting people coming to the event** – sending invitations and tickets; dealing with telephone and email queries
- **preparing the venue** – decorating the venue and dealing with queries from suppliers

Project Management

- ***host guests and performers*** – *arranging transport or giving directions*
- ***supporting staff after the concert*** – *taking care of lost property; taking unused programmes back to the office; dealing with queries*
- ***evaluating the success of the concert*** – *reviewing sales; responding to feedback, complaints and comments; helping to sort receipts and analyse the costs; assess monies generated*

The tasks undertaken are focused on the project and follow the plans and objectives of the project. They are not part of the regular, routine work of the organisation. Once the project is over, the tasks stop.

Working to strict timescales is critical. Things must be done on time as delays can have a knock-on effect on other people and tasks connected with the project.

Key stages in the lifecycle of a project

The lifecycle of a project follows the natural sequence of the project itself. The project will need to be started, comprehensive planning will then be required before the project is delivered and subsequently it will need to be evaluated and reviewed.

The key stages in a project are therefore:

- *initiation*
- *comprehensive planning*
- *project delivery and control*
- *closure and review*

Project Management

Initiation

At the initiation stage, the purpose of the project needs to be clarified before planning and preparation can take place.

Working to an agreed purpose helps to focus everyone involved with the project. It helps to stop them being distracted, especially if the project becomes very intense and they are working under pressure.

In the example, the agreed purpose of the charity dinner is to raise funds for the charity.

Before the planning gets fully underway, the decision-makers also need to agree the scope of the project.

The scope is defined as the broad outline of what is needed to achieve a satisfactory result. It is good practice to include details about what is not included within the scope of the project, so that people can see the parameters clearly.

In the example, the organisers need to agree, for example:

- **the size of the venue they think they can fill** – *the factory canteen can seat 75 people; a village hall can seat 125 whilst a local conference centre can accommodate 250.*
- **the catering services available** – *inhouse, outside caterers, contract caterers*
- **the type of entertainment they can afford and are able to organise** – *discos, local bands and entertainers or well-known bands*
- **what they can achieve with the resources they have available**

Project team members, especially the main decision-makers, need to agree the scope of their particular role in the project – e.g., how much time and expertise they can contribute.

They will look carefully at the reason for the project – the planned outcomes, costs and benefits to the organisation – and how the project fits into the activities, culture and objectives of the organisation as a whole.

The aims and objectives of the project all need to be agreed so that everyone understands where they will be going with the project, and what they will have to do to make it a success at every stage.

In the example, the purpose of the charity dinner is to raise money for the charity.

The aim is to run a concert that makes a decent profit that can be given to the charity.

The objectives along the way could include, for example:

- *raising the profile of the charity*
- *bringing public attention to the charity's work*

Project Management

- *increasing the number of supporters*
- *giving the guests a really good and memorable night*
- *career development for staff, by increasing their skills, knowledge and experience*

Comprehensive Planning

When planning and preparing for a project, there are several things that need to be agreed to make sure that:

- *the project is planned appropriately*
- *people understand what is expected of them and the project team*
- *sufficient resources are put in place*
- *sufficient budgets are put in place*
- *stakeholders' expectations are met*

In the planning stages, project managers need to consider:

- *timescales*
- *resources*
- *budgets*
- *risk assessments*
- *contingency plans*

When planning and preparing for a project, the timescales need to be agreed so that all of the different elements can be brought together on time. Very often, different parts of the project are interdependent meaning one part of the project cannot go ahead until the previous stage has been completed, so a delay at any stage can delay the whole project or lead to its failure.

For the example agreed timescales could include, for example:

- *starting the planning and preparation in February*
- *booking caterers, bands, resources, etc. and a venue for a date in August*
- *having the invitations and tickets ready for April*
- *launching the publicity for the concert in March*
- *sending out tickets from June onwards*
- *recruiting and training staff and volunteers to help at the concert between July and August*

Project managers also need to plan the resources that are going to be needed, for example:

Project Management

- ***human resources*** – *staff, volunteers and agency workers*
- ***physical resources*** – *accommodation, transport, seating, lighting, stationery, telephones and communication equipment*

These must be agreed at the beginning of a project as resources need to be planned in line with budgets and timescales. The project manager will need to have a total overview of resources and costs, and anyone working on the project team needs to be aware of any limits or deadlines.

In the example, when planning the resources for volunteers who will help at the concert, the organisers will agree things like:

- *the number of volunteers that they are going to need*
- *the budget that is allocated for their uniforms, training, welfare, travel and other costs*
- *the locations to be used for training sessions*

When planning or preparing a project, the overall budget may already be set. The organisers might have already allocated funds and the people running the project will have to deliver it within the budget they have been given. Early in the process, they need to check the budget to make sure that they can achieve what is expected. Alternatively, the event may need to be self-financing where there is upfront funding to support the planning, but the whole costs of the event must be deducted from the money generated by the event. As a consequence, an event such as the example will only generate a charitable contribution if there is money left over after all the costs of the event have been paid.

For other projects, part of the planning process might be to research the likely costs and to forecast the budget that will be needed to deliver the project. The project managers will then negotiate and agree budgets with the organisation before starting on the main planning, preparation and delivery of the project.

Most projects have a contingency budget that is also agreed at the beginning. This is a separate budget to cover unexpected problems – e.g., last minute change to entertainment due to sickness.

Budgets need to be agreed and allocated to different elements of the project – e.g., staff costs, stationery costs, catering and hospitality.

Part of project management planning is to make contingency plans to cover unforeseen costs, last-minute problems and unforeseen events or issues that have an impact on the project. For our example, the organisers would have contingency plans for extreme weather around the time of the dinner, for example: to provide dry access to the venue, provide sufficient umbrellas, lighting for photography, etc.

Project Management

Project managers need to have a contingency budget set aside to cover their contingency plans. This makes it easier to make quick decisions to get the project back on track if funds, and limits of authority to use them, have been agreed in advance.

Project Delivery and Control

After a great deal of planning and many meetings, the time comes to deliver the project. This is when everything is put into practice.

Decision-making and problem-solving skills will be needed to deal with queries and problems that could threaten to alter the progress of the project.

Progress needs to be monitored and measured so that any potential problems are identified as soon as possible, maybe against SMART targets, planners, flow-charts budgets and risk assessments.

Monitoring and controlling a project can involve performing internal and external audits.

All of this information will then be put into a brief, along with terms of reference to provide the basic structure for the planning stage.

Regular progress reviews and team meetings during a project will help to identify actual and potential problems as they arise. By reviewing flow-charts, task lists, planners, project plans, objectives and so on, the team can see the problems, reprioritise and allocate resources to deal with the issues.

Closure and Review

As the project moves into its final phase, it is time to evaluate against the agreed aims and objectives to see how it met and / or exceeded expectations. Projects need to be closed down and lessons need to be learned and recorded for future research and development.

The review stage is extremely important as it gives people the chance to make notes, give and receive feedback and record information for future projects whilst issues, problems and successes are still fresh in the memory.

Project closure needs to be managed well so that:

- *people who worked on the project feel valued and appreciated*
- *the clients or other decision-makers who authorised the project appreciate its value, see what has been achieved and feel confident about commissioning further projects*
- *contacts made within the supply chain feel valued and are kept up to date*
- *all stakeholders can see the benefits and positive results of the project before they move onto the next activity*

Project Management

Roles within the Project Team

Project teams can have many different members. They might work on the project full time, they might only be involved in one particular stage, or their role may only require their involvement from time to time. People on a project team can include, for example:

- *board members*
- *sponsors*
- *managers*
- *team leaders*
- *team members*
- *subject specialists*
- *administrators*

Board members
There may be board members who have direct or indirect functions on a project team. In the charity dinner example, input from board members might have included:

- **the managing director** – *providing initial ideas and overall strategy; weekly progress meetings to monitor and evaluate progress and plans; main contact to agree budgets at organisational level*
- **charity trustees** – *on the board to oversee operations from a distance and ensure compliance with regulatory requirements of the Charities Commission and the charity's own constitution*
- **shareholder representative** – *to monitor shareholders' interests and funds*
- **sales director** – *with an interest in sales revenue*

Sponsors
Some projects have sponsors who make contributions of finance and/or expertise. In national sports clubs, for example, sponsors pay for advertising their own businesses around the pitch, on shirts and other merchandise, and in marketing materials. They also use the venue for entertaining their own guests and customers and enjoy special privileges.

If a football club's project is to rebuild one of the stands, for example, a major sponsor may agree to cover the costs and be closely involved with the whole project, form initiation to closure and review.

Managers
Direction may come from the board, but the main planning, delivery and controlling of project plans will be the responsibilities of various managers. There may be:

- **a senior project coordinator** – *with overall authority over budgets and important decisions for several projects*

Project Management

- **the project manager** – *the main manager for the project; the main point of contact for most decisions and problems; has overall control of everyday activities for the whole project*
- **department managers** – *such as an HR or health and safety manager who are only involved with certain aspects of the project*

In organisations whose core business is project management, and in some other large organisations, there may be several full-time managers. Managers will deal with the different business functions and coordinate their activities with the project managers who have the overall view and control.

Team Leaders

As the project is broken down into different components, there may be team leaders in charge of each section. They will answer to the project manager and be responsible for their sub-teams and special areas only, which could include, for example:

- **induction and training** – *new team members and volunteers*
- **a catering team** – *looks after one of the food court areas in a large venue*
- **running one of the bars** – *one of ten bars in the large venue*
- **a customer service team** – *dealing with customer queries at information points*
- **a media team** – *that looks after press, TV and radio coverage*

Team Members

Team members can be, for example, employees, agency workers, freelance workers, or volunteers. They might be allocated to, for example:

- **the project full time** – *working in the planning office for the whole project*
- **the project part time** – *spending a regular two days a week on the accounts and budgets*
- **short-term roles** – *directing cars in a car park for a two-day event*

They will all work within the limits of their authority and refer to the team leader for everyday queries and problems.

Subject specialists

Subject specialists can be called in from time to time when the project manager needs specific skills, usually during the planning and delivery stages. Specialist could be called in to deal with:

- **health and safety assessments** – *e.g., in unusual work areas or environments*
- **fireworks display for an event**
- **designers for stationery, posters and other marketing materials**
- **branding** – *e.g., for sponsorship coverage*

Project Management

- **specialist equipment that is not normally used or owned by the organisation** – e.g., staging, marquees, lighting or sound systems
- **accounts and audits**

Such subject specialists might:

- **work for other departments within the organisation** – and be asked to assist with specific parts of the project only
- **work as freelancers** – and be engaged for particular roles on a consultancy basis
- **be part of specialist organisations** – working as part of an independent external team that is tasked to do specific activities
- **be a full team member for the duration of the project**

Subject specialists are often separate from the main team, so the lines of communication and responsibility need to be clearly defined. They are likely to be answerable to the project manager, who acts as a line manager, and have access to more senior decision-makers when required.

Administrators

Administrators perform a wide range of tasks in project management, such as:

- *processing receipts and invoices*
- *keeping accounts records up to date*
- *processing sales records and enquiries*
- *archiving information*
- *keeping Gantt charts and other monitoring systems up to date*

Administrators might work for other departments within the organisation, such as the accounts department, and be asked to assist with specific parts of the project only. Others may be part of the project team full time, performing administrative tasks for the project only.

As for other project management roles, administrators can be, for example:

- **freelancers** – engaged for particular roles on a consultancy basis
- **employed by specialist external organisations** – working as part of an independent team that is tasked to do specific activities
- **employed by the organisation on a temporary basis** – for the duration of the project
- **employed by the organisation on a permanent basis** – working on the project team part or full time

Project Management

Project Governance

Project governance is the alignment of the project with stakeholders' needs or objectives. It is critical for achieving organisational goals. It enables organisations to manage projects consistently and exploit the benefits of a project. It provides a framework which helps the project manager and sponsors to make decisions that suit both stakeholder needs and organisational objectives or deal with situations where they may not be aligned.

Stakeholder Involvement

A stakeholder is an individual, group, or organisation who may affect, be affected by, or perceive itself to be affected by a decision, activity, or outcome of a project. Stakeholders are either directly involved in the project or have interests that may be affected by the project's outcome. It normally includes the members of a project team: project managers, project sponsors, executives, customers, or users.

It is beneficial and advisable to know about good stakeholder management skill and communicate constantly with stakeholders in order to collaborate on the project because after all, they are also affected by the product.

If a project is small in size, the number of stakeholders can be small. However, if it is large and expanded to a large area, one may have a huge number of stakeholders, including communities or the general public. Also, all stakeholders are not alike. They have different expectations and needs. One must treat every stakeholder uniquely according to their needs or else the stakeholders might feel left out which can put the project in danger.

Different stakeholders often have opposing expectations that might create clashes within the project. Stakeholders may also interfere in the project, its deliverables, and the project team to fulfil their strategic business objectives or other requirements.

Types of Project Stakeholder

Project stakeholders can be classified into two types:

Internal Stakeholders: As the name suggests, these are the people involved in a project from within. They include:

- *A sponsor*
- *An internal customer or client* (if the project started due to an internal need of the organisation)
- *A project team*
- *A program or portfolio manager*
- *Management*

Project Management

- *Another team's manager of the company*

External Stakeholders: These stakeholders are not directly involved but are engaged from outside and are affected by the project outcome.

- **An external customer or client** *(if project started due to a contract from external party)*
- **An end user**
- **Subcontractors**
- **A supplier**
- **The government**
- **Local communities**
- **Media**

Why are stakeholders important for a project?

Stakeholders have different levels of duties and authority when contributing on a project. This level may differ as the project proceeds. It can range from occasional contributions to full project sponsorship.

Some stakeholders may also detract from the success of the project, either actively or passively. These stakeholders need the project manager's attention during the whole time of project's life cycle.

Stakeholder identification is a continuous process during the entire project life cycle. Identifying them, understanding their level of effect on a project, and satisfying their demands, needs, and expectations is essential for the success of the project.

Just as stakeholders can affect a project's objectives positively or negatively, a project can be perceived by the stakeholders as having positive or negative results.

One of the most important responsibilities of a project manager is to manage stakeholder expectations, which can be problematic as stakeholders often have very diverse or conflicting objectives.

Project Management

Project Stakeholders

- **Sponsor:** *A sponsor is the person or group who provides supplies and support for the project and is liable for assisting success. He may be external or internal to the organisation.*
- **Customers and users:** *Customers are the people or organisations who will approve and manage the project's product, service, or result. Users, as clear from the name, use the product.*
- **Sellers:** *Sellers, also known as vendors, are external companies that enter into a contractual agreement to provide services or resources necessary for the project.*
- **Business partners:** *They are external organisations that have a special relationship or partnership with the enterprise.*
- **Organisational groups**: *Organisational groups are internal stakeholders who are influenced by the actions of the project team. For example, human resources, marketing, sales, legal, finance, operations, manufacturing, etc.*
- **Functional managers:** *They are key individuals who play the role of management within an administrative or functional area of the business. For example, human resources, finance, accounting, etc.*
- **Other stakeholders:** *They are additional stakeholders which include financial institutions, government regulators, subject matter experts, consultants, and others, which have a financial interest in the project, contributing inputs to the project, or have in the outcome of the project.*

Stakeholders are people who get affected by your project or have any kind of interest in it. They can be internal, external, positive, negative, high power, low power, etc. However, to complete your project successfully you have to manage all these stakeholders and fulfil their prospects. If you fail to do so, your project may get jeopardised.

Project Management

Whether internal or external, all projects have stakeholders. One of the main reasons' projects fail is because the deliverables were not what the customer wanted, or they did not meet the customer's needs. To ensure project success, it helps that you know all of the key stakeholders on your project, how they prefer to communicate, what their needs are, and what the acceptable end results are.

Engaging stakeholders during—and especially at the beginning of—your project will help reduce and uncover risks and increase their "buy-in." When stakeholders are adequately engaged, their influence spreads far and wide. Some of the ways stakeholders are important to a project are as follows.

1. Providing Expertise
Stakeholders are a wealth of knowledge about current processes, historical information, and industry insight. Many times, these team members will have been at the company or on the project longer than the project manager or project team. It is important to involve all key stakeholders when gathering and documenting requirements to avoid missing major deliverables of the project. Project managers, or others who are in charge of deliverables, may not be experts on every project. Key stakeholders can provide requirements or constraints based on information from their industry that will be important to have when understanding project constraints and risks.

2. Reducing and Uncovering Risk
The more you engage and involve stakeholders, the more you will reduce and uncover risks on your project. When discussing initial requirements, project needs, and constraints, stakeholders may bring up issues or concerns about meeting those things. Uncovering risks and then discussing a plan to mitigate them before issues arise will dramatically increase the success of your project. Involving knowledgeable stakeholders during this process will help.

3. Increasing Project Success
By gathering and reviewing project requirements with stakeholders, you will get their "buy-in," which will in turn help increase project success. If you cannot meet stakeholders' needs, due to conflicting needs or priorities, set expectations early in the project life cycle. This will help you manage the relationship throughout the project instead of there being surprises at the end. Stakeholders should always be aware of the project scope, key milestones, and when they will be expected to review any deliverables prior to final acceptance.

4. Granting Project Acceptance
The more regularly you engage and involve stakeholders from the start, the more likely you will have a positive project conclusion. By the end of the project, the team members should have already been aware of delivery expectations, risks, and how to mitigate the risks. They also should have reviewed draft deliverables along the way. This process should help avoid any surprises at the end of your project. The final acceptance is just their final stamp of approval during the project closure phase.

Project Management

The Project Plan

A project plan, also known as a project management plan, is a document that contains a project scope and objective. It is most commonly represented in the form of a Gantt chart to make it easy to communicate to stakeholders.

Step 1: Understand the scope and value of your project

At its core, a project plan defines your approach and the process your team will use to manage the project according to scope. A project plan communicates vital information to all project stakeholders. If you approach it as something more than a dry document and communicate that aspect of it differently to everyone involved, it can and will be seen as integral to your project's success. The fact is a plan is more than dates. It is the story of your project, and you do not want it to be a tall tale! Like any well-written story, there are components that make it good. In fact, any solid plan should answer these questions:

- *What are the major deliverables?*
- *How will we get to those deliverables and the deadline?*
- *Who is on the project team, and what role will they play in those deliverables?*
- *When will the team meet milestones, and when will other members of the team play a role in contributing to or providing feedback on those deliverables?*

If your plan answers those questions and educates your team and clients on the project logistics, you are creating a viable, strategic game plan for your project.

At its core, a project plan defines your approach and the process your team will use to manage the project to scope.

Step 2: Conduct extensive research

Before you start creating a project plan, make sure you know all of the facts. Dive into the documents and communications relevant to the project. Go over the scope of work and related documents (maybe an RFP or notes from sales calls or meetings with your client team). Be thorough. Understand the details and ask thoughtful questions before you commit to anything. A good project manager is well-informed and methodical in the way he or she decides to write a project plan. At a minimum, you will be responsible for possessing a thorough understanding of:

- *The goals of the project*
- *Your client's needs and expectations*

Project Management

- *The makeup of your client team and their decision-making process (i.e., how they will review and approve your team's work), which might answer:*
- *Who is the project sponsor, and how available is he or she?*
- *Who is the PM, and will he or she be in constant contact with you? (They need to be).*
- *Who are the additional stakeholders your team should be aware of?*

Set time aside with your client to ask some tough questions about process, organisational politics, and risks.

Step 3: Ask the tough questions

In addition to all of your questions about your client team and their expectations, set some time aside with your main client contact and ask them some tough questions about process, organisational politics, and general risks before creating a project plan. Doing so will convey that your team has the experience to handle any type of difficult personalities or situation and that you care about the success of the project from the start.

Questions that may impact a project plan:

- *Has your team discussed how you will gather feedback?*
- *Who is the final sign-off? Or, who owns the project?*
- *Is there a stakeholder we need to consider who is not on your list? (A president, dean, the boss's spouse?)*
- *What is the project deadline? What are the factors or events that are calling for that date? (a meeting, an ad campaign, an event?)*
- *Are there any dates when you will be closed or not available?*
- *Will there be any meetings or points in the project where you will want us to present on the current project status to a larger group (i.e., a board meeting)?*
- *Has your team been through a project like this in the past?*
- *How did it go?*
- *Is there anything that would prevent the project from being successful?*
- *Is there a preferred mode of communication and online project planning tools?*
- *Are there any points in the process that some stakeholders might not understand that we can explain?*

Project Management

Step 4: Create your project plan outline

After getting the answers you need, take some time to think about the responses in light of the project goals and how your team might approach a similar project. Think about the tasks that are outlined in the scope of work and try to come up with a project planning and management approach by creating a high-level outline. All you need is a calendar to check dates.

A first outline can be very rough and might look something like a work breakdown structure.

Make sure your outline includes:

- *Deliverables and the tasks taken to create them*
- *Your client's approval process*
- *Timeframes associated with tasks/deliverables*
- *Ideas on resources needed for tasks/deliverables*
- *A list of the assumptions you are making in the plan*
- *A list of absolutes as they relate to the project budget and/or deadlines*

There will always be multiple ways to execute the work you are planning, and it is easy to focus on what the end product will look like. Do not go there. Instead, focus on the mechanics of how it will happen. Getting tied up in the execution will only confuse you and likely make you feel unimpressed by the final product because it is not what you envisioned.

Remember: You are there to plan and guide the project, not create it.

A project outline will help you to organise your thoughts, formulate what might work for the project, and then transform everything into a discussion. Take this time to build a simple project plan outline—it does not have to have all the details just yet. Doing so lays the foundations for a solid, sustainable project plan.

Step 5: Talk with your team

Starting a project must begin with clear communication of the project goals and the effort required to meet them. This comes with understanding the fact that a project manager cannot be the only one writing a project plan. Sure, you could try—but if you are interested in team buy-in, you will not. The reason you will not is because you do not want to put yourself or your team in an awkward position by not coming to a consensus on the approach before presenting it to your client. Doing that would be like stabbing every single one of your co-workers in the back.

It is also great to utilise the super-smart folks surrounding you to get their input on how the team can complete the tasks at hand without killing the budget and the

Project Management

team's morale. As a project manager, you can decide on waterfall or agile approaches, but when it comes down to it, you need to know that the team can realistically execute the plan.

You can also use your project plan review time to question your own thinking and push the team to take a new approach to the work. For instance, if you are working on a website design, can designers start creating visual concepts while the wireframes are being developed? Will it make sense for this project and for the team? Can you have two resources working on the same task at once?

Running ideas by the team and having an open dialogue about the approach can not only help you with building a project plan, it is also a big help in getting everyone to think about the project in the same terms. This type of buy-in and communication builds trust in a team and gets people excited about working together to solve a goal. It can work wonders for the greater good of your team and your project.

Step 6: Write your full project plan

When you have got all the info you need and you have spoken to all parties, you should feel more than comfortable enough to put together a rock-solid project plan using whatever tool works for you. Any good online project planning tool will help you to formalise your thoughts and lay them out in a consistent, readable way.

Make it readable

To make your project plan readable, use some formatting skills to make sure tasks, durations, milestones, and dates are crystal clear. Try to make a simple project plan—the more straightforward and easier to read it is, the better. No matter what tool you are using, you should include these features:

- **Include all pertinent project info:**
  Client Name, Project Name
  Version Number, Delivery Date
- **Break out milestones and deliverables in sections by creating headers and indenting subsequent tasks.** *(Reading one long list of tasks is really monotonous and can be mind-numbing even to the best of us.)*
- **Call out which team is responsible for each task.** *(Example: "CLIENT: Provide feedback")*
- **Add resources responsible to each task so there is no confusion about who is responsible for what.**
- **Be sure to show durations of tasks clearly. Each task should have a start and end date.**
- **Add notes to tasks that might seem confusing or need explanation. It never hurts to add detail!**

Project Management

- *Call out project dependencies. These are important when you are planning for the risk of delays.*
- *Include your company's logo and your client's logo if you are feeling fancy.*
- *Use your company's branded fonts if you are feeling really fancy.*

In addition to all of this, you should be as flexible as possible when it comes to how your project plan is presented. There is no absolute when it comes to how you represent your plan as long as you and your team understand what goes into one. Remember, people absorb information differently; while some people prefer a list-view, others might prefer to see a calendar, or even a Gantt chart. You can make all of those variations work if you have taken the steps to create a solid plan.

You should be as flexible as possible when it comes to how your plan is presented.

Step 7: Publish your plan

You are almost finished! You have done your research! outlined your approach, discussed it with your team, and built your formal project plan. Do yourself one quick favour and ask someone on your team to review it before you hand it over to your clients. There is nothing more embarrassing than being a project manager and delivering a plan with an error—like an incorrect date. It will take someone 10 minutes, and you will have peace of mind.

Step 8: Share your plan with the team and make sure they read it!

After you have put all of that work into creating this important document, you want to make sure that it has actually been reviewed. When you are delivering your project plan, make sure you provide a summary of it in prose format. A brief message that covers the overall methodology, resources, assumptions, deadlines, and related review times will help you to convey what the project plan means to the project and to everyone involved.

Do not be bashful about it: explain the thought that has gone into the process of building the project plan and open it up for discussion. It can be good to set up a call to review the plan line by line with a client. This ensures that your client will understand the process, and what each step in the plan means. Sure, you might have to explain it a few more times, but at least you are making the effort to help establish good project planning standards across the board and educate your clients on how your team works. And again, it shows that you care.

Project Management

Step 9: Prepare to keep planning

Some projects are smooth and easy to manage, and others are a complete nightmare that wake you up at 3 a.m. every other night (it happens). Regardless, plans will change. With a good team and a clear scope of work, you are on your way to making a solid plan that is manageable and well-thought-out. Having a solid project plan is your best defence against project chaos.

If you are an easy-going project manager who can adapt your approach and your plan to go with the flow while calling out the appropriate risks, you will find yourself happy. Otherwise, the daily changes will cloud your vision, and you will focus on things that will not help your team, your client, or the project.

Project Management

Project Management Methodology

All types of projects in project management follow a certain approach. There exists various methodologies through which project management can be carried out.

Critical Path Method (CPM)
This method was developed in the 1950s and is based on the idea that some tasks cannot be started until others are completed. This highlights task interdependencies. The critical path method identifies the most optimised work path to follow taking these dependencies into consideration so that you can finish your project in the least time possible.

Critical Chain Project Management (CCPM)
This methodology focuses primarily on the resources needed to complete a project and its tasks. The critical chain is identified which pinpoints the project's most critical tasks. In turn, the resources are reserved for these high-priority tasks.

The PMI/PMBOK "Method"
This methodology encompasses the breakdown of different types of projects into five project groups agreed upon by the Project Management Institute (PMI). Essentially it refers to the following the project management life cycle and each phase's demands.

Agile
This methodology was developed in 2001. It focuses on effective response to change, comprehensive documentation and individuals interacting over processes and tools. Continuous collaboration is a key feature between both team members and other project stakeholders.

Scrum
Is a variation from the Agile methodology and is its most popular framework. It is simple to implement and solves many problems that software developers have faced such as convoluted development cycles, delayed production and inflexible project plans. A small team is typically led by what is called a Scrum Master who clears all obstacles that prevent efficient work. Teams work in 'sprints' which are short cycles comprised of two weeks normally and typically meet daily to discuss the progress of the tasks of their project.

Kanban
Kanban is a methodology based on a team's capacity to do work. It originated from Toyota in the 1940s. It is a visual approach to project management and is useful for work that requires steady output. Here, teams move through the progress of their project visually and thus allows for clearer identification of any roadblocks or bottlenecks that may occur along the way.

Project Management

Assigning Tasks to Individuals

You want to make sure that everyone is fully occupied but on project tasks that play to their strengths.

From time to time that might mean that someone has to work on something that is not their core area of expertise, but provided they have the support required, that could be a good development opportunity.

However, assuming you have the luxury of being able to access a range of resources with varying skills, how should you allocate tasks?

Skill
Top of the list is skill – does the person have the skills required to actually carry out this project task and complete it successfully? If so, they are probably the best person for the job.

Experience
Has the resource in question done this sort of task before? If so, they will have the relevant experience and the confidence to do it again and probably will not need much support from you.

If they have not done it before, but you believe they have the skills to do the work, then they will need more support but could still complete the task successfully.

Interest
Just because someone has the skills and experience does not mean that they are interested enough in the work to do the task well.

If they have done the same task a thousand times before and really want to spend some time building their experience in other areas then you could allocate the work to them – but it might not be done to the highest standard, or in a timely fashion.

Talk to team members before giving them work in order to assess their level of motivation.

Cost
The person best placed to do the work may be far too expensive for your project budget, so you may have to compromise.

Equally, it is not worth using a highly paid programme manager to do basic admin tasks if you have someone on the team in a project co-ordinator or PMO support role who could do those for you.

Location
Where is the task going to be carried out? With a lot of project work it does not much matter and your team members could work from anywhere.

Project Management

But there are likely to be some tasks where location does play a part. For example, configuring servers on site, or working at a client location for a length of time.

You want to pick someone who is the best person for the job, but if you have a choice of resource, you could find that location plays a part in the decision-making process.

It is cheaper if you do not have to pay travel expenses and it is probably more convenient for the resource concerned if the work is local to where they are normally based.

Availability

Finally, you should take availability into account. OK, it is not the most important criteria when it comes to assigning work to team members, but it does matter.

There is not any point in assigning a task to someone who is already overloaded, while other team members sit around waiting for work to come in. Instead, it could be a good opportunity to improve the skills of someone else or to help others learn something completely new, like budget management.

In short, there are lots of factors that come into play when assigning project tasks to team members.

You probably do it unconsciously but every so often it does help to think through why you are giving a task to someone – as well as to check that they really are the most appropriate person for the job at that time.

Delivering the Project

It is true to say that no two projects are the same and everyone will have different objectives, parameters, budgets, constraints, outcomes, etc.

As a consequence, every project will need to be managed differently with different emphasis on different elements. There cannot therefore be a definitive guide as to how a project should be delivered and everyone should be assessed and planned on its own merits before a delivery plan is drawn up.

Key Project Documentation

As noted above, no two projects are the same and therefore a standard set of documentation cannot be prescribed to a project. The documentation will be unique to each project. Key pieces that may be used to deliver a project can include:

- *a brief and terms of reference*
- *project plans*

Project Management

- *definitions of project roles*
- *a risk log (RAID) or register*
- *project monitoring records* – e.g., Gantt charts or progress reports

Brief and Terms of Reference
During the initiation stage, a brief and terms of reference to provide a framework for the project must be produced. By agreeing these early in the process, everyone can agree their role and commitment to it, and the project managers can check whether or not the project is viable. This needs to be agreed before the organisation commits to planning and using its resources, finances and stakeholders' time.

It is important to show what is not covered by the project too. This is key in large organisations in particular, where people may look at a project and assume that it covers their area when it does not.

Project Plans
The project plans will include all aspects of the project, including:

- *timescales, deadlines and critical review points*
- *human and physical resources*
- *the budgets that relate to the project*
- *contingency plans*

The plan needs to go into detail about how the different timescales and tasks will overlap and affect each other.

Definitions of Project Roles
The various people involved with the project need to have their job descriptions in definitions of project roles. Having these together helps the project manager to have an overall view of who is tasked to do what, so that they can make sure that all aspects and tasks have been covered.

A Risk Log or Register
An important element of the planning stage is to prepare a risk log or register and put in measures to minimise risk. A risk assessment needs to be performed for each aspect of the project, and these are kept together in a risk log.

For example, organisations can use a RAID log for their projects:

- **Risks** – events that will have an adverse effect on the project
- **Assumptions** – factors that are assumed to be in place
- **Issues** – something that is going wrong on the project and needs managing

Project Management

- **Dependencies** – events or work that are dependent on the result of the project, or things on which the project will be dependent

Risks can be defined in many ways – e.g., financial risk when investing or borrowing money; reputation when making decisions that affect the organisation's image and good name; weather or other external influences; health and safety.

According to the Health and Safety Executive, there are five main steps to risk assessment. Many organisations use these as guidelines when designing and implementing their own risk assessments:

- *Identify the hazards*
- *Decide who might be harmed, and how*
- *Evaluate the risks and decide on precautions*
- *Record findings and implement them*
- *Review the assessment and update as necessary*

These risk assessment guidelines can be modified to apply to any type of risk as they help everyone to see and understand the potential hazards, and to take steps to reduce the chance of harm by having control measures in place.

A risk management log could include columns such as:

- **risk impact** – high, medium or low
- **probability of occurrence** – high, medium or low
- **risk descriptions**
- **project impact** – timescales or resources that may be affected
- **risk area** – budget, resources or schedule
- **symptoms** – human resources are not fully decided when a project is about to start
- **triggers** – 24 hours before bad weather is inevitable, contingency plans to cancel will come into effect
- **risk response** – mitigation
- **response strategy** – allocate extra resources, reschedule or cancel
- **contingency plan** – bring in qualified agency staff to cover short term

Project Monitoring Records

Once the project is underway, documents are needed for monitoring the project's progress against plans and objectives. These could include, for example, Gantt charts or progress reports.

Project Management

Managing Resources

When managing the project's resources, a range of the tools above can be used. They can help to provide an up-to-date, three-dimensional view of the project at all stages, which helps the project manager to:

- *make sure that resources are available on time for each stage of the project*
- *identify problems and potential risks as soon as possible*
- *find solutions to address problems, issues and risks*
- *make decisions about how to reallocate resources*
- *provide evidence to support requests for increased resources and timescales*
- *show more senior decision-makers how they are managing the project*

When managing resources, the purpose, scope, aims and objectives for the whole project need to be very clear. This gives a focus so that time, human and physical resources can be geared up to achieve goals without unnecessary waste.

Human resources
When managing human resources for a project, managers perform the usual functions associated with people management, for example:

- *planning and allocating work to match the skills, experience and knowledge of team members*
- *developing and maintaining a common sense of purpose and a positive working environment*
- *working to retain team members*
- *recruiting and training team members*
- *making sure everyone understands aims and objectives*
- *supporting team members in career and skills development*
- *ensuring compliance with legislation* – e.g., health and safety, data protection and equality and diversity
- *monitoring work and taking action to improve performance*

In addition to these management tasks, the project manager's main focus is to make sure that people with the right skills are available when required for each stage of the project. During the planning stage, they can:

- *identify exactly which human resources are going to be needed for specific parts of the project*
- *work out the lead times for preparing and recruiting staff*

Project Management

- *ensure that existing team members have the right skills*
- *recruit new team members, from inside or outside the organisation*
- *train and brief all team members in time*
- **emphasise the importance of timescales and quality** – *and how these can affect other areas of the project*
- **ensure that team members have the equipment they need to perform their duties** – *e.g., Hi-Viz jackets, stationery, laptops, tablets, travel tickets, radios or mobile phones*

During the delivery and control stage, these points need to be monitored, supported and reinforced, as necessary.

Physical resources

Projects are very focused and visible, which often means that the resources are under more scrutiny than in other business activities. As projects are usually stand-alone activities, every physical resource needs to be planned and allocated to them – e.g., venues, desks and stationery.

The project team is accountable and responsible for managing resources effectively and may have to answer to, for example:

- **senior managers and directors** – *who need the project to make a profit for the organisation*
- **clients** – *customers who have commissioned and paid for the project*
- **sponsors** – *companies who have associated their brand with the project*
- **government agencies** – *enforcing regulations on the environment or health and safety*

Due to the temporary nature of a project, with its beginning, middle and end, resources need to be flexible. This means that everything needs to be planned in great detail, which requires a considerable amount of management to keep things on track. For example, the project manager for our charity dinner example will have to manage:

- **the venue for the dinner** – *checking its capacity and suitability; booking it; setting up kitchens for the dinner; dismantling everything afterwards*
- **resources needed at the venue** – *sound and lighting systems; hiring toilets and changing rooms for the artists; parking facilities for staff and artists; rest areas, training rooms and catering facilities for volunteers*
- **office space for staff** – *at the venue and within the organisation's premises*
- **office equipment** – *integrated IT and telephone equipment at the venue and head office*
- **vehicles** – *hiring cars and vans for volunteers, artists and full-time staff to use*
- **catering and other resources for the artists** – *extra portable toilets; catering outlets; smoking areas*

Project Management

- ***sales, marketing and ticketing*** – *printing and distributing tickets, leaflets and posters*
- ***insurance and inspections of resources*** – *insurance for the venue, public liability, vehicles and rented equipment; dealing with the health and safety representatives from the local council who inspect the venue*

Every item has a cost and a lead time, so careful management is required to make sure that:

- *each item is fit for purpose and satisfies regulatory requirements*
- *it is available on time*
- *the quality is as agreed and expected* – *as set out in a service level agreement*
- *waste is kept to a minimum*
- *there is a plan for all resources at the end of the project* – *handing rented venues, equipment and machinery back in good condition; selling purchased items that are no longer required; returning equipment and supplies to head office*

Financial resources

Budgets are usually strictly controlled for projects and the project manager is accountable and responsible for agreeing, controlling and managing budgets. They need to consider:

- ***timescales*** – *to show when money is due to come in and out* – *when money from ticket sales and sponsors is likely to be available*
- ***priorities*** – *to target resources correctly to support the efficiency and effectiveness of the organisation* – *prioritising workforce costs; assessing and arranging payments for urgent, planned and essential purchases*
- ***financial resources*** – *to match funding with anticipated income and expenditure* – *helping to arrange business loans to finance long-term projects; dealing with increases and decreases in revenue and expenses*
- ***contingencies*** – *negotiating and setting aside budgets and resources for unpredictable and unforeseen circumstances*

Project Management

Managing Project Risks and Issues

Difference between Project Risks and Issues

Preparing a risk log or register is part of planning a project. As part of this process, it is important to be able to identify differences between risks and issues.

A **risk** is the probability of harm happening. It is only a 'what if' and the harm may not happen at all, especially if measures are put in place to minimise the risk of harm to the project. For example, there can be a physical risk of harm from:

- **slips, trips and falls** – due to unsafe flooring, obstructions, wires, badly-positioned equipment or other trip hazards
- **working at height** – up ladders or on scaffolds
- **cross-contamination when handling food and drink** – when staff do not wash their hands and pass on germs to customers
- **illness and injury** – from poor crowd control, excessive alcohol or excessive noise; if loose wires on machinery are not dealt with correctly

Projects may also be at risk due to:

- **failure of an event or task** – from insufficient planning
- **financial failure** – if revenue is too low or costs are too high
- **equipment failure** – due to inadequate maintenance
- **changes in external factors** – planning rules or employment laws; world prices; national or international political influence; weather; local community action
- **changes in internal factors** – reorganisation of premises, workforce or management structures; organisational culture

An issue that affects a project, has actually happened. It is something that is real and actually has an impact on the project. Despite every effort to minimise risk, there are some things that cannot be mitigated and they do cause issues for the project team.

If any one of the identified potential risks becomes a reality, it becomes an issue that the project management team needs to address. Examples of issues that affect projects include, for example:

- **weather** – leading to cancellation or reorganisation of an event; leading to increased costs from having to use extra resources to deal with the consequences
- **inability to recruit sufficient, good-quality team members** – due to insufficient local supply or competition from other organisations
- **illness or injury to team members or others** – following an accident in the workplace
- **increased prices of supplies** – due to a change in world prices of raw materials

Project Management

- ***decreased revenue*** *– as a result of bad weather*
- ***political change*** *– the UK deciding to leave the European Union*

As risks and issues can both affect how a project is run, they need to be managed and tracked. The project team need to do all that they can to minimise the risks of harm to the project, and to make plans and forecasts about how they will deal with issues that do arise.
The implications of failing to mitigate risks and plan how to deal with issues can be extremely serious – from physical harm to people to the failure of the whole project or the organisation.

Identifying and Mitigating Risks

When identifying and mitigating risks, the project manager needs to, for example:

- *identify potential hazards and risks during the planning stage*
- *create a risk log or register – and use it to mitigate risk*
- *maintain awareness of potential risks*
- *consult stakeholders to agree approaches to risk management*
- *use leadership skills to manage risks that materialise*
- *amend plans when risks have an impact on the critical path or other timelines*

The following table shows some suggestions about how the risks mentioned above could be identified and mitigated:

Project Management

Area of risk	How to identify the potential risks	Suggestions to mitigate the risks
Slips, trips and falls	Risk assessment of hazards – e.g., wires, wet floors, obstructions Observation Accident records	Have good health and safety working practices – e.g., keep wires out of the way; put yellow hazard warning signs up; inform people about hazard; improve general hazard awareness of staff; have procedures for reporting potential hazards quickly
Working at height	Identify times and tasks where working at height will be necessary	Provide regular 'working at height' training for relevant team members and contractors Provide correct personal protective equipment (PPE) – e.g., harness, hard hat, safety boots
Cross-contamination when handling food and drink	Identify critical control points – e.g., when catering staff handle customers' food	Provide food handling training to relevant staff Insist on good hygiene – e.g., hand washing Monitor temperature control Provide equipment needed – e.g., well-maintained fridges and other storage; heat lamps; PPE; thermometers Ensure that catering contractors are properly equipped and trained
Illness and injury	Risk assessments of all areas Accident records Industry experience	Health and safety training for all team members Ensure the environment is safe Deal with potential hazards immediately Enforce noise limits Restrict access to alcohol Arrange support from security and medical specialists – e.g., door staff to keep an eye on alcohol consumption; first-aiders and ambulance crews on standby
Failure of an event	During progress checks or reviews	Improve planning and communication between project team members and other stakeholders
Financial failure	Changes in sales or costs against forecast amounts	Review finances regularly – e.g., to identify problems and take action quickly Have a contingency plan and budget – e.g., to use as agreed in the planning stage Stick to budgets and escalate problems as soon as possible

Project Management

Area of risk	How to identify the potential risks	Suggestions to mitigate the risks
Equipment failure	Intermittent or complete breakdowns of equipment or machinery	Follow regular maintenance routines Train staff to report potential problems early – e.g., when they see a frayed wire or a crack Establish contacts who can fix and maintain equipment, especially in an emergency – e.g., IT or lighting specialists who can attend critical breakdowns that will affect delivery of the project
Changes in external factors	Changes that affect the resources used in the project – e.g., an increase in fuel costs	Review factors that may affect the project regularly – e.g., to identify potential problems and take action quickly Have a contingency plan and budget – e.g., to use as agreed in the planning stage Escalate problems that are outside the limits of authority as soon as possible
Changes in internal factors	Organisational meetings or communications about changes that could affect the project	Stay in touch with the whole organisation, not just the project team Check internal factors before committing to the project – e.g., to see if assumptions about resources and future plans are reliable and correct

Project Management

Managing Issues

When managing issues, the project manager needs to:

- **understand the nature of the issue** – *the reasons why recruitment of new team members is so difficult, maybe using a PESTLE analysis (to look at political, economic, social, technological, legal and environmental impacts)*
- **evaluate the scope of the issue** – *how big a problem this could be and how the recruitment problem could either ease or get worse*
- **evaluate the impact on the project** – *how the recruitment problems could cause extra work for current team members or complete failure of the whole project*

Doing a SWOT analysis as soon as an issue has been identified could be an effective activity to focus attention and aid the decision-making process. By looking at the strengths, weaknesses, opportunities and threats to progress of each possible solution, the project manager can evaluate the issue and work out how to limit or eliminate the impact of the issue.

For example, a project manager still needs another 50 stewards to run an event. They normally have trained volunteer stewards. However, with only one month to go, they do not have enough people to steward the event, and there is a legal requirement to have sufficient stewards on duty whenever the public are in the venue. All stewards need to have a full day's training if they do not hold a current Spectator Security qualification. The project manager does a SWOT analysis to help them identify the pros and cons of each option:

Project Management

	Option A – increase publicity to attract new applications from new volunteers – e.g., advertise, make public appeals, approach organisations that place volunteers	Option B – approach another organisation that has large numbers of trained volunteers who might help for this one event	Option C – employ an event company who use qualified, paid staff
Strengths	New team members add to the pool of talent for future events and projects Control over type of person selected Control over training and monitoring Low cost	Volunteers already used to working at large events Good to have relationship between organisations that can help each other out from time to time	Staff can be provided in time Identifiable costs The company's service history should indicate reliability Staff will be qualified and will know how to operate without further training Less input required from the project team as the event company will manage the 50 staff and associated resources
Weaknesses	Time taken to deal with advertising, applications, interviews and recruitment of new volunteers No guarantee that enough people can be found, recruited and trained in time Unknown numbers for uniforms and other resources until the last-minute Cost of advertising	Volunteers might not be available or willing to work with a new project team The other organisation might not want to lose its volunteers Restricted choice in the actual individuals who join the team Staff training time required	Need to rely on the event company to choose suitable individuals High costs Volunteers might resent paid staff doing the same job as them
Opportunities	Local radio is running a volunteer campaign next week One week to advertise, then two weeks to interview and recruit Training sessions for all volunteers booked in 4 weeks' time	Three or four well-known groups in the local area that could be approached Three weeks to sort out before training is due	Plenty of event companies and staff available if researched online and using trade networks Could be arranged quickly
Threats to success	Lack of time – leading to a high chance of failure, which would put the whole event at risk Other events might be competing to recruit volunteers	Lack of cooperation from others Other events might be competing to recruit volunteers	High costs might not be covered by contingency budget Other events might be competing to recruit staff for the same day

Project Management

Following the PDCA cycle devised by J Edwards Deming can also help the project manager to focus on how to manage issues:

- **Plan** – identify the problem and root causes; collect data; set objectives; allocate resources and training
- **Do** – implement the plan and take action
- **Check** – review and measure progress against objectives; analyse strengths and weaknesses of the plan
- **Act/Adjust** – praise success; identify further improvements; communicate any changes to the people involved

The most important thing to do, though, is to act promptly when a potential or actual hazard, risk or issue is identified, and to take steps to minimise or eliminate the causes before the effects become even more serious. A combination of actions may be required that might include, for example:

- **reallocating human resources** – e.g., to cover emergencies or sickness
- **reallocating physical resources** – e.g., moving equipment to where it will be used more efficiently
- **negotiating extra funds or time** – e.g., a contingency budget or an extension on a deadline
- **asking people for help and advice** – e.g., team members, colleagues or industry contacts due to an emergency
- **escalating issues** – e.g., when decisions are outside the limits of authority, or the project is in danger of failing

Management Tools for Monitoring Progress

By using management tools, the project manager can monitor progress and see when it is time to implement the next stage of delivery of the project. The example of the volunteers working at the charity dinner, the sequence might include:

- *establishing the uniform sizes needed for the new recruits*
- *giving a provisional order to the supplier – so that they can start to prepare*
- *finishing recruitment of volunteers*
- *confirming the uniform sizes that are needed and making the final order a month before the dinner – the company needs two weeks to print and deliver the uniforms*

Until the volunteer recruitment has been finalised, it is not possible to make the final uniform order. As a contingency, a few extras of the standard sizes will be ordered. By tracking all of this information using, for example, a PERT diagram or a Gantt chart, the project manager can identify critical points and make sure that everything is on track.

Project Management

Using the project management tools mentioned before, here are some suggestions about how they might be used to monitor progress in the recruitment and training of team members in the charity dinner example:

Management tool/ method	Suggestions of how this could be applied to monitoring progress
SWOT analysis	To track the strengths and weaknesses of recruitment policies compared to expected targets; to review the opportunities for finding the right people if there are issues; to review the threats to progress to make sure that they are still relevant
Work Breakdown Structures (WBS)	To monitor the job descriptions set out in the initial WBS to make sure that the right people are being selected; to monitor training programmes set out in the WBS to make sure that they are relevant and suitable
PERT diagrams	To have a visual record about how a delay in advertising vacancies has a knock-on effect on applications, interviews and training
SMART objectives	To review levels of recruitment and training against the SMART targets on a regular basis
Gantt charts	To see how the recruitment and training elements of the project are progressing in relation to all other aspects of the project, such as physical resources and finance
Plan on a Page	To prepare a quick overview for progress meetings and interim management reports
RACI matrix	To use as a guide to make sure that communication is as expected and agreed between different stakeholders – to ensure that the relevant directors and external stakeholders are being informed of progress

Another useful tool to use when monitoring a project's progress is to show the **RAG** status – **red, amber, green**. During the planning stage, the planning team can set parameters about what the colours mean, for example:

- **Red** – major problems that will affect the viability of the whole project and cannot be resolved by the project manager – the matter should be escalated to the project board member
- **Amber** – problems that have a negative effect on one or more aspects of the project's viability and performance – problems can be dealt with by the project manager and their team, who then notify the board about progress
- **Green** – the project is performing to plan – all problems are within tolerances and expectations and can be dealt with within normal limits of authority

There can be drawbacks to the traffic-light system; it can oversimplify a project's progress and it is very dependent on the integrity of the information that can turn an element from

Project Management

red to amber or green. As a visual aid, it is effective as it draws attention to the problem areas and shows when everything is on track.

It can really help to keep everyone involved and motivated by letting them know how things are going. If the news is not very good, it can help to reassure everyone, so that they work harder to get back on track and understand the problems behind problems and potential issues. If things are going well, the team and other stakeholders benefit from knowing and getting some positive praise and feedback. This lifts morale and helps to keep people motivated and focused.

Reviewing Project Performance

The project manager needs to evaluate a project and look at all of the data that has been collected, so that the team can, for example:

- **compare the outcomes with the original objectives** – *to see if the project has achieved its intended aims and the correct quality standards*
- **understand how the project has achieved its purpose** – *or why it has failed*
- **identify how the project used human resources** – *to analyse the skills used and identify career development opportunities*
- **identify how efficiently the project used physical resources** – *comparing budget forecasts with actual costs; reviewing the levels of waste*
- **identify problems and potential improvements**
- **advise stakeholders and decision-makers** – *about how to repeat, develop or improve actions and plans for future projects*
- **identify needs for further project work** – *to set up a new project to solve major issues that were discovered when working on the first project*

When evaluating a project, the data needs to be reliable and relevant to be of use. We need to consider what we want to know, and what we want to measure, to be able to identify what data we need and how we will collect it. Organisations will have their own ways of evaluating a project, which could include, for example:

- **comparing estimated costs with actual costs** – *to evaluate the budget allocations and identify the causes of variance*
- **collecting and reviewing feedback from customers and other users of the services and products covered in the project** – *e.g., independent surveys, feedback forms, forum comments, focus groups or satisfaction surveys*
- **analysing operational data** – *e.g., looking at patient records in a hospital to evaluate changes in services*
- **reviewing progress reports** – *e.g., final 'wash-up' reports from staff and other stakeholders about their experiences and recommendations*
- **analysing sales patterns** – *e.g., to see when tickets were purchased and by whom; to see if business changes have affected sales as expected*

Project Management

- *analysing changes in activity and comments on websites and social media –* e.g., to illustrate a change towards Internet shopping following a project on online sales

The methods selected will depend upon who needs and wants to see the evaluation of project performance. The media, for example, might only be interested in the initial financial impact of changes made by the project, whereas the organisation's HR department will be more interested in evaluating the impact on staff skills, experience, training and career development. Reviews of project performance need to be presented in ways that satisfy the needs of stakeholders.

In general, the project team's review needs to:

- *show the successes of the project*
- *praise everyone who contributed to the success*
- *identify areas of weakness and lessons that can be learned for future projects*
- *illustrate the project team's value to support bids for future projects*

Chapter 9: Project Planning

Project Planning

Planning for a Project

The Project

A project will start when the sponsor (the person who has asked for the research to be done) first identifies the need for change. If the project fits in with their business plans, they will pursue it.

The next step would be to work out how much it will cost to make the change and compare it to the benefit which will be gained as a result. This is called a cost benefit analysis. A cost benefit analysis is simply a list of all the costs with a total at the bottom and a list of the benefits to be expected as a result of the change. Not all projects result in an increase in income or profit, however there are other benefits to gained from running the project which would be difficult to place a value on. A better working environment for example, might improve staff motivation resulting in less sickness, reduced stress and a happier workforce which usually leads to greater productivity. This may be difficult to work out in financial terms, it is sometimes better to look at the cost of not doing the project – in this case increasing staff turnover, more recruitment costs, low morale, poor productivity, etc. If the result is acceptable the project will be given the go ahead and the first stages of planning the project will begin.

It should be stated at this point that:

> *the biggest part of any project is not actually doing the work – but planning the work and how it will be done*

The first document produced is the Project Charter.

Project Charter

The Charter outlines the purpose of the project, how it will be structured and how it will be executed. It will contain details about the vision, objectives, scope and deliverables along with a description of the responsibilities for the project team and stakeholders.

The charter will also list the roles and responsibilities of the project team and identify the project's customers and stakeholders.

Although it seems to contain a great deal of information, the project charter is a very brief document which covers only the headline details of the project. It may only be one or two pages, depending on the size and scale of the project.

The charter will include the following details:

Project Planning

- The appointed project manager
- A definition of the project scope
- The budget
- The defined milestones
- A list of the important / key stakeholders
- The technical characteristics of the project deliverable

The Charter is sometimes called the "Project Definition Document." It gives the project manager the authority to direct and complete the project.

The project manager is involved in developing the project charter, but cannot approve it

Structure of a Project Charter

The following is the outline of a typical project charter. Not all of the content may be needed for every project, and it is the responsibility of the Project Manager to decide what should and should not be included for each project. It should be remembered that this is a document being used to "sell the idea" of the project, so the more comprehensive the document, the fewer questions may be asked, which will reduce the level of objections held by the decision makers.

1. Executive Summary

This section summarises each of the sections in this document concisely by outlining the project:

- Project Definition
- Organisation and plan
- Risks and issues
- Assumptions and constraints

a. Project Definition

This section describes what the project sets out to achieve. It outlines the vision for the project, the key objectives to be met, the scope of work to be undertaken and the deliverables to be produced.

Vision
Describe the overall vision of the project. The vision statement should be short, concise and achievable.

Examples of vision statements include:

Project Planning

- *To deliver a robust, scalable financial management system to the business*
- *To procure new work premises with adequate capacity and functional surrounds*
- *To successfully introduce new customer service processes to the marketplace*

Objectives
List the key objectives of the project. Objectives are statements which describe in more detail what it is that the project is going to achieve. All objectives listed should be Specific, Measurable, Achievable, Realistic and Time-bound (SMART).

Business Objectives
List the business-specific objectives to be achieved. For example:

- *To deliver new accounts payable and receivable and payroll processes, thereby reducing financial processing timescales by at least 30%*
- *To build brand new work premises with 50% more space, 30 more cark parks and 20% fewer operational costs than the existing premises*
- *To provide a new customer complaints service to enable customers to issue complaints on-line and receive a direct response from the company within 24hrs*

Technological Objectives
List the technology-specific objectives to be achieved. For example:

- *To install new accounts payable and receivable and payroll system modules within the existing accounting system, thereby achieving 99.5% system up-time*
- *To relocate existing technology infrastructure at the new building premises within 2 days elapsed time and with no impact on customer service delivery*
- *To build a new website which allows customers to enter and track complaints through to resolution.*

Scope
Define the scope of the project in terms of the business:

- *Processes which will change*
- *Organisational areas which will be affected*
- *Locations which will be impacted on*
- *Data which will be altered*

Project Planning

- *Applications which will be installed and/or altered*
- *Technologies which will be deployed and/or decommissioned*

Where relevant, identify the related business areas which will <u>not</u> be affected as a result of this project.

Deliverables
Summarise the key project deliverables in a table as shown below which includes examples

Item	Components	Description
New premises	New physical building Interior fit-out Telecommunications	1200 sq. m premises near city centre with outdoor facilities, parking and signage Open plan environment with 5 offices, 3 meeting rooms and a staff games room Voice / data telecoms infrastructure and video conference facilities
New financial system	Accounts payable module Accounts receivable module Payroll module	A new system module which enables staff to quickly enter accounts payable transactions A new system module which enables staff to quickly enter accounts receivable transactions A new system module which enables staff to quickly enter payroll information
New customer complaints process	Complaints website Complaints resolution process Complaints measurement process	New website with customer complaints forms, a complaint tracking page and company contact information New full-time staff complaints role and process for resolving complaints made New process for assessing complaint characteristics (such as numbers, business areas and resolution timescales)

b. Project Organisation

Customers

Project Planning

Describe the customers who will use the deliverables produced from the project. Customers may be individuals or groups within or outside of the company. The success of the project will be primarily based on whether or not the deliverables produced match the requirements of the customers identified in this table.

Customer	Representative
Customer Group	Customer Name

Stakeholders

List the key stakeholders for this project. A 'stakeholder' is simply a person or entity outside of the project who has a key interest in the project. For instance, a company financial controller will have an interest in the cost implications of the project, a CEO will have an interest in whether the project is conducted in accordance with the vision of the company. Examples of stakeholders include:

- Company Executives
- Legislative bodies
- Regulatory bodies.

Complete a similar table to the one below (includes examples):

Stakeholder	Interested in
CEO	Alignment with company vision and strategy
Financial Controller	Alignment with company budget
Health and Safety Office	Alignment with health and safety standards
Government body	Compliance with legislation
Industry body	Compliance with codes of practice

Roles

Identify the roles required to undertake the project. Examples of typical roles include project:

- Sponsor
- Review Group
- Manager
- Team Member

Project Planning

For each role identified, list the resource likely to fill each role and their assignment details by completing the following table:

Role	Organisation	Resource Name	Assignment Status	Assignment Date
Role	Organisation	Person	Unassigned / Assigned	xx/yy/zz

For larger projects with more than 10 resources, list only the key roles in the above table. Include a detailed listing and description of all roles within a separate Resource Plan document if required.

Responsibilities

List the generic responsibilities for each role identified. A full list of the responsibilities, performance criteria and skills required should be documented within a separate *Job Description* for each project role.

Project Sponsor

The Project Sponsor is the principal 'owner' of the project. Key responsibilities include:

- *Defining the vision and high-level objectives for the project*
- *Approving the requirements, timetable, resources and budget*
- *Authorising the provision of funds / resources (internal or external)*
- *Approving the project plan and quality plan*
- *Ensuring that major business risks are identified and managed*
- *Approving any major changes in scope*
- *Receiving Project Review Group minutes and taking action accordingly*
- *Resolving issues escalated by the Project Manager / Project Review Group*
- *Ensuring business / operational support arrangements are put in place*
- *Ensuring the participation of a business resource (if required)*
- *Providing final acceptance of the solution upon project completion.*

Project Review Group

The Project Review Group may include both business and 3rd party representatives and is put in place to ensure that the project is progressing according to plan.

Key responsibilities include:

Project Planning

- *Assisting the Project Sponsor with the definition of the project vision and objectives*
- *Undertaking Quality Reviews prior to the completion of each project milestone*
- *Ensuring that all business risks are identified and managed accordingly*
- *Ensuring conformance to the standards and processes identified in the Quality Plan*
- *Ensuring that all appropriate client/vendor contractual documentation is in place prior to the initiation of the project*

Project Manager
The Project Manager ensures that the daily activities undertaken on the project are in accordance with the approved project plans. The Project Manager is responsible for ensuring that the project produces the required deliverables on time, within budgeted cost and at the level of quality outlined within the Quality Plan.

Key responsibilities include:

- *Documenting the detailed Project Plan and Quality Plan*
- *Ensuring that all required resources are assigned to the project and clearly tasked*
- *Managing assigned resources according to the defined scope of the project*
- *Implementing the following project processes: time / cost / quality / change / risk / issue / procurement / communication / acceptance management*
- *Monitoring and reporting on project performance (re: schedule, cost, quality and risk)*
- *Ensuring compliance with the processes and standards outlined in the Quality Plan*
- *Reporting and escalating project risks and issues*
- *Managing project interdependencies*
- *Adjusting the detailed plan as necessary to provide a complete picture of the progress of the project at any time.*

Project Team Member
A Project Team member undertakes all tasks necessary to design, build and implement the final solution.

Key responsibilities include:

- *Undertaking all tasks allocated by the Project Manager (as per the Project Plan)*

Project Planning

- *Reporting progress of the execution of tasks to the Project Manager on a frequent basis*
- *Maintaining all documentation relating to the execution of allocated tasks*
- *Escalating risks and issues to be resolved by the Project Manager.*

Structure

Depict the reporting lines between each of the key roles described above within a Project Organisation Chart. An example follows:

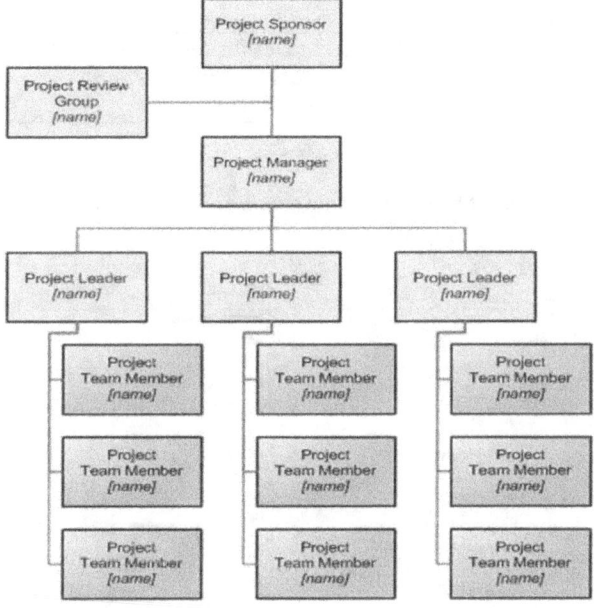

Project Planning

Summary Project Plan

Approach

Describe the approach to be taken to implement each of the phases within the project.

Phase	Approach
Initiation	Outline the method by which the project will be further defined, the project team appointed and the Project Office established.
Planning	Define the overall planning process to ensure that the phases, activities and tasks are undertaken in a co-ordinated fashion.
Execution	Describe the generic phases and activities required to build, test and implement the deliverables of the project.
Closure	Describe the steps required to release the deliverables to the business, close the project office, reallocate staff and perform a Post Implementation Review of the project.

Overall Plan

A more detailed Project Plan will be drawn up during the "Planning" phase of the project.

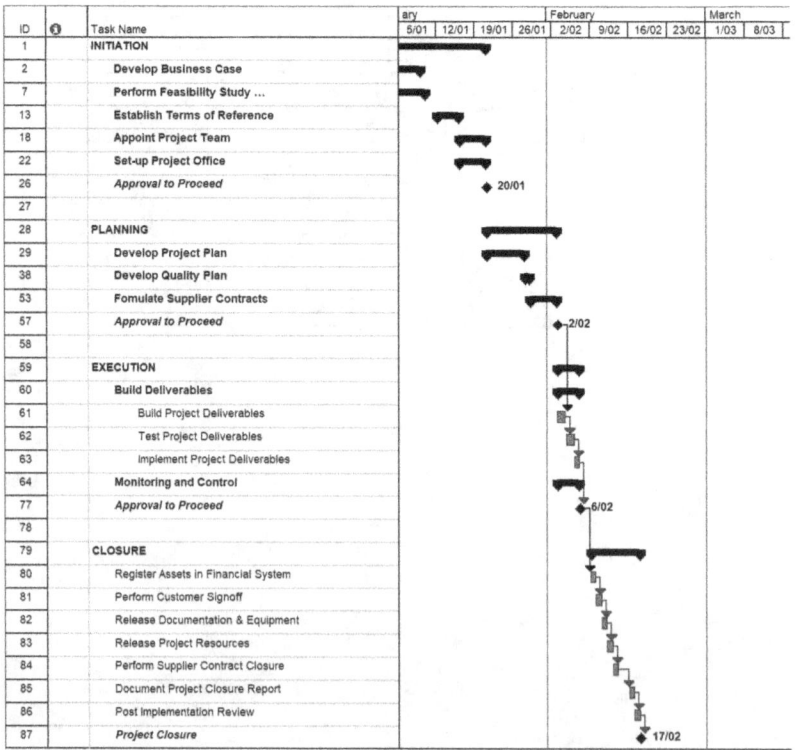

Project Planning

Milestones
List the major project milestones and the required delivery dates. A 'milestone' is a significant event or stage to be completed. Explain why each milestone is critical to the project, as follows:

Milestone	Date	Description
Milestone Title	xx/yy/zz	Explain why milestone date is critical to business

Dependencies
List any project activities which:

- Will impact on another activity external to the project
- Will be impacted on by the non/delivery of another activity external to the project

Project Activity	Impacts on	Impacted on by	Criticality	Date
Planned Activity	External Activity	External Activity	Low/Medium/High	xx/yy/zz

Resource Plan
Summarise the duration and effort required for each project team member, as follows:

Role	Start Date	End Date	% Effort
Project Role	xx/yy/zzzz	xx/yy/zzzz	xx/yy/zzzz

A detailed Resource Plan will be drawn up during the "Planning" phase of this project.

Financial Plan
Summarise the project budget approved (within the Business Case) as follows:

Project Planning

Category	Cost	Value
People	Salaries of project staff Contractors and outsourced parties Training courses	£ x £ x £ x
Physical	Building premises for project team Equipment and materials Tools (computers, cabling, phones...)	£ x £ x £ x
Marketing	Advertising / branding Promotional materials PR and communications	£ x £ x £ x
Organisational	Operational downtime Short-term loss in productivity Cultural change	£ x £ x Describe

A detailed Financial Plan will be drawn up during the "Planning" phase of this project.

Quality Plan
Briefly describe the various processes to be undertaken to ensure the success of the project.

Process	Description
Quality Management	Summary of how the process will be undertaken
Change Management	
Risk Management	
Issue Management	
Configuration Management	
Document Management	
Acceptance Management	
Procurement Management	
Financial Management	
Timesheet Management	
Project Reporting	

Project Planning

A detailed Quality Plan will be drawn up during the "Planning" phase of this project.

c. Project Considerations

Risks

Summarise the most apparent risks associated with the project. Risks are defined as "any event which <u>may</u> adversely affect the ability of the solution to produce the required deliverables". Risks may be Strategic, Environmental, Financial, Operational, Technical, Industrial, Competitive or Customer related. Complete the following table:

Description	Likelihood	Impact	Mitigating Actions
Inability to recruit skilled resource	Low	Very High	Outsource project to a company with proven industry experience and appropriately skilled staff
Technology solution is unable to deliver required results	Medium	High	Complete a pilot project to prove the full technology solution
Additional capital expenditure may be required in addition to that approved	Medium	Medium	Maintain strict capital expenditure processes during the project

To complete this section thoroughly, it may be necessary to undertake a formal Risk Assessment (by documenting a *Risk Management Plan*). To reduce the likelihood and impact of each risk's eventuating, clear 'mitigating actions' should be defined.

Issues

Summarise the highest priority issues associated with the project. Issues are defined as "any event which currently adversely affects the ability of the solution to produce the required deliverables". Complete the following table:

Project Planning

Description	Priority	Resolution Actions
Required capital expenditure funds have not been budgeted	High	Request funding approval as part of this proposal
Required computer software is only at 'beta' phase and has not yet been released live	Medium	Design solution based on current software version and adapt changes to solution once the final version of the software has been released
Council approval must be sought to implement the final solution	Low	Initiate the council approval process early so that it does not delay the final roll-out process.

d. Assumptions

List the major assumptions identified with the project to date. Examples include:

- *There will be no legislative, business strategy or policy changes during this project*
- *Prices of raw materials will not increase during the course of the project*
- *Additional human resources will be available from the business to support the project*

Constraints

List the major constraints identified with the project to date. Examples include:

- *The financial budget allocated is fixed and does not allow for over-spending*
- *There are limited technical resource available for the project*
- *The technical solution must be implemented after-hours to minimise the operational impact on the business.*

e. Appendix

Supporting Documentation

Attach any other documentation which is relevant to the Project Charter, including:

- *Curricula Vitae (CVs) for key project staff*
- *Research Materials*
- *External quotes or tenders*
- *Detailed financial planning spreadsheets*

Project Planning

- *Other relevant information or correspondence.*

A project charter builds a solid foundation for a project. It gives a common understanding of the objectives.

Benefits of a Project Charter

The following are a few benefits of a project charter:

- *It gives the project manager the authority to complete the project*
- *It explains the project's existence*
- *It shows management's support for the project*
- *It defines the outcome*
- *It aligns the project with the organisation's objectives*
- *It gives team members a transparent reporting system*
- *It saves you from scope creep and gold plating*
- *It helps you avoid disputes*

The project charter is key to the project's success. It provides stakeholders with a common understanding of the project. It is an agreement between the key stakeholders, and it communicates the project manager's authority. It is at the absolute core of the project as everything else will but created from this.

Project Planning

Producing the Project Plan

A project plan is used to plan a project from its initial stages through to its planned conclusion. It is produced by the project manager who will have spent a great deal of time ensuring every detail and element of it is correct and they will use their expertise and judgement to do this.

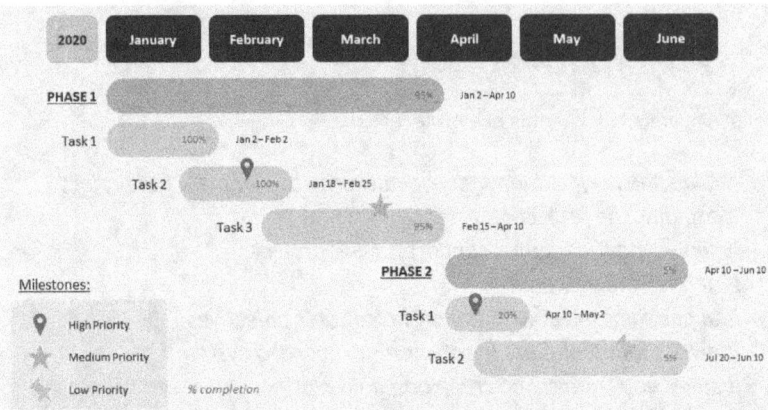

The project plan is not one single document but rather a compound document made up of a number of other documents each of which have a specific role and purpose.

Every project is unique in what it addresses, the scope, scale, value, etc. which means there cannot be a single, standard, document which can be created and tailored to suit each project, however, there are some specific elements which should be included in every project plan. This will help to avoid confusion and forced changes during the project execution phase.

Project Plan	
The Project Charter	Budget
Project Goals	Human Resources Plan
Project Scope	Risk Register
Milestones and Major Deliverables	Communications Plan
Work Breakdown Structure	Change Management Plan
Stakeholder Management Plan	Timeline

Project Planning

Project Goals

Project goals are defined in the project charter, but they should be included in the project plan as well to explain the goals of the project or be included the charter as an appendix to the plan.

No matter how a project manager chooses to incorporate the goals into the project plan, the important thing is to maintain a clear link between the project charter—a project is first key document—and the project's second key document, its project plan.

> *A project goal is a tangible statement of what a project should achieve.*

The project goal defines the questions that will be asked at the end of the project. What has the project accomplished? That is the project goal.

Examples:

- *Improve employee satisfaction by introducing flexible working hours.*
- *Introduce mobile devices for sales staff to reduce average order time and increase customer satisfaction.*
- *Upgrade network infrastructure to increase bandwidth and eliminate network outages.*

A project goal should be tied to a higher purpose.

- *increase sales*
- *cut cost*
- *increase profitability*
- *increase safety*
- *protect the health of people*

This is where the goal can be linked to the Mission, Value and Goals of the organisation. If the goal is not tied to these, it may just end up as another wreck at the bottom of the sea. Simply because it did not bring the results it was supposed to deliver.

Project Goals

Importance:	Goal	Ownership
1.	Build a new warehouse in the Northern region to better serve our customers in the Borders and Scotland.	Project Team

Project Planning

Project Scope

Like the project goals, the scope of the project is defined in the charter and should be further developed and refined in the project plan. By defining the scope, the project manager can begin to show what the project's goal or finished product will look like at the end. If the scope is not defined, it can get expanded throughout the project and lead to cost overruns and missed deadlines.

Example:

> if you are leading a marketing team to create a brochure for a company's product line, you should define how many pages it will be and provide examples of how the finished product might look.

For some team members, a corporate brochure might mean two pages, while others might consider ten pages to be more appropriate. Defining the scope can get the entire team on the same page at the outset.

This should be written as a definitive of statement of what the project will achieve and what it will not achieve. It should be written in a style which can be understood by all – it should not assume and prior technical knowledge.

Project Scope

What is included:
What is Not included:

Milestones and Major Deliverables

The key stages in a project are called milestones and the work which is achieved at these key stages is called a major deliverable. They both represent the big components of work on a project. A project plan should identify these items, define them, and set deadlines for their completion.

If you were building a house, a key stage is when the roof is completed. So, the completed roof would be a major deliverable. This would be identified in the project plan, stating when it must be delivered (completed) by.

Following those, the project could have milestones for internal completion, electrical testing, client acceptance testing, and the date for the handover of the keys. These milestones have work products associated with them, but they are more about the processes than the products themselves.

Project Planning

Milestone and major deliverable deadlines do not have to be exact dates, but the more precise, the better. Precise dates help project managers break down work structures more accurately.

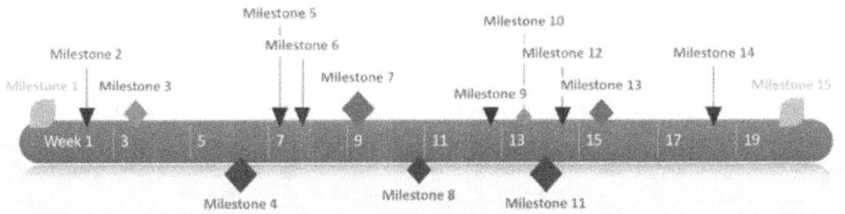

Milestones and Major Deliverables

Week	Milestone	Description
1	1	Formation Meeting
1	2	Planning application submission

Typical Milestones in a Project

Project Approval
While not as commonly noted as other project milestone examples, the first milestone in the course of any project is the initial approval that allows the project to move forward.

For internal projects, this milestone often comes in the form of an approval from a department director or other high-level stakeholder. For other projects, this milestone is usually marked by the completion of a sales contract and scope of work. Once the project is approved, project managers begin inputting elements of the project into their chosen project management tool.

Requirements Review *(Major projects)*
Most enterprise projects involve a lengthy process in which the project requirements are defined and gathered through a series of meetings, review sessions, and document exchanges. The project team then typically interprets and consolidates their notes and presents the client with a detailed description of the requirements as they understand them.

When the client or customer agrees that the requirements are accurately documented, another major project milestone has been reached.

Design Approval *(Major projects)*
After gathering the customer's requirements, a project team needs to design a solution that will meet the requirements and fulfil the terms of the scope of work.

Project Planning

When the initial design is complete (which often takes months or even years for large projects), the customer needs to review the proposed solution and confirm that it will satisfy the project objectives.

This design approval is a significant milestone for projects in fields as diverse as software, construction and marketing, just to name a few.

Project Phase Milestones
Once the project team begins to actually build or implement the proposed solution, the project manager will typically define project-specific milestones related to the components of the work being done.

In a construction project, for example, the project manager might need to mark milestones (and arrange milestone payments) for the completion of phases such as framing, concrete pouring, plumbing installation and interior finishing.

Final Approval
The most significant of all project management milestones, of course, is the one that marks the completion of a project. This milestone typically comes at the end of an extensive testing and inspection process, and a final review session in which all stakeholders agree that the work is complete and meets the project requirements.

Upon reaching this milestone, successful project managers typically hold a follow-up meeting with the team to discuss what worked, what could have been better and how to work even more efficiently and effectively on the next project.

Project Planning

Work Breakdown Structure

A work breakdown structure (WBS) breaks down the milestones and major deliverables in a project into smaller chunks so one person can be assigned responsibility for each chunk or element. In developing the work breakdown structure, the project manager will consider many factors such as the strengths and weaknesses of project team members, the interdependencies among tasks, available resources, and the overall project deadline.

Work Breakdown Structure is defined as a:

> *"Deliverable oriented hierarchical decomposition of the work to be executed by the project team."*

Project managers are ultimately responsible for the success of the project, but they cannot do the work alone. The WBS is a tool the project manager uses to ensure accountability on the project because it tells the project sponsor, project team members, and stakeholders who are responsible for what. If the project manager is concerned about a task, they know exactly who to meet with regarding that concern.

The WBS is a hierarchical reflection of all the work in the project in terms of deliverables. In order to produce these deliverables, work must be performed.

A typical approach in developing a WBS is to start at the highest level, with the product of the project. For example, you are assigned as the project manager of a New Product Development project. The new product you are developing is a new toy for children. The objective of this product development project is to increase the revenue of the organisation by ten percent.

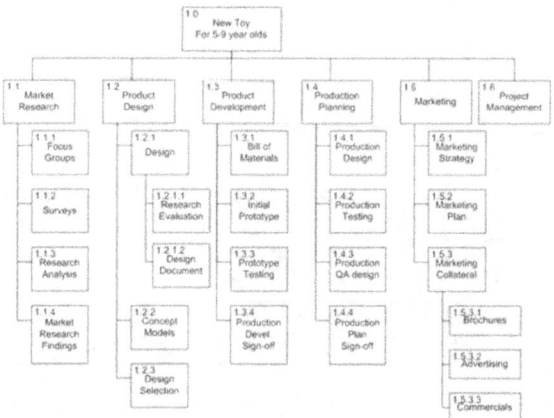

Above is an example of a WBS for a new toy. Each level of the WBS is a level of detail created by decomposition. Decomposition is the process of breaking down the work into smaller, more manageable components. The elements at the lowest level of the WBS are

Project Planning

called tasks. In the example above, brochures, advertising and commercials are all work packages or tasks.

The decomposition of a schedule will continue at varying rates. 'Brochures' is a task identified at the fourth level of decomposition, while the 'marketing plan' is also a task but defined at the third level of decomposition.

As a project manager, the level of decomposition will be dependent on the extent to which you will need to manage. The expectation is that each task will have a single owner and the owner is expected to manage and report on the work necessary to deliver the task. This person is called the 'task owner.' If you cannot assign a single owner, or you need to have additional visibility into the progress of that task, additional decomposition is recommended.

Once all the deliverables of the project have been identified, tasks will be performed in order to create the deliverables. In some cases, these activities are the physical deliverables, but in other cases they are the actions that need to be performed. A physical deliverable, for example, might be an image (an actual file) that is needed for the brochure. Listing out each of the tasks to be performed will result in an activity list as demonstrated below.

Work Package	WBSID	Activity	Predecessor	Duration in Weeks	Resource Type
Focus Group	1.1.1.1	Identify Focus Group Targets			
Focus Group	1.1.1.2	Prepare Focus Group Objectives			
Focus Group	1.1.1.3	Perform Focus Group			
Surveys	1.1.2	Perform Survey			
Research Analysis	1.1.3	Perform Analysis			
Market Research Findings	1.1.4	Create Market Research Findings			
Research Evaluation	1.2.1.1.1	Review Market Research Findings			
Research Evaluation	1.2.1.1.2	Develop Design Options			
Research Evaluation	1.2.1.1.3	Present Design Options			
Design Document	1.2.1.2.1	Draft Design Document			
Design Document	1.2.1.2.2	Design Document Review			
Design Document	1.2.1.2.3	Final Design Document			
Concept Models	1.2.2	Develop Concept Model			
Design Selection	1.2.3	Review Concepts			
Bill of Materials	1.3.1	Create Initial Bill of Materials			
Initial Prototype	1.3.2.1	Develop Initial Prototype			
Initial Prototype	1.3.2.2	Revise Initial Prototype			
Prototype Testing	1.3.3	Test Prototype			
Production Design	1.4.1	Design Production Process			
Production Testing	1.4.2	Design Production Testing Process			
Production QA design	1.4.3	Design Quality Assurance Tests			
Marketing Strategy	1.5.1	Develop Marketing Strategy			
Marketing Plan	1.5.2.1	Develop Initial Marketing Plan			
Marketing Plan	1.5.2.2	Final Marketing Plan			
Brochures	1.5.3.1	Create Brochures			
Advertising	1.5.3.2	Create Ads			
Commercials	1.5.3.3	Create Commercials			
Production Plan Sign-off	1.4.4	Production Plan Sign-off			
Production Devel. Sign-off	1.3.4	Production Devel. Sign-off			
Project Management	1.6	Project Management Activities		LOE	

Project Planning

Budget

Project budget management is a process of formally identifying, approving and paying the costs or expenses incurred on the project. Project budget management involves using purchase order forms to state each set of project expenses, such as training, consulting services, equipment and material cost, etc. Usually in the process, the project manager plays the role of "Approver" (a person who approves a budget for a project) and the finance unit (e.g., Finance Department) acts as a "Recorder" (an organisational unit that tracks and audits budgeting activities and reports to the project manager).

Project Budget

WBS ID.	Work Element	Salaries and Wages		Cost		Materials and Equipment	
		Rate - £/hr	Hours	Budget	Actual	Amount	Cost
1.1.1.1	Identify focus group targets	£25.75	6	£154.50			

Budgeting Process

The process of determining budget for a project is an activity of combining the cost estimates of individual activities, or a work package, to develop the total cost estimate that allows setting a formal minimum cost for that work package.

This minimum cost figure may differ from the figure which is finally recorded as the Project Manager may decide to add money into the minimum cost in case there are changes to the planned prices or the project hits a problem and is delayed. These are known as contingencies. This will be repeated for each work package until all the planned activities have been identified and funded. These values will then be used as a way to control the budget and provide valuable data to the project resource management process.

The project budgeting process is conducted at the initial steps of project planning, and typically it is performed in parallel with the project scheduling process. The steps of the process are highly dependent upon the cost estimations, task durations and allocated resources. The process is also known as "the project budgeting process". The budgeting serves as a cost control mechanism that allows comparing actual project costs to the items of the authorised project budget. The process allows developing a budget considering key cost factors associated with time durations of project tasks.

Project Planning

When working on the project budgeting activities, the project manager should collaborate with people responsible for managing the work efforts as well as for estimating project costs (the cost estimating team). They will develop and give the cost estimates of individual activities, or work packages, so that the project manager can actually start performing budgeting activities.

The project manager should use the Work Break Down Structure (WBS) of the project, the cost estimates, historical data and records, resource information, and policies in order to identify the monetary resources required for the project.

Budgeting and Budget Risk Management

The budgeting process will not be complete and effective if no risk assessment and assignment have been applied. Without assessing risks surrounding the project, uncertainties and threats that happen regularly during the project implementation will affect the project's bottom line. Cost estimates should be developed with reference to conducted risk assessing activities but identified risks should not be considered a factor influencing the increase in the overall price of the budget. Risk assessing activities allow representing risks as actual costs incurred over the course of project development. Usually, risk assessments cover such areas as development team experience, reliability of the technology used, time shortages, availability of project resources, etc.

Once analysed, a scope and percentage can be assigned to each identified risk.

Human Resources Plan

The human resources plan shows how the project will be staffed. Sometimes known as the staffing plan, the HR plan defines who will be on the project team and how much of a time commitment each person is expected to make. In developing this plan, the project manager negotiates with team members and their supervisors on how much time each team member can devote to the project. If additional staff are needed to consult on the project, but are part of the project team, that is also documented in the HR plan. Appropriate supervisors are consulted, as necessary.

Human Resources Plan

	Project Manager	Design Engineers	Implementation Manager	Training Leads	Functional Managers	Dept. Managers
Requirements Gathering	A	R	R	C	C	I
Coding Design	A	R	C		C	I
Coding Input	A	R				
Software Testing	A	R	C		I	I

Project Planning

Network Preparation	A	C	R		I	I
Implementation	A	C	R	C	C	C
Training	A			R	C	C

Key:
R – Responsible for completing the work
A – Accountable for ensuring task completion/sign off
C – Consulted before any decisions are made
I – Informed of when an action/decision has

Risk Register

Many things can go wrong on a project. While anticipating every possible disaster or minor hiccup is challenging, many pitfalls can be predicted. In the risk management plan, the project manager identifies risks to the project, the likelihood those scenarios will happen, and strategies to mitigate them. To formulate this plan, the project manager seeks input from the project sponsor, project team, stakeholders, and internal experts.

Mitigation strategies are put into place for risks that are likely to occur or have high costs associated with them. Risks that are unlikely to occur and ones that have low costs are noted in the plan, even though they do not have mitigation strategies.

A risk register is used to identify potential risks in a project or an organisation, sometimes to fulfil regulatory compliance but mostly to stay on top of potential issues that can derail intended outcomes. The risk register includes all information about each identified risk, such as the nature of that risk, level of risk, who owns it and what are the mitigation measures in place to respond to it.

A risk assessment needs to be performed for each aspect of the project, and these are kept together in a risk log.

Organisations can use a RAID log for their projects:

- **Risks** – events that will have an adverse effect on the project
- **Assumptions** – factors that are assumed to be in place
- **Issues** – something that is going wrong on the project and needs managing
- **Dependencies** – events or work that are dependent on the result of the project, or things on which the project will be dependent

Risks can be defined in many ways – e.g., financial risk when investing or borrowing money; reputation when making decisions that affect the organisation's image and good name; weather or other external influences; health and safety.

Project Planning

According to the Health and Safety Executive, there are five main steps to risk assessment. Many organisations use these as guidelines when designing and implementing their own risk assessments:

- *Identify the hazards*
- *Decide who might be harmed, and how*
- *Evaluate the risks and decide on precautions*
- *Record findings and implement them*
- *Review the assessment and update as necessary*

These risk assessment guidelines can be modified to apply to any type of risk as they help everyone to see and understand the potential hazards, and to take steps to reduce the chance of harm by having control measures in place.

A risk management log could include columns such as:

- **risk impact** – high, medium or low
- **probability of occurrence** – high, medium or low
- **risk descriptions**
- **project impact** – timescales or resources that may be affected
- **risk area** – budget, resources or schedule
- **symptoms** – human resources are not fully decided when a project is about to start
- **triggers** – 24 hours before bad weather is inevitable, contingency plans to cancel will come into effect
- **risk response** – mitigation
- **response strategy** – allocate extra resources, reschedule or cancel
- **contingency plan** – bring in qualified agency staff to cover short term

Producing a Risk Register

Identify the Risk
Risk cannot be resolve if the risk is not known. There are many ways to identify risk. The data is collected in a risk register.

One way is brainstorming or even brainwriting, which is a more structured way to get a group to look at a problem. Use the resources to hand such as the team, colleagues or stakeholders.

Find those individuals with relevant experience and set up interviews to gather the information needed to both identify and resolve the risk.

Look both forward and backwards. That is, imagine the project in progress. Think of the many things that can go wrong. Note them. Do the same with historical data on past projects. This will allow the list of potential risk to grow.

Project Planning

As risk is identified ensure the risk register is not filling up with risks that are not really risks at all. Make sure the risks are rooted in the cause of a problem. Basically, drill down to the root cause to see if the risk is one that will have the kind of impact on the project that needs identifying.

When trying to minimise risk, it is good to trust intuition. It can point to unlikely scenarios that may be assumed could not happen. Use process to weed out risks from non-risks.

Analyse the Risk

Once potential risks are identified, they can be listed in the risk register. The next step is to determine how likely each of those risks are to happen. This information should also go into the risk register.

When assessing project risks, many impacts can ultimately and proactively be addressed, such as avoiding potential litigation, addressing regulatory issues, complying with new legislation, reducing exposure and minimising impact.

Analysing risk is hard. There is never enough information to be gathered. A lot of that data is complex, but most industries have best practices, which can help with the analysis.

The risk is analysed through qualitative and quantitative risk analysis. That means the risk factor is determined by how it impacts the project across a variety of metrics.

Those rules applied are how the risk influences the activity resources, duration and cost estimates. Another aspect of the project to think about is how the risk is going to impact on the schedule and budget. Then there is the project quality and procurements. These points must be considered to understand the full effect of risk on the project.

Prioritise the Risk

Not all risks are created equally. The risk needs to be evaluated to know what resources will be needed to resolve it when and if it occurs. Some risks are going to be acceptable. The project could grind to a halt and possibly not even be able to finish it without first prioritising the risks.

Having a large list of risks can be daunting. But this can be managed by simply categorising risks as high, medium or low. Once the risk is viewed in context, planning for how and when risks will be addressed can begin.

Some risks are going to require immediate attention. These are the risks that can derail the project. Other risks are important, but perhaps not threatening the success of the project.

Then there are those risks that have little to no impact on the overall project's schedule and budget. Some of these low-priority risks might be important, but not enough to waste time on. They can be all but ignored.

Project Planning

Assign an Owner to the Risk
All the hard work identifying and evaluating risk is for nothing if someone is not assigned to oversee the risk. Who is the person who is responsible for that risk, identifying it when and if it should occur and then leading the work towards resolving it?

That determination is up to the project manager. There might be a team member who is more skilled or experienced in the risk. Then that person should lead the charge to resolve it. Or it might just be an arbitrary choice. Of course, it is better to assign the task to the right person, but equally important in making sure that every risk has a person responsible for it. The person responsible should be identified in the risk register.

By not fulling addressing all risks at this stage leaves the project open to more risk in the event t should occur. It is one thing to identify risk, but if it is not managed then the project is not fully protected.

Respond to the Risk
For each major risk identified, there should be a plan to mitigate it. There should be a developed strategy which includes a preventative or contingency plan. The risk is acted upon by how it was prioritised. Communications should be established with the risk owner and with the project manager, decide on which of the plans to implement to resolve the risk.

Monitor the Risk
Whoever owns the risk will be responsible for tracking its progress towards resolution. The project manager will need to be updated to have an accurate picture of the project's overall progress to identify and monitor new risks.

Set up a series of meetings to manage the risks. Make sure the means of communications to do this has been agreed. There should be various channels dedicated to communication.

Face-to-face meetings may be used, but some updates might be best delivered by email or text or through a project management software tool. They might even be able to automate some, keeping the focus on the work and not busywork.

Whatever the choice, always be transparent. Everyone in the project must know what is going on, so they know what to be on the lookout for and help manage the process.

Project Planning

Communications Plan

A communications plan outlines how a project will be communicated to various audiences. Much like the work breakdown structure, a communications plan assigns responsibility for completing each component to a project team member.

In this step, it is important to outline how issues will be communicated and resolved within the team and how often communication will be opened to the team and the stakeholders or the boss. Each message has an intended audience. A communications plan helps project managers ensure the right information gets to the right people at the right time.

Communications Plan

Project:	Project Renew
Summary:	Redesign Website to support new brand image

Communication Goals:
Keep Stakeholders informed of project timeline, budget and project needs
Provide a clear insight into any decision's needed or roadblocks
Provide structured opportunities for feedback from stakeholders
Give to stakeholders as needed to gain acceptance of the project

Stakeholder Information

Person	Role Title	Frequency	Format / Channel	Notes
Dave Smith	Assistant CEO	Major Milestones	High Level budget by email	Prefers audited and approved files
Joan Greaves	HR Lead	Weekly	Weekly F2F meeting & emails	Must authorise additional labour

Producing a Communications Plan

Perform a Situation Analysis.
Conduct an audit to evaluate the communications status. Gather and analyse all relevant information within the organisation. To conduct the communications audit, do the following:

- *Brainstorm with communication staff.*
- *Conduct surveys and focus groups.*
- *Talk to other departments in your company.*

Project Planning

Define the Objectives.
After the information has been collected and evaluated, define the overall communications objectives. What results need to be achieved? What is to be accomplished by implementing this communication plan? The objectives should be SMART.

Define the Key Audiences.
The recipients for the messages must be identified. List all the key audiences of the organisation. These may include the following:

- *Members/non-members.*
- *Clients.*
- *Related associations.*
- *Educators.*
- *Local government officials.*
- *Media representatives.*

Identify Communication Channels
Plan to deliver messages to key recipients through multiple media channels. Decide which media channels would be the most effective to get the message delivered to the target audiences.

Establish a Timetable.
In order to achieve the communications objectives, plan and time the communication steps for the best results. Based on the research and resources, develop a solid timing strategy to execute the steps of the communication plan.

Evaluate the Results.
It is always important to measure the results to understand whether the objectives have been met. If the results are unsatisfactory, make necessary adjustments in order to perform better next time. The evaluation might take the form of the following:

- *Annual reports.*
- *Monthly reports.*
- *Progress reports.*
- *Reports from other departments.*

Developing a written communication plan will take some effort – but it is worth it. A communication plan is the main tool for successfully delivering the messages to the key audiences in order to develop mutually beneficial relationships.

Project Planning

Stakeholder Management Plan

A stakeholder management plan identifies how stakeholders will be used in the project. Sometimes stakeholders only need to receive information. That can be taken care of in the communications plan. If more is needed from stakeholders, a stakeholder management plan outlines how it will be obtained.

Because of how much power Stakeholders wield, the project manager needs to balance the requirements from key stakeholders with finesse.

What are their primary goals with this project? What are they hoping to invest? The more you can tease out what each of their goals and requirements are from the outset, the better.

Because there are many different types of stakeholders, you will want a well-rounded stakeholder management plan.

Stakeholder Register

Name	Title	Role	Power	Interest	Requirement	Concern
R Jones	Accountant	Sponsor	H	H	Maintain strict budget controls	Expenses only received monthly
M. Shah	Programmer	Team	L	H	Complete stage 14 by planned date	Network Issues

List the Stakeholders

Internal stakeholders are easy to identify. They are typically those within the organisation that have a key interest in the completion of a project. They are usually department heads, such as heads of Marketing, IT, Development, Operations and more. These stakeholders can affect the project either directly or indirectly by influencing the direction of their department on the given project.

Project Planning

External stakeholders are not typically part of the organisation itself but are made up of investors, users/customers, the media, neighbouring businesses or governmental oversight authorities.

Prioritise the Stakeholders
Prioritise which stakeholders are going to have a bigger influence over the project and note at which stage their influence becomes lesser or greater.
Start by considering how to manage the stakeholders on your project, and then start prioritising their demands and goals. Understand that those priorities can flex at different project points. For example, at certain points, say, during a website design project, the stakeholder with a special interest in the design will have their goals prioritised. Then, as you move into the development phase, the stakeholders with a special interest in development will have their goals elevated over design.

Interview the Stakeholders
Working with new stakeholders can be tricky at the start—some are easier to manage than others. Depending on the type of project, there will either be many voices from outside the company with different personalities and demands, or many voices inside the company with competing goals.

Try to get a solid understanding of whether or not the stakeholders feel positively or negatively about the project, and at what stages their perspectives might shift. Also, identify which ones have a stronger set of views and which ones are more flexible and open to compromise. This will help to mitigate any possible stop gaps down the road.

Develop a Matrix
A quick mock-up of a quadrant to sort the findings will help easily distinguish those with high interest, high priority versus low interest, low priority. It will also help to sort all those in between.

For example, those with a high interest but a low priority are typically the best confidants. They are ready to get work done and will cheerlead the project on. Those with low interest and high priority might be the squeakiest wheels—keep the lines of communication open with them but keep a firm boundary so as to not spend all the time focusing on them.

They say the squeaky wheel gets the grease, so remember that even those in the low priority, low interest or high priority, low interest still need to be continually communicated with to ensure that their voices are heard throughout the project.

Set & Manage Expectations
Once the matrix is outlined and priorities and interests have been identified, create the project plan. Clearly identify which stages each key stakeholder will be involved in, and timelines by which their feedback is needed.

Project Planning

Include a schedule of office hours for them to easily make contact so that they can have time to provide feedback either in a private setting or in a group. As always, be realistic, transparent and honest at every project phase—the stakeholders can tell and will be thankful for it.

Risks of not having a Stakeholder Management Plan
Since stakeholders usually involve multiple key contacts across many different avenues, it is important to communicate with them effectively and efficiently. Not having interviewed them ahead of time or gauging their priority or interest, could mean spending a great deal of time trying to validate the requirements of a stakeholder with low priority and low interest, leaving those with a high priority feeling frustrated at the process.

Project Change Management Plan

A change management plan lays out a framework for making changes to the project. (This should not be confused with the Change management in a Human Resources context which may run in parallel to the project itself)

Although project managers tend to want to avoid changes to the project, they are sometimes unavoidable. The change management plan provides protocols and processes for making changes. It is critical for accountability and transparency that project sponsors, project managers, and project team members follow the change management plan.

There are several steps involved in writing a change management plan.

Demonstrate the reasons for the change.
Make sure that the reasons for the change effort are clearly defined. When stakeholders have a clear understanding of why the change is needed and how it will improve business or the way they work, they are more likely to support rather than resist the change.

Determine the scope
The next step in writing the change management plan is determining who the change will affect. Also determine what the change will impact, including policies, processes, job roles, and organisational structure.

Identify stakeholders
In large projects a change management team may be created to deal with changes to the project in smaller projects it will be the role of the Project Manager. The composition of this team is extremely important and it must be led by a credible leader. The change management team interacts with stakeholders, addresses concerns, and oversees a smooth change transition. Roles within the team require clear definition, including outlining each member's responsibilities.

Clarify the expected benefits
These benefits should be clearly delineated so that everyone involved understands the advantages of proceeding with the change.

Project Planning

Establishing well-communicated and achievable milestones are vital to the success of any change plan. These milestones become symbols to employees that the plan is working, progress is happening, the direction is still right, and the effort is worth it."

Create a change management communication plan.
There are three basic elements to communications in the context of change management.

- *Identify the stakeholders and those impacted by the change.*
- *Schedule regular face to face interactions and email communications to keep stakeholders updated on progress.*
- *Communications should be consistent, thorough, and regular. Communications should also clearly explain the change, define the reasons for change, present the benefits of the change, and always include change owner's contact information*

Project Monitoring

Project monitoring is a crucial element of all project management plans.

It refers to the process of keeping track of all project-related metrics including team performance and task duration, identifying potential problems and taking corrective actions necessary to ensure that the project is within scope, on budget and meets the specified deadlines. Without it, you cannot see where or why projects fail. It essentially comes down to keeping tabs on all project-related measurements, proactively recognising possible problems and taking the necessary steps to guarantee the project is completed on budget, on time and in scope.

The process of project monitoring begins during the planning phase of the project. During this phase, it is important to define how the project success will look like and how the goals can be measured using KPIs (Key performance indicators).

Project monitoring exists to make sure you are implementing a project as competently as possible. It should always be a cohesive and constant part of project management, and vital decisions should never be made without it.

The project management lifecycle has five phases: initiating, planning, executing, monitoring, and closing.

During the initiating & planning phase, the project receives the necessary approvals, a plan has been created, and the work actually begins on the tasks.

The executing phase and the monitoring phase happen concurrently. This means that you are monitoring your progress while you are completing tasks.

Project Planning

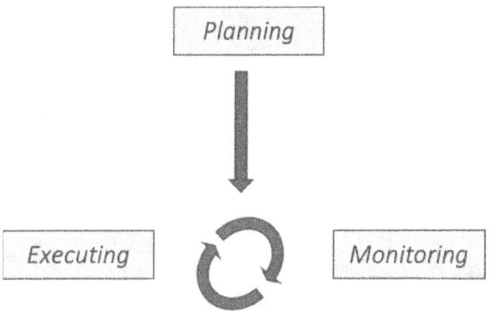

Executing and monitoring of projects happen concurrently.

Once the project plan is finalised and approved, the project manager monitors the progress making sure that the tasks are completed accordingly.

It is vital to monitor projects diligently and use the data you gathered both before and during the project to come up with intelligent decisions. Here are some questions answered through project monitoring:

- *Are tasks being carried out as planned?*
- *Are there any unforeseen consequences that arise as a result of these tasks?*
- *How is your team performing at a given period of time?*
- *What are the elements of the project that needs changing?*
- *What is the impact of these changes?*
- *Will these actions lead you to your expected results?*

Project Monitoring can be implemented via:

- *Staff Meetings, which can be conducted on a Weekly, Monthly or an Annual basis.*
- *Partner's meeting, Learning forums (FGD, Surveys) or Retreats.*
- *Participatory reviews by the stakeholders*
- *Monitoring and Supervision Missions that can be Self, Donor or Joint.*
- *Statistics or Progress reports*

Project monitoring aids various purposes. It brings out the problems which occur, or which might occur during the implementation of the project and which demands solutions for smoother progress in the project. Effective monitoring helps in knowing if the intended results are being achieved as planned, what actions are needed to achieve the intended results during the project execution, and whether these initiatives are creating a positive impact towards the project execution.

Project Planning

- **To assess the project results:** To know how the objectives are being met and the desired changes are being met.
- **To improve process planning:** It helps in adapting to better contextual and risk factors which affect the research process, like social and power dynamics.
- **To promote learning:** It will help you learn how various approaches to participation influences the outcomes.
- **To understand stakeholder's perspectives:** Through direct participation in the process of monitoring and evaluation, learn about the people who are involved in the research project. Understand their values and views, as well as design methods to resolve conflicting views and interests.
- **To ensure accountability:** To assess if the project has been effectively, appropriately and efficiently executed, so that they can be held accountable.

Implementing Project Monitoring and Control

Monitoring and control processes continually track, review, adjust and report on the project's performance. It is important to find out how a project's performing and whether it is on time, as well as implement approved changes. This ensures the project remains on track, on budget and on time.

On the surface this sounds simple enough, until one stops to think about the depth and breadth of the monitoring and controlling activities described throughout the PMBOK® Guide, which include:

- *Comparing planned results with actual results*
- *Reporting performance*
- *Determining if action is needed, and what the right action is*
- *Ensuring deliverables are correct based on the previously approved definitions and/or requirements*
- *Acquiring sign-off on deliverables by authorised stakeholders*
- *Assessing the overall project performance*
- *Managing risks*
- *Managing contracts and vendors*

In other words, project managers use the monitoring and controlling processes to translate project execution data from information into knowledge. This knowledge is then used to make the right management decisions and to take the right actions at the right time. Generally speaking, project managers face two choices in most situations:

- *Recommend the implementation of appropriate changes, which are planned and approved by the change management process*
  or
- *Allow the project to function "as is"*

Project Planning

Project Control

Project control is:

> *"a project management function that involves comparing actual performance with planned performance and taking appropriate corrective action (or directing others to take this action) that will yield the desired outcome in the project when significant differences exist."*

Project controls are a series of tools that help keep a project on schedule. Combined with people skills and project experience, they deliver information that enables accurate decision making.

The project control process mainly focuses on:

- *Measuring planned performance vs actual performance.*
- *Ongoing assessment of the project's performance to identify any preventive or corrective actions needed.*
- *Keeping accurate, timely information based on the project's output and associated documentation.*
- *Providing information that supports status updates, forecasting and measuring progress.*
- *Delivering forecasts that update current costs and project schedule.*
- *Monitoring the implementation of any approved changes or schedule amendments.*

Monitoring and control keep projects on track. The right controls can play a major part in completing projects on time. The data gathered also lets project managers make informed decisions. They can take advantage of opportunities, make changes and avoid crisis management issues.

Put simply, monitoring and control ensures the seamless execution of tasks. This improves productivity and efficiency.

Monitoring and control methods

When setting up a project's monitoring and control process, first establish the project baselines. This includes the scope, schedule and budget. Use this information to benchmark the project's progress throughout the lifecycle.

Use a Work Breakdown Structure (WBS) to break a project down into small units of work, or sub-tasks. This makes the work easier to manage and evaluate. This enables easier

Project Planning

detection of issues, keeps the project under control and allows for easier progress verification. It also helps prevent team members from feeling overwhelmed.

There is a range of monitoring and control techniques that can be used by project managers, including:

- *A Requirements Traceability Matrix (RTM) maps or traces, the project's requirements to the deliverables. The matrix correlates the relationship between two baseline documents. This makes the project's tasks more visible. It also prevents new tasks or requirements being added to the project without approval.*
- *A control chart monitors the project's quality. There are two basic forms of control chart – a univariate control chart displays one project characteristic, while a multivariate chart displays more than one.*
- *Review and status meetings further analyse problems, finding out why something happened. They can also highlight any issues that might happen later*